# Framing Film Festivals

Series Editors
Marijke de Valck
Department of Media and Culture Studies
Utrecht University
Utrecht, Netherlands

Tamara Falicov
Department of Film and Media Studies
University of Kansas
Lawrence, KS, USA

Every day, somewhere in the world a film festival takes place. Most people know about the festival in Cannes, the worlds' leading film festival, and many will also be familiar with other high profile events, like Venice, the oldest festival; Sundance, America's vibrant independent scene; and Toronto, a premier market place. In the past decade the study of film festivals has blossomed. A growing number of scholars recognize the significance of film festivals for understanding cinema's production, distribution, reception and aesthetics, and their work has amounted to a prolific new field in the study of film culture. The Framing Film Festivals series presents the best of contemporary film festival research. Books in the series are academically rigorous, socially relevant, contain critical discourse on festivals, and are intellectually original. Framing Film Festivals offers a dedicated space for academic knowledge dissemination.

More information about this series at
http://www.springer.com/series/14990

Stuart James Richards

# The Queer Film Festival

Popcorn and Politics

palgrave
macmillan

Stuart James Richards
University of Melbourne
Melbourne, Victoria
Australia

Framing Film Festivals
ISBN 978-1-137-59034-3          ISBN 978-1-137-58438-0    (eBook)
DOI 10.1057/978-1-137-58438-0

Library of Congress Control Number: 2016960897

Printed on acid-free paper

This Palgrave Macmillan imprint is published by Springer Nature
The registered company is Nature America Inc.
The registered company address is: 1 New York Plaza, New York, NY 10004, U.S.A.

*To Mum and Dad with love*

# ACKNOWLEDGEMENTS

This project began as my PhD dissertation. I was warned numerous times at how difficult and lonely the experience was going to be. While, indeed, these last few years have been a challenge, I have found this period anything but isolating. The support I have received from family and friends has been incredibly gratifying, and it is imperative for me to take a moment to say thank you.

First and foremost, I would not have produced this work if it were not for the guidance from my supervisors Audrey Yue and Fran Martin from the School of Culture and Communication at the University of Melbourne. Their advice and encouragement have been invaluable and made me the researcher I am today. Thank you to the administrative staff both past and present from the School of Culture and Communication, particularly Annemarie Levin. I would also like to thank RMIT University, particularly Alexia Kannas, Allan Thomas, Brian Morris, and Stephen Gaunson for their support. Thank you to those who provided me with academic guidance throughout my tertiary years. Particular mentions must go to Barbara Creed, Felicity Coleman, Wendy Haslem, Chris Healy, Tom Apperley, Rimi Khan, Timothy Laurie, and Helen Young. I'm significantly grateful for the mentorship and friendship of Angela Ndalianis, who never failed to keep me positive during this experience.

This project would not have been possible if it weren't for the openness, hospitality, and support from my case studies the San Francisco Frameline International LGBTQ Film Festival, the Melbourne Queer Film Festival, and the Hong Kong Lesbian and Gay Film Festival. Special mention must go to Lisa Daniel from MQFF and everyone at Frameline, particularly Sarah Deragon and Sarah Jelinsky of Team Sassy (!), Alexis Whitham, Lares Feliciano, and Harris Kornstein for their friendship. All the interview subjects who took part have enriched this research. Thank you also to the Rowena Parade Corner Store for allowing the café to be my second home.

Thanks to my fellow graduate researchers for the company. Particular mentions go to Sarah Comyn, Felicty Ford, Amanda Trevisanut, Louise Sheedy, Luke Heemsbergen, Dion Kagan, and Simone Gustafsson. To all my other friends, thank you. To the Mutineers, Pandorans, and any other team I have been a part of, the lols were plentiful, thank you. Thanks to John Wilson for assisting me with the cover design. To Dion Kagan, Katherine Copsey, Claire Miller, Mikhaila Clemens, Jeannie Lee, and Liz Mutineer, thank you for proof reading my work and for your friendship. I must give special mention to Liz, whose friendship over the years has helped me have the sense of humour I have today.

To my brothers Brendan and Cameron and sister Jennifer, thank you for your love and support. To my other sisters, Nuala Bethel and Olivia Monaghan, I simply could not have done this without either of your advice.

Finally to my parents Marcus and Linda Richards, your love and encouragement has been limitless and for that I thank you. This project is dedicated to you.

# CONTENTS

# LIST OF FIGURES

# LIST OF TABLE

CHAPTER 1

# Introduction

From grassroots screenings organised by community activists to commercially minded organisations, the queer film festival has always been an integral player in the development of queer film. Beginning as underground radical and experimental film festivals that directly challenged dominant ideologies of sexuality and gender identity, queer film festivals have grown to become part of an elite film institution with an influential position in queer cinema. These festivals provide space for the lesbian, gay, bisexual, transgender, and intersex (LGBTI) community to access films otherwise unavailable. However, in order for the festivals to achieve their social missions, they must achieve financial sustainability. The blossoming of professional queer film festivals highlights the relevance of the *social enterprise* as a conceptual framework for an analysis.

The rubric of the social enterprise will be used to unpack the manner in which the queer film festival employs market-focused activities to serve its social goals of providing quality cinema and a communal experience. The social enterprise is a non-profit organisation that will engage in economic strategies to fulfil its social mission, where the social entrepreneur will engage with various income streams to create sustainable social transformations (Dees et al. 2001; Westall 2001; Nicholls 2006; Doherty et al. 2009). This is a dramatic development from the early inceptions of the queer film festival, many of which began as community art events. This transition from community-based organisations to elite film institutions will be explored within the conceptual framework of cultural policy and the development of the creative industry in order to illuminate the queer film festival's road to

© The Author(s) 2016
S.J. Richards, *The Queer Film Festival*,
DOI 10.1057/978-1-137-58438-0_1

professionalisation. The queer film festival no longer depends on subsidies or philanthropic gestures, as it can now be recognised as providing specific creative value to their respective cities. This discussion will place the queer film festival within existing scholarship pertaining to the relationship between art and commerce. In light of this consideration, this book will be an important addition to current scholarship, both in its inclusion of audience studies and in its analysis of how social and economic values interrelate. The extent to which these two seemingly opposing objectives can coexist will be a focus of this study.

Three case studies will be presented for analysis, highlighting this book's concerns with the specific spaces within which queer films are exhibited. The first case study will be the Melbourne Queer Film Festival (hereafter MQFF), a festival for which I have been a selector of for the past six years. Second, the Hong Kong Lesbian & Gay Film Festival (hereafter HKLGFF) will be an interesting case study as it is emblematic of Hong Kong's cosmopolitan identity. These festivals will be compared to the largest and oldest film festival of its kind internationally, the Frameline San Francisco International LGBTQ Film Festival (hereafter Frameline); while MQFF had its inaugural film festival in 1991 and HKLGFF in 1990, Frameline commenced in 1977. These case studies will allow for a robust discussion of the contemporary state of queer film festivals. While Frameline screens many of its films in San Francisco's famous gay ghetto the Castro, MQFF has its home in the central business district (CBD) of Melbourne. HKLGFF screens films in both Central and Kowloon. All are creative cities. The developments of their cultural milieus have influenced these film festivals. This research will aim to identify common themes in each of these festivals with the central research question being thus: in the exhibition of films at the queer film festival, can economic value and social empowerment coexist? This raises various questions relevant to the relationship between theory and contemporary sexual politics.

## FROM GAY POLITICS TO QUEER THEORY

A development of significant relevance to this book is the widening theoretical gap between the terms "gay" and "queer." Much has been written academically about the definition of queer, and it now has a firm placing in academia. It is not the aim of this book to provide an in-depth discussion of the history of queer theory. It is, however, necessary to begin with a commentary on the current state of what queer means. A key position of this project is a queer critique of sexual normativity, while acknowledging the current ambiguity around the use of the word.

Queer politics and theory were born out of the limitations of the gay and lesbian liberationist movement. Whereas it was once a radical political force alongside the student radicals, black militants, and anti-war activists fighting conservative notions of sexuality and gendered behaviour, gay activism began to concentrate on "securing equality for (the) homosexual population defined in terms of same-sex object choice" (Jagose 1996, 58). This was a political transformation from opposing the social institutions that marginalised and pathologised homosexuality to assimilation within the dominant institutions of society. This saw the hegemonic binary of homosexual versus heterosexual identity affirmed. This formation of a clearly defined, socially assimilationist gay and lesbian community has been termed "the ethnic model" of gay and lesbian difference (Seidman 1994).

The ethnic model's aim was to establish the gay and lesbian community as a legitimate minority group, similar to an "ethnic group." This established visible and commodified lesbian and gay urban communities and legitimised "lesbian" and "gay" as categories of identification.[1] For the most part, this was considered successful; however, there was a lack of fluidity within the maintenance of normative identity categories, thus creating a hegemonic rigid binary between heterosexual and homosexual identities. This resulted in limited room for those that did not neatly fit into these categories, such as differences in socio-economic status, race, and so on. This was a significant departure from the gay and lesbian liberationist era of politics. Gay liberation demanded a radical exodus from traditional sex and gender categories, whereas the onset of the ethnic model formulated an assimilationist mindset. This was a transition "from a broadly conceived sexual and general liberation movement" to the "agenda of the male-dominated gay culture ... winning civil rights" (Seidman 1993, 117). These contradictory desires of liberation versus legitimation hindered the gay and lesbian movement (Vaid 1995). The "equal but different" mentality saw equal rights sought under an order that many originally thought to be corrupt. While visible communities were established and solidified, many pre-existing inequalities (such as race, age, and ability) were rearticulated within the ethnic model. Ironically, Jagose argues (1996), "the ethnic model's gay and lesbian subject was white" (62). The ethnic model was based on an essentialist notion of identity, that is, the idea that our sexuality and gender are a set of innate characteristics as opposed to the queer idea of the possibility of identity being fluid and made and unmade through performance.

In her aptly titled book *Queer Theory* (1996), Jagose discusses queer as an early 1990s movement away from the identity politics that underpin these notions of the lesbian and gay identity. While previous gay and lesbian movements saw identity politics as integral to progress, queer theory developed a post-structuralist critique that highlighted the limitations of identity categories. Foucault (1988) shaped the beginnings of a contemporary queer approach to identity where sexual identities are seen as discursive productions as opposed to a natural inherent condition. Ultimately, this plays into the ideological difference between essentialism and constructionism, where queer theory challenges the essentialist notion that sexuality and gender are fixed. Instead, queer theorists argue that identity is socially constructed and that we are subjects of our own culture. In this sense, queer marks a suspension of identity as something fixed, coherent, and natural, and can be seen to give voice to previously obscured voices within the hetero/homo binary. Queer theory critiques identity as problematic. Writes Jagose:

> The suspicion that normative models of identity will never suffice for the representational work demanded of them is strengthened by the influential postmodern understandings of identity, gender, sexuality, power and resistance. These provide the context in which queer becomes an intelligible … phenomenon (Jagose 1996, 71).

Queer can be used to describe an open-ended community whose shared characteristic is not identity itself but an anti-normative positioning with regard to sexuality. Thus, queer need not materialise in any specific form; rather, queer exists as a critical resistance to normality. Warner's theory on heteronormativity is representative of this type of thinking. Conceptually developed in his introduction to *Fear of a Queer Planet* (1993), heteronormativity identifies the view that any sexual relations that are not between a monogamous man and woman are deemed to be deviant. An instrument of queer critique, heteronormativity recognises the extent to which heterosexual privilege saturates our everyday life:

> Because the logic of the sexual order is so deeply embedded by now in an indescribably wide range of social institutions, and is embedded in the most standard accounts of the world, queer struggles aim not just at toleration or equal status but at challenging those institutions and accounts. The dawning

realisation that themes of homophobia and heterosexism may be read in almost any document of our culture means that we are only beginning to have an idea of how widespread those institutions and accounts are (Warner 1993, 6).

Warner's work is an articulation of what it means to be queer and is a departure from gay and lesbian identity politics. Likewise, many scholars of the time, such as Gayle Rubin, Adrienne Rich, and Eve Kosofsky Sedgwick, began to rethink the relationship between gender and sexuality. The development of queer politics is a critique of sexual oppression and power—*including* expressions of power in the name of gay identity.

A *homonormative* critique is an extension of Warner's work on heteronormativity by looking at the uneven power relations within the LGBTI community. Duggan asserts that homonormativity is a product of neoliberalism and involves assimilationist politics rather than confrontation. According to Duggan, homonormativity:

Does not contest dominant heteronormative assumptions and institutions, but upholds and sustains them, while promising the possibility of a demobilized gay and lesbian constituency and a privatized, depoliticized gay culture anchored in domesticity and consumption (Duggan 2003, 65).

She continues by stating that homonormativity recodes key terms in gay politics. In an age where the American LGBTI rights movement has primarily been concerned with access to conservative institutions such as marriage and the military, "freedom" is transformed into "inequalities in commercial life and civil society" (65). Freedom and equality, it seems, are not distributed evenly to all members of the LGBTI community. Contemporary queer cinema exists within these constantly negotiating positions on identity and community.

## The Queer Film Festival

The underlining definition of the queer film festival is a series of film screenings that primarily focus on queer themes. The labels associated with these festivals range from lesbian and gay (such as Hong Kong), queer (such as Melbourne), LGBTQ (such as Frameline in San Francisco) to names that don't explicitly state an association with the LGBTI community, such as MIX NYC, Image, and Nation in Montreal, or Side by Side in

St Petersburg. The primary purpose of these festivals is to provide a space for the exhibition of films that would otherwise struggle to secure a large audience. The development of queer cinema from a radical impulse to a niche market (Rich 2000) has been propelled by the increased professionalism of the queer film festival. The queer film festival has a mission statement in serving the queer community and promoting social empowerment while still remaining financially viable. There is a limited but a gradually expanding array of scholarly literature written on the queer film festival. It is widely assumed among scholars that the queer film festival is a space for films that are by/for/about queers to be exhibited and discussed (Ferrelli 1999; June 2003; Ford 2014); "Such zones are part of a concerted political project to seize the means of self-representation in the face of widespread cultural invisibility and stereotyping" (Pidduck 2003, 267). The queer film festival plays a significant role in any queer community, where it is a "destination to which folks make pilgrimages to fix memory and reclaim history, a sort of moving-image version of, say, Gettysburg" (Rich in Straayer and Waugh 2006, 624). These are spaces for reflection and social engagement.

From the outset, it is important to clarify that the very nature of a film festival is so much more than the films being exhibited, particularly when discussing a queer film festival. Siegel (1997) argues that the location and festival sites play a key role in the cultural politics of the queer film festival— "from purchasing tickets to cruising the lines milling about in the lobby spilling out onto Castro Street" (132).[2] When researching a film festival, we must go beyond the theatres.

Most scholarship on the queer film festival concerns itself with queer cinema's journey into the mainstream and how this can result in a homogenised array of films programmed. Clarke (1999) highlights the risk of niche marketing with the queer film festival becoming homogenised, that a homosexual phantom normalcy will dissipate any semblance of diversity. B. Ruby Rich is unusually cynical when she writes:

> Audiences don't want disruption. They don't want "difference." Instead they hunger for sameness, replication, reflection. What do queers want on their night on the town? To feel good. To feel breezy and cheesy and commercial and acceptable and stylish and desirable. A six-pack and *Jeffrey* (Christopher Ashley 1995). A six-pack and *Bound* (Wachowskis 1996). They just wanna have fun [*sic*]. And if the occasion is serious, then it had better be predictable: the AIDS quilt or lesbian adoption rights (Rich 1999, 83).

These concerns all arose within the "Queer Film and Video Forums" published in *GLQ*, which have become staple readings for any critical analysis of the queer film festival. The forums acted as a triptych discussion of the queer film festival. The forums heard from a diverse array of players on the circuit with curators "speaking out" in the first forum (2005), critics in the second (2006), and artists rounding up the forums in the third (2008). Taken as a collective dialogue, we can see major dichotomies arise: while experimental works and short films are political, standard narrative features are more apolitical. While a queer critique of the mainstream results in visibility and a critical destabilisation of sexual identity, elements of queer images becoming too "mainstream" are both heteronormative and homogenised. While queer film festivals can be limiting in their queer exclusivity, they also play a significant role in the development of the queer community.

Furthermore, there is concern over the queer film festival existing in a framework with Western imperialism being employed as "a global discourse in the name of international multiculturalism" (Gretsch 1997). Fung (1999) has concerns over race and the queer film festival, arguing for the need to avoid dedicated programming when exhibiting race-related films— "it's Asian, so let's put it with other Asian work and include *rice* in the program title" (91). Problematically, in light of these concerns, the global queer film festival circuit is often seen as a "transnational queer public" and discussed as a "collective identity" (White 1999, 74). This does not taken into account the complex nuances of local influences on sexuality and gender identity in some regions.

While some film festival scholars have argued that the film festival occupies a position of power within the film industry occupying an influential position in alternative film distribution (de Valck 2007) and acting as cultural "gate-keepers" (Stringer 2003, 43), Loist (2011) points out that it is folly to assume that this prestige actually translates to the position of the film festival worker. Loist's analysis of the precarious position the film festival worker occupies specifically refers to those that work for smaller, more local, film festivals (especially in the queer community). This discussion of film festival staff as cultural workers prompts us to consider the queer film festival specifically as a project within the contemporary creative industry. While the cultural workers deal with low pay and temporary positions, they are rewarded by flexible schedules, mobility, and so on (Hesmondhalgh 2008). It will become evident that this was a key influence on my own research, where many staff members interviewed have since moved on from their positions.

Like many other community arts organisations, the queer film festival has traversed the arduous journey from being an informal event to a professional organisation. Rhyne details the history of the queer film festival, highlighting four significant periods. First, 1977–1990 saw the growth from informal screenings into non-profit organisations. Second, the period of 1991–1996 saw new relationships between film festivals and both corporate sponsorship and the commercial film industry. Third, from 1997 to 2001, the queer film festival circuit expanded dramatically into new markets in East Asia and Eastern Europe. Finally (keeping in mind Rhyne's dissertation was published in 2007), the period from 2001 onwards saw the development of alternative digital distribution networks such as pay per view television and online circulation. For my own forthcoming analysis, Rhyne's dissertation is a key reference as it traces the queer film festival's economic growth alongside the development of the "ideal gay subject." From the outset, Rhyne chooses not to address the films programmed in her case studies (both Frameline and the NewFest in New York) as they have already received scholarly attention. Instead Rhyne examines the institution of the queer film festival itself. This project's analysis will consider Rhyne's work while also examining the films programmed and how economic growth in the queer film festival (as outlined in both Rhyne's work and my early chapters) affects the films programmed. Describing the queer film festival as a circuit is problematic, however, as collaboration does not necessarily occur between festivals. While Frameline holds a very influential position with festival directors attending Frameline to acquire films for their own festivals (including MQFF's former director Lisa Daniel), the networked nature of the queer film festival does not extend beyond this.

This growing dependence on sponsorship is a key theme in Gamson's essential work (1996), where he discusses the construction of collective identities in New York queer film festival programming, where the environment has dramatically changed. Gamson's analysis is based upon the claim that "collective identities... are continually filtered and reproduced through organisational bodies" (235). While these festivals:

> Take actions on behalf of "communities," they do so also as organisations largely autonomous from those populations. As such, they must negotiate and move within particular institutional environments and are dependent on a variety of parties for support and legitimacy (235).

Nowadays there is less reliance on grants and more corporate interest from sponsors. The ideological implications of this are profound. Gamson pessimistically questions whether this organisational path has turned the film festival patrons from being political to a consumer. Basing his analysis within a conceptual framework of social movement theory, he argues that the "collective identity formation is an ongoing (political) process, and it is a process in which multiple, overlapping identities inevitably conflict" (236). In order for these festivals to continue to exist, Gamson argues that they must create equilibrium between its relationships to "the community" and its relationships to sponsors. This is a "double bind within these socially formed spaces" (236). While the experimental MIX NYC has moved away from gay and lesbian labels with "an organisational shift to garner connections to the elite art world while expanding racially" (258), the more commercial NewFest has adopted an increasingly multicultural approach towards identity affirmation. MIX NYC is part of a wider trend in queer film festivals to distance itself from identity models, such as BFI Flare in London and Image + Nation in Montreal (Galt and Schoonover 2014). While MIX NYC does deconstruct identity for a more fluid collective identity, Gamson concludes that both have become to "resemble one another, both structurally... and ideologically" (256) as both adopt curatorial approaches that reflect the changing organisational field. As Anderson points out in an analysis of the evolution of Inside Out in Toronto and Ottawa, "the queer film festival must be able to adapt to the changing nature of queer media as the changing nature of queer participation has resulted in a renewed emphasis on community involvement and access" (Anderson 2012, 52). The queer film festival circuit is an organisational field that must always be ready to adapt to queer politics, sponsorship, and quality in media.

It is important to note the diversity of queer film festivals on the international circuit. Frameline, MQFF, and HKLGFF are all major queer film festivals aiming to provide exhibition space for LGBT films. MIX NYC, the New York Queer Experimental Film Festival, states that it makes art for itself and its community, not for museums or any other commercial interests. The Side-by-Side (*Bok o Bok*) Lesbian and Gay International Film Festival based in St Petersburg, Russia, aims to provide a safe, open space for LGBTI Russians. The festival has faced significant challenges within a Russian culture that is deeply conservative. Likewise, Q! Film Festival in Jakarta has faced severe backlash from the Islamic Defenders Front, a conservative religious organisation. According to former festival director John Badalu:

It's quite a challenge every year even just to put it together. The first edition, we didn't really know what to expect and it turned out well. There are times when we didn't have money at all. There was a year where the turnover of the organisers was really high that we literally almost started from scratch again. There was also a time where we did make it big and screened films in the public cinemas. And there was a time where we became a national headline and were protested by some Islamic fundamentalist groups (Badalu 2015).

Queer film festivals are significantly varied worldwide, each with numerous strategic forces driving its organisational development. Factors that influence the management of the Q! Film Festival in Jakarta would be very different to that of Frameline.

In considering the queer film festival, there is a complex interplay between queer theory, queer politics, and the queer film festival as the term "queer" seems to mean different things in different contexts. As highlighted earlier, queer developed out of radical theory and activism (with organisations such as Queer Nation and ACT UP), yet has been used in watered-down moments such as television shows *Queer as Folk* and *Queer Eye for the Straight Guy,* where queer is merely synonymous with gay. Before being co-opted by activists, the label "queer" was a derogatory label, which has resulted in many being hesitant to adopt the label as a positive term (Reed 1993). This hesitance comes from those that are "neither interpellated by the term nor persuaded that the new category describes or represents them" (Jagose 1996, 103).[3] The label "the queer film festival" itself seems to be using queer only as an umbrella term for LGBTI. Is a film festival that has distinct and segregated films for the boys and girls really that queer?

This results in another hesitance towards the label, where some fear the erasure of the labels lesbian and transgender. In the early 1990s, Wolfe and Penelope (1993) argued that we cannot "afford to allow privileged patriarchal discourse (of which post-structuralism is but a new variant) to erase the collective identity Lesbians have only recently begun to establish" (5). These contestations of the label queer coincide with the queer film festival being part of the creative industry shift in contemporary neoliberal cultural policy, where its manifestation is becoming more and more corporate. The queer film festival's status has grown from that of a community arts organisation to the ranks of the more elite international film festival.

## THE COMMUNITY ARTS ORGANISATION
## AND THE NEOLIBERAL TURN

The double bind mentioned earlier is a key concern in a discussion of the queer film festival, as its roots are in the community arts form. In *From Nimbin to Mardi Gras: Constructing Community Art* (1993), Gay Hawkins discusses the formation of such communities and the community arts aesthetic in her analysis of the Community Arts Program of the Australia Council. Community art was initially placed "within the realm of self-expression, not Culture ... While everyday creativity was accepted it did not necessarily have anything to do with art. In fact, it was most often equated with well-being; like exercise they were good for people" (118). Community art was originally associated with social inclusion and self-expression as opposed to more highbrow notions of what constitutes arts and culture, which produced a "cultural scenario in which everyone was involved, everyone was a cultural producer ... in the drive to collapse the social distance between artists and audiences community arts became some-thing that everybody did and nobody watched" (132).

The commitment to a collective identity is integral to the success of such organisations. In her account of the history of Desh Pardesh, the Toronto-based South Asian gay and lesbian arts and cultural festival, Fernandez (2006) highlights the strength of the collective process in such community arts organisations. Through arts and activism fostering the collective pro-cess, the festival was able to "break down barriers and identify what capacity benefits were needed for its multiple communities" (18). Fernandez continues:

> What emerges from Desh's mandate is just how fundamental this sensitive interplay between creative expression, public participation, and the empow-erment of the communities involved was to the Desh organizers. This deep commitment to and interest in links and relationships at numerous levels helps to explain how out of a fringe identity-based support group in Toronto, a multidisciplinary celebration that would spread across the country and even-tually the globe was initially imagined and subsequently realized (22).

Fernandez concludes her essay with the proposition that in the context "of marginalisation, it is only through the synergetic solidarity of collectivity that this fight for cultural recognition and political clout can begin" (30).

This synergy of the multiple identities at play in the queer community is a quintessential goal for any LGBT or queer organisation.

This is a key focus in Drucker's work on the effect that neoliberalism has had on the LGBT community where he asks: "how will LGBT communities and movements be structured in a time of increasingly divergent identities?" (Drucker 2011, 28). The neoliberal cultural economy sees an upward distribution of power through self-governance in order to cater to economic interests. This has resulted in a distinct fracturing of the LGBTI community:

> In developed capitalist countries, while commercial scenes are more accessible to even lower income LGBTs, growing economic inequality has meant increasingly divergent realities in LGBT people's lives. Alienation has mounted among some LGBT people from the overconsumption increasingly characteristic of many aspects of the commercial gay scene, which inevitably marginalises many LGBT people (6).

This is where the growth of the queer film festival becomes complex as ultimately this development is informed by the neoliberal shift in cultural policy, a line of thinking which will be explored in Chaps. 2 and 3.

For cultural theorists, neoliberalism sees a paradigm shift in social, cultural, political practices, and policies towards a use of the language of markets, consumer choice, and individual autonomy to shift risk from governments and corporations onto individuals and to extend this kind of market logic into the realm of social and affective relationships (Ong 2006). For McGuigan (2004), cultural policy being informed by such language forces culture to be saturated with a market-oriented mentality that closes out alternative ways of thinking and imagining as "neoliberal globalisation has compounded the divergences and inequalities that uneven capitalist development had helped to produce" (828). Given that neoliberalism "reinforces and reproduces inequalities" (Mtewa 2003: 39), is it a paradox then that the queer film festival, a socially progressive organisation, is working within this economic attitude which overrides a view of the film festival as simply a community arts organisation that provides social inclusion?

There has been a recent boom in academic interest in this neoliberal shift into the creative industries. The term "creative industry" can "capture significant 'new economy' enterprise dynamics that such terms as 'the arts,' 'media' and 'cultural industries' do not" (Cunningham 2004, 1). Through the production and exploitation of creativity, wealth and job creation can occur. For Hesmondhalgh and Pratt (2005), the implications of these changing paradigms go beyond policy. It is the commercialisation of cultural production:

> This explosion of writing and thinking about the cultural and creative industries is of course partly influenced by policy developments, but it goes beyond policy too, for the cultural industries raise questions about shifting boundaries between culture and economics, and between art and commerce—relationships that have been central to a number of recent developments in social theory and other academic areas (1).

In terms of the film festival, the development of the creative industries has reshaped relationships between art, commerce, and more importantly, social activism. Loist (2011) implores film festival scholars to examine the queer film festival in larger terms, such as in relation to flows of cultural and finance capital, especially in regard to who gains from these flows. This passage of the queer film festival from informal screenings to functioning within the matrix of the creative industries in a neoliberal framework leads us to examine the very nature of the film festival itself.

The contemporary film festival exists within a complex creative industries structure that is heavily influenced by regional attitudes to the economisation of the arts. The USA, Hong Kong, and Australia have all made movements towards incorporating neoliberal trends in the arts, which has been demonstrated by Rhyne (2007) for the USA in particular. This is not consistent throughout Europe, however. Western Europe, for instance, provides a different environment for the creative industries, where a "greater resistance towards commercial sponsorship in the arts is in place" (Loist 2014, 232). Loist provides case studies in Germany and Austria to demonstrate the diversity of festival organisations that are hesitant to welcome the neoliberalisation of the arts. As such, the approach I offer here to the queer film festival may not be applicable to *all* queer film festivals. Some queer film festivals remain volunteer-collectives with a "greater resistance towards commercial sponsorship in the arts" (232). Currently, however, I am primarily concerned with queer film festivals that are facing this neoliberal double bind.

## THE INTERNATIONAL FILM FESTIVAL

This approach to the queer film festival boils down to how social and economic values play out in the film festival. De Valck (2014) offered a similar approach in her article on film festivals and the commercialisation of art cinema. Here, she conducts a Bourdieusian analysis by looking at "how social agents negotiate the tension between an art for art's sake ideology and a commercializing subfield" (41) at the International Film Festival Rotterdam. Here there are two contrasting schools of thought in constant negotiation; film festival organisational decisions that are autonomous—purely artistic—and ones that are heteronomously organised within a commercial economy. While film festivals are "embedded in society and susceptible to outside influence – such as commercialisation, globalisation and the recent economic crisis" (56), it is imperative to fight for the autonomy of art cinema. The motivations of this analysis are in a similar mindset. While queer film festivals must acknowledge the economic reality of the contemporary creative industries, the social importance of an exhibition space of queer cinema must always be considered.

Much of the existing critiques of the international film festival can be thematically organised into two separate categories, looking at the festival either in terms of its organisational structure or in terms of its audience. Both approaches fail to address how the inherent objectives of the queer film festival's social empowering capacity and financial sustainability influence one another. To be clear, pre-existing scholarship on the film festival does engage in the social dynamics at play; however, how these social undercurrents influence (and in turn are influenced by) the demand for fiscal responsibility remains underdeveloped. Like de Valck, I am considering two schools of thought in constant negotiation: films that are social empowering and films that are commercially viable.

## THE FILM FESTIVAL'S ORGANISATIONAL STRUCTURE

We need to consider the notion of the film festival circuit as a multitude of connections, where these *circuits* are integrated into existing media industries. While Elsaesser (2005) and De Valck (2007) both highlight the film festival as initially being a European phenomenon, we need to consider the "hierarchical tiers and parallel/sub-circuits" of film festivals globally (Loist 2016, 60). Film festivals have been at the forefront of historical shifts in film culture and, as such, exist in a plurality of circuits. I would also add that the queer film festival in particular was not born as a European phenomenon but originated in San Franciscan political circles. Each queer film festival is heavily influenced by their respective socio-political contexts.

Existing scholarship on the organisation of the film festival inadequately addresses the role economics plays in social empowerment and political movements. The film festival has often been discussed, most notably by Elsaesser (2005) and De Valck (2007), in terms of actor-network theory (ANT), a theory developed by scholars Callon (1986) and Latour (1987) and sociologist Law (1987), that tries to explain how material-semiotic networks come together to act as a whole. The logic here implies that the social and the technical are inseparable. ANT states that every actor in the network, whether it be an organisation, person, or object, is equally important in the coextensive network.

The actors in film festival networks exist on different levels. First, the professional stakeholders involved with the organisation and the audience members have direct influence in shaping the outcome of the festival. Second, actors exist on a material level, such as the films, festival venue, or host city. Third, and perhaps most importantly, actors can exist on a cognitive level. In the instance of queer film festivals, the films exhibited and the stakeholders involved all exist in the network with their own ideologies on sex and gender. According to Elsaesser (2005), film festivals "consist of a number of cooperating and conflicting groups of players, forming together a dense latticework of human relations, temporally coexisting in the same time-space capsule. They are held together, not by the films they watch, but by the self-validating activities they engage in" (101). Simply put, these stakeholders come together in the one environment not necessarily for the films they watch but for their own personal and professional fulfilment. This ANT approach to social and technical actors being inseparable will be a starting point for my application of the social enterprise model, but *not* an end point. The social enterprise model will allow this research to investigate the collective consequences of this relationship with regard to the complexities of the LGBT community.

Another quite similar approach to discussing the film festival in terms of a network is the concept of the field-configuring event. Lampel et al. (2008) define the field-configuring event as a "temporary social organization that encapsulates and shapes the development of professions, technologies, markets and industries" (1026). The film festival is a field-configuring event in that various stakeholders—journalists, filmmakers, film lovers, programmers, distributors, and so on—assemble on a temporary basis to further develop the film industry to "construct social networks, recognise accomplishments, share and interpret information and transact business" (1026). Ultimately, the film festival can be defined as a network of stakeholders, who all come from diverse organisations with diverse purposes (Rhyne 2009). This networking can create opportunities for social interaction including the construction of reputation and status. Furthermore, an increasing amount of film festivals engage with film production and distribution (Iordanova 2015). Rüling argues that while the film festival is establishing its identity, the stakeholders jointly create a "common meaning system by defining standards ... and by positioning the field in relation to entities outside of it" (2009, 51). This emergence of a field creates an institutional identity with "dominant field norms and logics, and to the protection and reinforcement of field identity" (51). The field-configuring event is an interesting approach to film festival analysis. However, while it allows for a discussion of how stakeholders create social networks, it cannot adequately address the role of film. While the field-configuring event is a useful tool to interrogate the effectiveness of conventions and events (Hardy and Maguire 2010; Schüßler et al. 2013), it cannot sufficiently address the complex social and political relationship audiences have with the films programmed. The field-configuring event approach would address how social networks manifest at Frameline and MQFF to shape and change the institutional field; however, this organisational analysis does not extrapolate the role queer cinema has on the cultural geography of their respective cities.

A third approach to film festival organisational analysis centres on the debate over whether the festival circuit is a network or not. According the Iordanova, the global film festival circuit is not inherently networked. As such, they are a "discrete phenomena that spring up independently rather than as part of an orchestrated move" (26). The film festival will establish only a *loose* network once it has a firm placing within its local community. De Valck (2007) sees that festivals can continue proliferating due to specialisation and that there is an apparent division of tasks, where "a small number of major festivals have leading positions as marketplace and media event and the remaining majority may perform a variety of tasks ranging from launching young talent to supporting identity groups" (45). Elsaesser too believes that festivals can flourish even further as "it has capillary action and osmosis between the various layers [and] is highly porous and perforated" (87). In other words, the network structure of the film festival is open to the transmission and exchange of information between differing festival networks and stakeholders. This specific point allows this book to examine the relationship queer film festivals have with other film and community organisations in their respective cities. For example, film festival selectors for MQFF are in constant contact with the much larger Melbourne International Film Festival (MIFF; their offices are separated only by three floors in the same building!). So when a queer film such as *Prodigal Sons* (Kimberly Reed 2008) is screened at MIFF with a rather small audience, it will still be programmed by MQFF. Another example on this point is how Frameline has developed relationships with other media organisation groups in the Bay Area, such as the Centre for Asian American Media (CAAM).

The film festival's description as an alternative distribution network is problematic. This perhaps simplistic view is questioned in various interrogations of the film festival (Elsaesser 2005; Iordanova 2009). How viable is the film festival compared with Hollywood, especially in regard to the various facets of the film business—distribution, production, and exhibition? While the film festival obviously doesn't have the financial power of Hollywood, there are still some glaring power differences at play as there are in Hollywood, such as the power of the festival director over the film director, and the real power being held by the film distributor. While the film festival does expose film content that the Hollywood market normally hides, large-scale film festivals are becoming less a site of cultural celebration of art-house cinema, with more and more blockbuster films (that are usually out of competition), celebrities, glitzy red carpets, and accredited journalists (Iordanova 2009). Iordanova's conclusion that the film festival is more an alternative exhibition network than an alternative distribution network seems more apt. This is especially relevant to this book, as many films programmed don't receive commercial exhibition outside of the realm of the queer film festival.

In relation to the queer film festival, the network can go only so far. While discussing the film festival as a network, whether it be through ANT, the field-configuring event, or the film festival as an alternative distribution network, this conceptual framework fails to highlight how social empowerment occurs nor does it allow for the cultural complexity that programming around sexuality and gender identity actually entails. LGBTI and queer programming strategies are markedly different from those other types of film festival, as early incarnations owe much to the activism of earlier social movements (Loist 2012). The relationship between the queer film festival and social empowerment is complex in nature. While one can exult over the UN-style diversity in the queer film festival programme, does this actually change the inequality evident *within* the LGBTI community? The multi-faceted influence programming times, neighbourhood locations, and audience needs to be addressed in order to identify *how* social empowerment transpires in the queer film festival environment. An organisational approach would not adequately allow this. As such, this requires further research into other areas of the film festival.

The film selection process and programming strategy can be critiqued further by applying Pierre Bourdieu's analysis (1984) of the social mechanisms behind taste and distinction in a discussion of value and critical capital (and in turn the power behind this capital):

> By broadening the palette of competitive and non-competitive sections festivals are not only democratizing access. New power-structures are introduced and other differentials operate: for instance, delegating the selection for certain sections to critics or to other bodies inevitably creates new forms of inclusion and exclusion, and above all new kinds of hierarchies, hidden perhaps to the spectators, but keenly felt by producers and makers (Elsaesser 2005, 96).

This broad palette of competitive and non-competitive sections of the film festival creates two types of film festivals. According to Peranson (2008), we have the prestigious business film festivals, such as Cannes and Sundance, whose audiences are control groups for distributive purposes. Second, we have the audience-friendly festivals, such as Vancouver and Buenos Aires, which are lauded as representative of utopian objectives. We can see a distinct difference in terms of the organisation's motivation. The purpose of the film festival is either to propel the industry forward or to provide an entertaining or otherwise enriching experience for the festival audience. This book will examine whether these objectives are mutually exclusive.

Key programming choices can be heavily influenced by the commercial sponsorship of festivals. In her analysis of the Hong Kong International Film Festival (HKIFF) making the transition from being government funded to corporately funded through sponsorship, Ruby Cheung (2009) argues that the "influx of commercial sponsorships that were introduced to replace public funding challenged the high art aspirations of the festival, turning it into a more populist film industry-driven market oriented event" (99). This transition has not helped films considered "high art" to gain distribution outside of the festival circuit as more populist films seem to be taking the spotlight.

Sponsorship should not be considered a philanthropic act but a financial exchange for advertising and promotion. Sponsorship decisions are made according to promotional benefits determined in advance. A successful sponsorship performance is judged in terms of visibility and awareness. In other words, how many consumers are receiving the message? For Cheung, the issue with supply and demand may mean that there will be no room for more edgy and experimental work. Although corporate sponsorship may financially strengthen a festival, programming freedom may become limited, and artistic integrity may become compromised.

This unstable balance cannot be thoroughly explored if we merely discuss the film festival in terms of its organisational practices as it ignores one quintessential aspect: the role of both the collective audience and the individual spectator in this environment. How has this development of the queer film festival shaped the audience member, in terms of being a consumer and engaging in a political activity? Discussing the queer film festival as a cultural organisation that has to balance both resource generation *and* delivering a socially relevant product to its audience will fill this void.

## The Audience

The queer film festival audience can be a powerful collective. The film festival audience is unique, being greatly unlike a general moviegoer, as "festivals do not just showcase cinema, they actively build audiences and communities" (Rastegar 2012, 312). In her analysis of the Glasgow Film Festival, Dickson finds that audience members tend to define their experience in terms of space and corporeality rather than cinema itself (Dickson 2015). She concludes that attendance at these events is an embodied practice, and, as such, more film festival research needs to address how being in the "physical presence in space with 'other bodies' is one of the most gratifying aspects of festival culture" (718). Festival programmes interpellate audiences in temporary events. The audience has the power to affect the subjectivity of the film through the film festival screenings being liminal "spaces of flow" (Harbord 2009), for example Midi Onodera's *Ten Cents a Dance* (1986), which created a riot amongst its predominately lesbian audience at the Roxie Theatre during Frameline in 1986. This event forever changed the subjectivity of the film as its most significant contribution to the queer community was inciting anger amongst its lesbian audience. Harbord defines a film as a recorded document of something past, which is then screened in the present. She sees that the "choreography of a dance between the live event on one hand and the recorded, pre-fixed film on the other is the manufactured time of the festival. The alchemy resulting from these different temporalities, the now and the then, characterizes the potency of the film festival as event" (44). The audience is an important player in the queer film festival environment as they have the power to imprint newer meaning onto the films being screened. We simply cannot separate the festival's meaning from its particular location. The specific moment of the screening attaches itself to the "notoriety" of the film, whether it wins an award or has a negative reaction with the audience.

These film festival screenings can shape marginalised identities into a collective imagined community. The "imagined community" was coined by Benedict Anderson in his book *Imagined Communities: Reflections on the Origin and Rise of Nationalism* (1983), which claims that the rise of nationalism and the imagined community are linked to increasing equitable access to national print media. The imagined community is the idea that each member will not necessarily meet face-to-face but still feel a shared collective identity. Anderson acknowledges that regardless of the "actual inequality . . . the nation is always conceived as a deep, horizontal comradeship" (7). Iordanova (2010) points out the difference between print media's role in the construction of identity and that of the film festival. Anderson states that the regularity of the newspaper addresses the reader as part of the imagined community within their respective nation, even though everyone reads the paper separately and at different times. This is somewhat different for the film festival as members of the community actually do come face-to-face at the same time. According to Iordanova, the film festival suspends "the 'imagined' element of the community by substituting it with a real one that is, nonetheless, configured around the same axis of imagination that drives the ideas of nation and nationalism" (13). However, how appropriate this description of the community being face-to-face is, remains to be seen, as gay and lesbian films are often programmed concurrently. There is also a secondary act of imagination occurring here, that of the relationship between the audience and the subjects on screen. There can be a self-identification with the subjects on the screen, even if they are fictional characters. The queer subjects on screen are available to be seen as a microcosm of "our" community. Thus, the community-oriented film festival realigns the symbolic boundaries conventionally associated with the imagined community. Anderson defines the nation as being a socially constructed community, imagined by members who perceive themselves to be part of that kinship, while Iordanova pushes this concept of community beyond the boundaries of the nation-state.

Iordanova's approach here can be deployed to situate the imagined queer community as an alteration of Anderson's original argument. Iordanova claims that audiences of transnational film festivals are asked to experience an "undisguised act of imagination, as an extension of a community that is 'headquartered' somewhere else but to which they, by virtue of their very attendance at the festival, now relate to through a mental image of affinity and through the act of their very real togetherness" (13). A majority of films programmed in any queer film festival would be from outside of the city the film festival calls home. However, by watching these films at the queer film festival, audience members are imagining an affinity with someone somewhere else (be they a subject in a documentary or a fictional character). Iordanova positions the transnational film festival as existing in plurality as opposed to singularity. By discussing MQFF and Frameline as taking place in cosmopolitan global cities, we can begin to unpack the intersectional nature of an imagined queer community that might entail as "festivals also work toward extending the 'imagined communities' by developing their very different geography and temporality in mediating transnational identities in a new way" (13).

Defining just what exactly the imagined queer community is can be difficult as the very notion of identity is a slippery one. For Howe (2008), they are similarities between the queer identity and nationalism as "both speak to political aspirations based on a shared sense of identity. However, although membership in a nation can only in certain circumstances be chosen, membership in a queer 'nation' is almost certainly chosen" (41). This "choice" of queer identity is clarified as actively based "on sexual practices, self-conscious forms of marking, and political positioning" (41). Participating in various activities such as political rallies or attending a film festival screening with one's fellow queers further consolidates this active group membership. This active participation with fellow queers can create mutual empowerment.

This reminds us that the queer film festival at its core is an *actual* festival. Elsaesser (2005) proposes that the festival is a site of self-celebration and self-performing. The audience plays an ancient role, that of the self-celebration of community (examples used are a community at harvest time or the arrival of spring), and also a modern and utopian one, the audience is the forum where "the people perform their sovereignty" (101). Both these aspects are applied to Luhmann's model of autopoiesis:

"the tendency of a system to set up close-circuit feedback loops with which it is stabilized internally, while also protecting itself from the surrounding environment" (102). This "closed-circuit feedback loop" represents the intimacy of the community and the audience, and the festival is stabilised internally by the sheer exclusivity of the film festival and the concept of a limited screening. Each film will often have only one or two screening sessions, and most films sell out.

Elsaesser's discussion on European film festival aids in an analysis of the queer film festival when we consider that the queer film festival *is* a festival for a specific community. For Elsaesser, the festival is a site of celebration:

> Festivals require an occasion, a place and the physical presence of large numbers of people. The same is true of film festivals. . . . Given their occasional levels of excess—one thinks of the topless starlets of Cannes in the 1960s and 70s, the partying, the consumption of alcohol, and often the sheer number of films—they even have something of the unruliness of the carnival about them (94–95).

While it is not my intention to downplay the festivities of the European film festival, the very essence of the queer film festival *is literally* a celebration of community. Frameline, for instance, coincides with the LGBT Pride festivities. Many screenings have after-parties or celebrations afterwards, such as the annual *Transtastic* shorts party or in 2010 where the band Le Tigre performed after their self-titled documentary. These carnivalesque celebrations are at the very core of the queer film festival, and it is this celebration of the "community" identity that makes the queer film festival a valuable alternative to the rigid power dynamics of Hollywood-produced commercial films with LGBT characters. Such festivals create public spheres, where they:

> Promote cinemas that articulate different experiences and expressions, and in doing so, they constitute alternative public spheres/counter-publics where ideas, often-times repressed or ignored in larger contexts, are exchanged and explored. These festivals do not see art as the ultimate goal of cinema (Wong 2011b, 160).

Here a queer counter-public allows for an existence apart from "the official publics of opinion culture and the state, or through the privatized forms normally associated with sexuality" (Berlant and Warner 1998, 558). The queer film festival can offer its patrons something Hollywood cannot: a collective identity. As such, this notion of the queer film festival audience being a counter-public requires this book to identify just *how* these audiences differ from traditional film festival attendance.

This book will examine how the queer community comes together during the queer film festival. Dayan (1997), a media scholar who looked at the Sundance Film Festival from an anthropological perspective, asked two questions. First, "how did different groups become an audience?" (Dayan as qtd in Elsaesser 2005, 95). And, second, "what were the inner dynamics of short temporary communities, such as they form at a festival, in contrast to kinship groups' behaviour at birthdays, religious holidays or funerals?" (95). Dayan discovered that film festivals worked with a higher fluidity of scripts as compared to other kinship events. The film festival is also not so much "defined by the films" but more by the media and "buzz" surrounding the festival that "has the double function of performative self-confirmation and reflexive self-definition, creating "verbal architectures" that mould the event's sense of its own significance and sustain its self-importance" (95). The queer film festival's audience is an amalgamation of various subgroups coming together for the festival, albeit usually for different screenings. Exactly how this performance and confirmation of identity occurs will be illuminated through this book.

These approaches to the film festival audience remind us that we must recognise the important role that the queer community and its organisations play in the queer film festival. In his aforementioned article on New York queer film festivals, Gamson (1996) argues that the collective identity of the audience is "filtered and reproduced through *organizational bodies*" (235, his emphasis). Individuals can take part in the imagining of their community, *and* their collective identity is actively constructed and settled upon by these communities (Taylor and Whittier 1992). Here, identities are constructed within an institutional environment (Scott and Myer 1991). Social movement theory asserts that the "collective search for identity is a central aspect of movement formation" (Johnston et al. 1994, 10) and that these movements are inherently socially and culturally motivated (Scott 1990). The very purpose of a group's social movement is the creation of a collective identity (Melucci 1996). This formation is an ongoing process that can at times cause conflict. Tension between "identity – putatively singular, unitary, and integral – and identities – plural, crosscutting, and divided – is inescapable at both individual and collective levels" (Calhoun 1994, 27). Gamson concludes that the social movement based on the collective identity of the queer community in New York is filtered through the organisational bodies of the film festivals through a balancing act:

> Between the 'top-down' structural imposition and the 'bottom-up' voluntaristic construction of collective identities sit there organizational bodies, filtering identity formulations. They do their filtering quite strategically, if often without conscious intent, as they attempt to strike a balance between the pressures of community standing and the pressures of their resource generation (257–258).

Ultimately, this interplay between commerce and art is a direct result of the advancement of neoliberal cultural policy, which I have discussed earlier in terms of queer cinema. Neoliberal cultural policy itself emphasises the economic pay-off of supporting and preserving culture; rather than culture for culture's sake, it underlines job creation, tourism, and income tax revenue (Gibson 2005). This international negotiation of culture and policy identifies the film festival as a "cultural contact zone" (Nichols 1994, 16) and a site of competition among new global cities (Stringer 2001). Rhyne (2009) sees the festival circuit as "maintained through the discourse and economic articulation of a discrete and new cultural industry" (10). Identifying the sometimes-messy relationships between various stakeholders (distributors, journalists, filmmakers, the audience, sponsors) in regard to neoliberal cultural policy within the institution of the film festival is crucial to understanding the sometimes-unstable balance of art, finance, and politics. This organisational outlook is ultimately a balancing act, which can be fleshed out further with the conceptual framework of the social enterprise, as conservative programming is the result of the relationship between financial viability and social empowerment. The framework of the social enterprise will allow me to interrogate how the queer film festival accomplishes its social mission and how it strengthens the queer community in terms of economic viability.

## THE SOCIAL ENTERPRISE

A common theme we have seen reoccur in film festival studies is the delicate balance of commerce and culture. This has never been more evident when we look at the queer film festival, which has to programme films that represent the diverse array of identities that are at play in the queer community, while still remaining financially sustainable. To interrogate how this balance plays out, I will use the framework of the social enterprise. Loosely defined, the social enterprise refers to market-focused activities serving a social goal (Doherty et al. 2009). What makes the social enterprise different from other business ventures are the intentions behind these organisations. Here we have mission statements concerning social activities whose financial surpluses are "principally reinvested for that purpose in the business or in the community rather than being driven by the need to maximise profit for the shareholders and owners" (26). For the non-profit organisation, the possibilities of what the social enterprise entails are exciting. Westall claims that the Social Enterprise is:

> A loose umbrella term which rouses the awareness of a variety of organizations that highlight alternative ways to do business that directly incorporate social and environmental concerns. This gives the possibility of creating revenue streams that enable an organisation to create sustainable social change without being reliant on time-limited funding or charitable donations (2001, 1).

While always having an unrelenting drive to achieve their objective, social entrepreneurs will seek out funding opportunities, financial relationships, and avenues for resources that many non-profit organisations would avoid. Social entrepreneurs will "engage simultaneously with government, philanthropic institutions, the voluntary sector, banks, as well as the commercial market to secure funding and other support where necessary" (Nicholls 2006, 10). This is where the careful balancing act between the mission and the money comes into play. While these various income streams make the organisation more self-sufficient, how far "reliance on the market can support sustainability is contested" (10). Furthermore, how far social enterprises can rely on the commercial market without compromising the social mission can also become an uneasy predicament.

The aim of the social enterprise is to create sustainable social transformations, where through the use of applicable business skills, there are both an innovative social impact and a mobilisation of resources (Alvord et al. 2004). Successful social enterprises create cultural and social change in regard to the original problem that the organisation's social purpose identifies. In other words, social enterprises address key market failures that don't meet supply and demand within a marginalised community or sector. What allows the social enterprise to create the possibility for dynamic change is that their "networks demonstrate an unrelenting focus on systemic social change that disregards institutional and organizational norms and boundaries" (Nicholls 2004, 10). The social enterprise's equal evaluation of both economic investment and cultural change is the catalyst for this transformation. For Alvord, Brown, and Letts, this social transformation concerns three key concepts. First, developmental studies that focus on the economic, social, and political change; second, organisation theory that helps us understand the core strategies for effectiveness; and finally, new social movement theory that looks at characteristics of social action, resource mobilisation, and the shifting of social identity formation.

A key dilemma that social enterprises face is the assumption that social and economic values must work in opposition. How can we measure both the creation of economic value and its social equivalent equally when measuring such social impact requires different methods from conventional economic practices (Nicholls 2006)? The intersection between financial investment and social returns is hazy and difficult to define. Traditionally, investors either want to make a profit or "give back" to the community. We work for either a non-profit or a for-profit organisation, and the social enterprise blurs this boundary between the two (Dart 2004). Furthermore, the middle ground between the two polar opposites is an area still not agreed upon by academics (Mair et al. 2006). Moreover:

> All investments are understood to operate simultaneously in economic, social, and environmental realms. There is no "trade off" between the three, but rather a concurrent pursuit of value—social, financial, and environmental. Regardless of the equation involved, the parts operate together, in concert, at all times. They cannot be separated and considered as distinct propositions, but are one and the same (Emerson 2003, 45).

These three different realms are not opposing but inseparable. All results from investments create significant worth that is economic, social, *and* environmental—a blended result. The cultural and political transformative possibilities of the social enterprise are just as important as the economic investment into projects with social missions. Economically orientated academics usually explain the social enterprise as a rational and functional solution to public sector funding and philanthropic resource constraints (Dees et al. 2001). This however eclipses the important opportunity for social movement as a result of successful social enterprises.

Raymond Dart (2004) believes that the *moral legitimacy* of the social enterprise should enable these organisations to be immune from economic-based evaluations. This form of legitimacy is the moral evaluation of business practices according to social norms and value systems (Suchman 1995). By being morally legitimate, these organisations are "normative and based on an evaluation of whether an activity of a focal organization is the proper one (relative to external norms) rather than whether it specifically benefits those who are making the evaluation" (Dart 2004, 416–417). Therefore, these organisations should not (necessarily) produce financially valued results and should not undergo rigorous financially based criticism. The social enterprise is enforced through its "pervasive political and ideological ideas about valid organizational models" (419). The social enterprise is a fitting conceptual framework, within which my analysis of the effectiveness of the queer film festival's social change can be further enhanced.

## APPROACH

Intensive fieldwork was carried out at my three primary case studies. I travelled to San Francisco to attend Frameline 35 in 2011. While subletting in the Mission District near Dolores Park, I had ample opportunity to experience the neighbourhoods of both the Mission and the Castro. Frameline 35 ran for 11 days from June 16 to June 26. This falls into the peak of San Francisco's Pride month. Earlier, I interned for Frameline's programming and hospitality department in 2009, which organised the attendance of more than 500 industry guests. This earlier stay in San Francisco helped forge the initial foundations for this research. While at Frameline in 2011, I attended screenings and industry parties and also joined friends in their usual Frameline outings, that is, see a film and have a drink at a nearby bar in the Castro. Carrying out fieldwork in Melbourne was significantly more straightforward as it's my hometown. I have been on the selection committee for the Melbourne Queer Film Festival since 2009. Given this background, I cannot classify myself as an ethnographic outsider in either fieldwork outings due to my close connections to both festival scenes. While I am observing social meanings and activities in "naturally occurring settings or fields" (Brewer 2000, 6), I am still directly involved and engaged in these settings. While reflexivity is important in acknowledging one's own biases (Nightingale and Cromby 1999), I consider myself both an observer and a participant in this research. In September 2014 when I attended HKLGFF, I did consider myself as an outsider. This was my first time visiting Hong Kong, and I did not previously know the participants I interviewed.

Interviews were carried out during this fieldwork. They were semi-structured in nature and featured both those professionally involved with the organisation (or stakeholders) and audience members. The length of the interviews varied from 15 minutes to some that went over an hour. All locations were in a setting of the interviewee's choice. Locations ranged from their office, their home, and cafes, or sometimes even on a beach or in Dolores Park, San Francisco. Audience interviews are imperative for this analysis as reception studies tell us that the meaning of texts (and in this case also festival spaces) is not inherent and fixed but decoded according to the viewer's cultural background (Hall 1973). This highlights the subjective quality of arts and entertainment experiences. While stakeholders had the choice to remain anonymous, all allowed for the names to be used in this research. All audience members were given pseudonyms for their own privacy. Interviews with audience members consisted of friends and acquaintances and aimed to reflect diversity in age and sexuality and gender identity. Eight stakeholder interviews were conducted in Melbourne. Their positions given were their job titles when they were interviewed. Many have since changed positions within the festival or have since left. They were:

Lisa Daniel, former festival director.[4]
Rowena Doo, former festival general manager.
Crusader Hillis, former festival director.
Rohan Leppert, City of Melbourne councillor.
Liz Mutineer, selection panel member.
Shaun Miller, festival sponsor.
Mark Pace, selection panel member.
Madeline Swain, former festival director.
Paul Tonta, festival selection panel member.

Twelve stakeholder interviews were conducted in San Francisco. Their position descriptions are given for the time of the interview. Many have since moved on from Frameline. They were:

Sam Berliner, volunteer intern
Des Buford, director of programming.
Sarah Deragon, head of distribution.
Lares Feliciano, volunteer coordinator.
Jennifer Kim, director of development.
Nisa Poulson, volunteer intern.

Harris Kornstein, former communications and outreach manager.
Jennifer Morris, festival director.
K.C. Price, executive director.
Philip Walker, sponsorship associate.
Frances Wallace, sponsorship coordinator.
Alexis Whitham, programming and hospitality associate.

From HKLGFF, I conducted semi-structured interviews with the following:

Joe Lam, festival director
Gary Mak, festival co-organiser

To complement this fieldwork, archival research was also undertaken. Previous Frameline festival programmes were stored at the head office and were readily available upon request. All MQFF programmes are accessible online. I received old HKLGFF programmes from Gary Mak. Further archival research was carried out at the Victorian Gay and Lesbian Archives. This archival research greatly assisted in contextualising the history of these festivals. Archival research consisted of examining old programmes, posters, and other festival-related material. The festival programmes for both festivals were analysed in depth; specifically, Frameline's programmes from Frameline 31 in 2007 through to Frameline 35 in 2011, MQFF's programmes from 2008 through to 2012, and HKLGFF's programmes from 2011 through to 2014. Film festival ephemera are pivotal in the research of film festivals and must not be considered "beneath the value of serious documents, such as correspondence, financial statements, or internal operating orders" (Zielinski 2016, 140). Queer film festival programmes are critical to the archives of social movements.

## CHAPTER OUTLINE

This monograph has two central research questions. First, how has the queer film festival developed into a social enterprise? Second, how does this need for financial sustainability influence the programme? Chapter 2 focuses on the development and structure of the three film festivals. The development from traditional cultural policy to the creative industries forms the conceptual framework for my analysis of their history. The purpose of using this approach is to contextualise their transformation. Frameline was established in 1977 and was primarily a community art event. In the early 1990s, Frameline was unwillingly involved in the "Culture Wars," which saw Republicans attack the National Endowment for the Arts (NEA) funding projects that they found abhorrent. This resulted in Frameline losing this NEA funding and forced them to rely more on ticket sales and corporate sponsorship. Since then, the festival has grown to be a leading film institution. While Frameline's growth largely paralleled the conceptual shift from cultural policy to the creative industry, MQFF was very much born into the creative industry. MQFF's inaugural festival was in 1991 as part of the larger Midsumma festival[5] and was supported by a mix of government funding and corporate sponsorship, a significantly different beginning to Frameline. Finally, HKLGFF began as a niche cultural event at the Hong Kong Arts Centre and was revitalised in 1999 to be a commercial event. The three historical accounts are divided into stages of the festival's growth, which positions key advances alongside policy developments.

Chapter 3 examines the festivals in terms of six key characteristics of the social enterprise. This analysis draws on semi-structured interviews I carried out with festival staff members and associated stakeholders. Examination of the organisational structure of the festivals also supports this analysis. Chapter 4 marks the beginning of the second area of examination for this book. My second significant research question concerns the festival's programming. How does the social enterprise's need to balance financial and social values produce homonormativity in the festival programmes (if at all)? Chapter 4 considers homonormativity as a key term for analysis. This extrapolates the connection between the conceptual framework of the social enterprise and homonormativity. This forms the crux of this project. How does the need to balance social and economic values produce conservative programming? Can socially progressive films find their voice when they are a "hard sell"? This chapter offers textual analyses of the films programmed. For brevity sake, primary focus is on Frameline and MQFF. The feature-length narratives of each programme are examined in terms of the key features of homonormativity, with a select few undergoing a close scene analysis to demonstrate how both homonormative and socially empowering films are present in the festival's programming. These films will be decoded in accordance to three characteristics of homonormativity—depoliticisation, domesticity, and a hierarchy of sexual identity. This textual analysis is to be supported by audience interviews.

In Chap. 5, data from these semi-structured interviews is used to interrogate the space of the festival. One's experience at a film festival is so much more than merely watching the film. Space plays a key role in the experience of film. Both content analysis and interviews provide a multifaceted approach to how the films are programmed and experienced. Audience analysis for this project is twofold as perceptions of audience formation from the perspective of the festivals are examined alongside responses from audience members. These chapters, and ultimately this book as a whole, attempt to investigate whether there is a link between defining the queer film festival as a social enterprise and any conservative elements in the films programmed.

## Conclusion

On a disciplinary level, this research provides an innovative interrogation into several fields of study and adds a significant contribution to film festival studies, queer cinema, and social enterprise studies. Film festival studies are becoming an area of interdisciplinary interest for both film and cultural studies, which this research capitalises on. The film festival has developed into a cultural institution that provides value to the creative city. Exactly *what* this value entails will be explicated in this research. The development of the creative industry logic is discussed as having an impact on the queer film festival. In light of this, cultural policy's influence on the films programmed is examined. In terms of the creative industry, examining queer arts organisations makes for an interesting analysis as they have grown from being a marginalised grassroots minority that existed on the peripheral to being a valuable asset to any major arts event calendar. This analysis acts as an intervention into the topic of sustainability for queer organisations.

Finally, the contemporary diversity in queer cinema being exhibited is put under the spotlight. Queer cinema has developed to a heterogeneous collection of films, which is evident in contemporary queer film festival programme offerings. This book emphasises the diversity of LGBT cinema, from conventional homonormative gay and lesbian romantic comedies to edgier queer films akin to the underground experimental work shown in the early days of Frameline. I argue that maintaining this diversity is the key to the possibility of financial viability and social empowerment coexisting in the queer film festival. Ultimately, this book identifies the complex nature of queer film festival programming. To say that such programming is homonormative merely because the majority of the programming is divided along the gender binary is far too simplistic. The forthcoming analysis of the queer film festival problematises such simplistic assumptions as it moves beyond the analysis of film form and narrative to include the importance of the audience and the socio-geographic environment in political empowerment.

The queer film festival highlights the possibility for social empowerment to occur within the neoliberal framework of the contemporary creative industry. The queer film festival boom throughout the 1990s was a result of community organisations engaging in the economically minded creative industries. At surface level, the queer film festival is structured according to films for the boys and films for the girls—hardly a recipe for innovative programming. However, this book's exploration will identify that there are both complex economic and social factors involved in the production of these spaces.

## NOTES

1. Quintessential examples of commodified urban gay communities are the Castro District of San Francisco and Greenwich Village in Manhattan.
2. Specific histories of both Frameline and MQFF will be presented in Chap. 2.
3. On a personal note, I have the same hesitance when acquaintances use the term "faggot" in a similar vain.
4. Lisa Daniel was the director of the festival at the time of the interview.
5. Midsumma is a Melbourne LGBT arts and cultural festival in summer.

## WORKS CITED

Alvord, Sarah H., L. David Brown, and Christine W. Letts. 2004. Social Entrepreneurship and Societal Transformation. *The Journal of Applied Behavioural Sciences* 40(3): 260–282.

Anderson, Benedict. 1983. *Imagined Communities: Reflections on the Origin and Spread of Nationalism*. London: Verso.

Anderson, Joceline. 2012. From the Ground Up: Transforming the Inside Out LGBT Film and Video Festival of Toronto. *Canadian Journal of Film Studies| Revue Canadienne d'Études Cinématographiques* 21(1): 38–57.

Berlant, Lauren, and Michael Warner. 1998. Sex in Public. *Critical Enquiry* 24(2): 547–566.

Bourdieu, Pierre. 1984. *Distinction: A Social Critique of the Judgement of Taste*. Trans. Richard Nice. Cambridge, MA: Harvard University Press.

Brewer, John D. 2000. *Ethnography*. Buckingham: Open University Press.

Calhoun, Craig. 1994. *Social Theory and the Politics of Identity*. Cambridge: Blackwell.

Callon, Michel. 1986. Some Elements of a Sociology of Translation: Domestication of the Scallops and the Fishermen of St Brieuc Bay. In *Power, Action and Belief: A New Sociology of Knowledge*, ed. John Law, and Paul Kegan, 196–233. London: Routledge.

Cheung, Ruby. 2009. Corporatising a Film Festival: Hong Kong. In *Film Festival Yearbook: The Festival Circuit*, ed. Raghan Rhyne, and Dina Iordanova. St Andrews: College Gate Press.

Cunningham, Stuart. 2004. The Creative Industries after Cultural Policies: A Genealogy and Some Possible Preferred Futures. *International Journal of Cultural Studies* 7(1): 105–115.

Dart, Raymond. 2004. The Legitimacy of Social Enterprise. *Nonprofit Management and Leadership* 14(4): 411–424.

Dayan, Daniel. 1997. In Quest of a Festival (Sundance Film Festival). *National Forum*, September 22.

De Valck, Marijke. 2007. *Film Festivals: From European Geopolitics to Global Cinephilia*. Amsterdam: Amsterdam University Press.

———. 2014. Supporting Art Cinema at a Time of Commercialization: Principles and Practices, the Case of the International Film Festival Rotterdam. *Poetics* 42: 40–59.

Dees, Gregory, Jed Emerson, and Peter Economy. 2001. *Enterprising Nonprofits*. New York: Wiley.

Dickson, Lesley-Ann. 2015. 'Ah! Other Bodies!': Embodied Spaces, Pleasures and Practices at Glasgow Film Festival. *Participations: Journal of Audience & Reception Studies* 12(1) 703–724. Accessed on 15 July 2015 at: http://participations.org/Volume%2012/Issue%201/39.pdf

Doherty, Bob, et al. 2009. *Management for Social Enterprise*. London: Sage Publications.

Drucker, Peter. 2011. The Fracturing of LGBT Identities under Neoliberal Capitalism. *Historical Materialism* 19(4): 3–32.

Duggan, Lisa. 2003. *The Twilight of Equality: Neoliberalism, Cultural Politics, and the Attack on the Democracy*. Boston, MA: Beacon Press.

Elsaesser, Thomas. 2005. *European Cinema: Face to Face with Hollywood*. Amsterdam: Amsterdam University Press.

Emerson, Jed. 2003. The Blended Value Proposition: Integrating Social and Financial Results. *California Management Review* 45(4): 35–51.

Fernandez, Sharon. 2006. More than an Arts Festival: Communities, Resistance, and the Story of Desh Pardesh. *Canadian Journal of Communications* 31(1).

Ferrelli, Joseph. 1999. *Celebrating Our Media Heritage with FILMOUT: The San Diego Lesbian, Gay, Bisexual, and Transgender Film Festival: Queer by Any Other Name*. Master's Thesis. San Diego, CA: San Diego State University.

Ford, Akkadia. 2014. Curating a Regional, Queer Film Festival. *Fusion* 4. Accessed on 15 July 2015 at: http://www.fusion-journal.com/issue/004-fusion-the-town-and-the-city/curating-a-regional-queer-film-festival

Foucault, Michael. 1988. Power and Sex. In *Politics, Philosophy*, ed. Kritzman, Lawrence D., 197–210. Trans. David J. Parent. New York: Routledge.

Fung, Richard. 1999. Programming the Public. *GLQ: A Journal of Gay and Lesbian Studies* 5(1): 89–93.

Galt, Rosalind, and Karl Schoonover. 2014. Minds, Bodies, and Hearts: Flare London LGBT Film Festival 2014. Festival review. *NECSUS: European Journal of Media Studies* 3(2), 217–224. Accessed on 15 July 2015 at: http://www.necsus-ejms.org/minds-bodies-hearts-flare-london-lgbt-film-festival-2014

Gamson, Joshua. 1996. The Organizational Shaping of Collective Identity: The Case of Lesbian and Gay Film Festivals in New York. *Sociological Forum* 11(2): 231–261.

Gibson, Chris. 2005. The 'Cultural Turn' in Australian Regional Economic Development Discourse: Neoliberalising Creativity? *Geographical Research* 43(1): 93–102.

Gretsch, Jenna. 1997. *San Francisco International Lesbian and Gay Film Festival and Its Global Discourse*. Master's Thesis. San Francisco, CA: San Francisco State University.

Hall, Stuart. 1973. *Encoding and Decoding in the Television Discourse*, vol 7. Birmingham: Centre for Cultural Studies, University of Birmingham.

Harbord, Janet. 2009. Film Festivals—Time Event. In *Film Festival Yearbook: The Festival Circuit*, ed. Raghan Rhyne, and Dina Iordanova, 3–4. St Andrews: College Gate Press.

Hardy, Cynthia, and Steve Maguire. 2010. Discourse, Field-Configuring Events, and Change in Organisations and Institutional Fields: Narratives of DDT and the Stockholm Convention. *Academy of Management Journal* 53(6): 1365–1392.

Hawkins, Gay. 1993. *From Nimbin to Mardi Gras: Constructing Community Arts*. St. Leonards, NSW: Allen & Unwin.

Hesmondalgh, David and Pratt, Andy. 2005. Cultural Industries and Cultural Policy. In *International Journal of Cultural Policy* 11(1), 1-13.

Hesmondhalgh, David. 2008. Cultural and Creative Industries. In *The Sage Handbook of Cultural Analysis*, ed. Tony Bennett, and John Frow. Los Angeles, CA: SAGE.

Howe, Alyssa Cymene. 2008. Queer pilgrimage: The San Francisco homeland and identity tourism. *Cultural Anthropology* 16(1): 35–61.

Iordanova, Dina. 2009. The film festival circuit. In *The flim festival yearbook: The festival circuit*, ed. Ragan Rhyne and Dina Iordanova, 23–39. St Andrews, Scotland: College Gate Press.

Iordanova, Dina. 2010. Mediating Diasora: Film Festivals and 'Imagined Communities'. In *Film Festival Yearbook 2: Film Fesitvals and Imagined Communities*, ed. Dina Iordanova, and Ruby Cheung. St Andrews: St Andrews Film Studies.

———. 2015. The Film Festival as an Industry Node. *Media Industries* 1(3). Accessed on 15 July 2015 at: http://www.mediaindustriesjournal.org/index. php/mij/article/view/98

Jagose, Annemarie. 1996. *Queer Theory*. Carlton: Melbourne University Press.

Johnston, Hank, Enrique Larana, and Joseph Gustfield. 1994. *New Social Movements: From Ideology to Identity*. Philadelphia, PA: Temple University Press.

June, Jamie. 2003. *Is It Queer Enough?: An Analysis of the Criteria and Selction Process for Programming Films within Lesbian, Gay, Bisexual, Transgender, and Queer Film Festivals in the United States*. Master's Thesis. The University of Oregon.

Lampel, Joseph, and Alan D. Meyer. 2008. Field-Configuring Events as Structuring Mechanisms: How Conferences, Ceremonies, and Trade Shows Constitute New Technologies, Industries, and Markets. *Journal of Management Studies* 45(6): 1025–1035.

Latour, Bruno. 1987. *Science in Action: How to Follow Scientists and Engineers through Society*. Cambridge, MA: Harvard University Press.

Loist, Skadi. 2011. Precarious Cultural Work: About the Organization of (Queer) Film Festivals. *Screen* 52(2): 268–273.

———. 2012. A Complicated Queerness: LGBT Film Festivals and Queer Programming Strategies. In *Coming Soon to a Festival Near You: Programming Film Festivals*, ed. Jeffrey Ruoff. St Andrews: St Andrews Film Studies.

———. 2014. *Queer Film Culture: Performance Aspects of LGBT/Q Film Festivals*. Hamburg: Universität Hamburg, Institut für Medien und Kommunikation.

———. 2016. The Film Festival Circuit: Network, Hierarchies, and Circulation. In *Film Festivals: History, Theory, Method, Practice*, 49–64. London: Routledge.

Mair, Johanna, Jeffrey Robinson, and Kai Hockerts. 2006. *Social Entrepreneurship*. London: Palgrave Macmillan.

McGuigan, Jim. 2004. *Rethinking Cultural Policy*. Buckingham: Open University Press.

Melluci, Alberto. 1996. *Challenging Codes: Collective Action in the Information Age*. Cambridge, MA: Cambridge University Press.

Mtewa, Phumi. 2003. GLBT Visions for an Alternative Globalization. In *Globalization: GLBT Alternatives*, ed. Irene Leon, and Phumi Mtewa, 35–48. *Quito*: GLBT South-South Dialogue.

Nicholls, Alex. 2004. *Social Return on Investment: Valuing What Matters*. London: New Economics Foundation.

———. 2006. *Social Entrepreneurship: New Models of Sustainable Social Change*. Oxford: Oxford University Press.

Nichols, Bill. 1994. Global Image Consumption in the Age of Late Capitalism. *East-West Film Journal* 8(1): 68–85.

Nightingale, David, and John Cromby. 1999. *Social Constructionist Psychology*. Buckingham: Open University Press.

O'Clarke, Eric. 1999. Queer Publicity at the Limits of Inclusion. *GLQ: A Journal of Lesbian and Gay Studies* 5(1): 84–89.

Ong, Aihwa. 2006. *Neoliberalism as Exception: Mutations in Citizenship and Sovereignty*. Durham, NC: Duke University Press.

Peranson, Mark. 2008. First You Get the Power, Then You Get the Money: Two Models of Film Festivals. In *Dekalog 3: On Film Festivals*, ed. Richard Porton, 37. London: Wallflower.

Pidduck, Julianne. 2003. *New Queer Cinema: A Critical Reader*. Edinburgh: Edinburgh University Press.

Rastegar, Roya. 2012. Difference, Aesthetics and the Curatorial Crisis of Film Festivals. *Screen* 53(3): 310–317.

Reed, Christopher. 1993. 'Queer' a Sneer No More. *The Age*, June 30, 15.

Rhyne, Raghan. 2007. *Pink Dollars: Gay and Lesbian Film Festivals and the Economy of Visibility*. PhD Dissertation. New York: New York University.

———. 2009. Film Festival Circuits and Stakeholders. In *Film Festival Yearbook: The Festival Circuit*, ed. Raghan Rhyne, and Dina Iordanova. St Andrews: St Andrews Film Studies.

Rich, B. Ruby. 1999. Collision, Catastrophe, Celebration: The Relationship between Gay and Lesbian Film Festivals and Their Public. *GLQ: A Journal of Lesbian and Gay Studies* 5(1): 79–84.

———. 2000. Queer and Present Danger. *Sight and Sound*, 80, March. http://www.bfi.org.uk/sightandsound/feature/80

Rüling, Charles-Clemens. 2009. Festivals as field-configuring events: The Annecy International Animated Film Festival and Market. In *The flim festival yearbook: The festival circuit*, ed. Ragan Rhyne and Dina Iordanova, 49–66. St Andrews, Scotland: College Gate Press.

Schüßler, Elke, Charles Rüling, and Bettina Wittneben. 2013. On Melting Summits: The Limitations of Field-Configuring Events as Catalysts of Change in Transnational Climate Policy. *Academy of Management Journal* 57(1): 140–171.

Scott, Alan. 1990. *Ideology and the New Social Movement*. London: Unwin Hyman.

Scott, Richard, and John Meyer. 1991. The Organization of Societal Sectors: Propositions and Early Evidence. In *The New Institutionalism in Organizational Analysis*, ed. Paul DiMaggio, and Walter Powell, 180–140. Chicago: Chicago University Press.

Seidman, Steven. 1994. Queer-ing sociology, sociologizing queer theory: An introduction. *Sociological Theory* 12(2): 166–177.

———. 1993. Identity politics in a postmodern gay culture: Some conceptual and historical notes. In *Fear of a Queer Planet*, ed. Michael Warner, 105–142. Minneapolis: University of Minnesota Press.

Siegel, Mark. 1997. Spilling Out onto Castro Street. *Jump Cut* 41(May 1997): 131–136.

Straayer, Chris, and Thomas Waugh (ed). 2006. Queer Film and Video Festival Take: Critics Speak Out. *GLQ: Journal of Gay & Lesbian Studies* 12(4): 599–625.

Stringer, Julian. 2001. Global Cities and the International Film Festival Economy. In *Cinema and the City: Film and Urban Societies in a Global Context*, ed. Mark Shiel, and Tony Fitzmaurice, 134–144. Oxford: Blackwell Publishers.

Stringer, Julian. 2003. Neither one thing nor the other: Blockbusters at film festivals. In *Movie blockbusters*, ed. Julian Stringer, 202–214. London and New York: Routledge.

Suchman, Mark. 1995. Managing legitimacy: Strategic and instiutional approaches. *Academy of Management Review* 20(3): 571–610.

Taylor, Verta, and Whittier, Nancy. 1992. Collective Identity in Social Movement Communities. In *Frontiers in Social Movement Theory*, eds. Alon Morris and Carol McClurg Mueller. New Haven, CT: Yale University Press.

Vaid, Urvashi. 1995. *Virtual Equality: The Mainstreaming of Lesbian and Gay Liberation*. New York: Anchor Books.

Westall, Andrea. 2001. *Value Led, Market Driven-social Enterprise Solutions to Public Policy Goals*. London: Institute of Public Policy Research.

White, Patricia. 1999. Introduction: On Exhibitionism, in Queer Publicity: A Dossier on Lesbian and Gay Film Festivals. *GLQ: A Journal of Gay & Lesbian Studies* 5(1): 73–78.

Wolfe, Susan J., and Julia Penelope (ed). 1993. *Sexual Practice, Textual Theory: Lesbian Cultural Criticism*. Cambridge, MA: Blackwell.

Wong, Day. 2011b. *Visual Anthropology* 24: 152–170.

Zielinski, Gerald J.Z. 2016. On Studying Film Festival Ephemera: The Case of Queer Film Festivals and Archives of Feelings. In *Film Festivals: History, Theory, Method, Practice*, ed. Marijke de Valck, Brendan Kredell, and Skadi Loist, 138–158. London: Routledge.

## INTERVIEWS

Badalu, John, email message to author, 15 January 2015.

## CHAPTER 2

# The Queer Film Festival and the Creative Industries

In the Californian summer of 2009, I undertook an internship with the San Francisco Frameline International LGBT Film Festival as the programming and hospitality associate. Having never travelled to America before, it was a very exciting and tumultuous time in my life. I had no concrete idea what I wanted to do with my career; I had left a boyfriend back in Melbourne, and I was incredibly nervous as to whether I was up to the standards the festival required. Three months later, once the festival was over and I was saying goodbye to my new dearest friends in the Frameline office, I had grown both professionally and personally. My interactions with many of the staff and festival guests had shaped my understanding of queer media. Part of my role as the programming and hospitality associate was to organise all of the industry guests attending the festival. This included manually entering all of their details into festival database, and at over 400 guests, this took quite a while. One day while talking with a co-worker, I commented at how diverse the guests were. We had filmmakers, actors, distributors, journalists, programmers, and so forth coming from all over the world. My colleague simply replied, "of course they are, we are Frameline. If programmers from smaller festivals want to have a strong program, they need to be aware of what is going on internationally in the queer film festival circuit; and Frameline is a very influential player in that circuit." My own personal observations later came to support this opinion. At almost 40 years old and having a regular turnout of over 60,000 attendees, Frameline is the oldest and one of the largest queer film festivals worldwide. Being situated in San Francisco—a city with a strong vibrant history of queer activism—is another

© The Author(s) 2016
S.J. Richards, *The Queer Film Festival*,
DOI 10.1057/978-1-137-58438-0_2

factor that positions Frameline as a key player in queer media internationally. Frameline's growth makes the organisation a leading player and key example of an arts organisation embracing the creative industry. As the festival grew, the organisation was no longer reliant on philanthropic gestures or government funding but became an economically sustainable non-profit business.

My second case study for this chapter, the Melbourne Queer Film Festival (MQFF), has grown significantly over the last two decades from being organised out of the back of a bookstore to now being one of the largest queer film festivals in Australia. MQFF began as a small subsidiary event for Midsumma, a Melbourne gay and lesbian arts and culture festival. Through numerous changes in directors, the festival found its secure footing with director Lisa Daniel and board president Claire Jackson. The festival's growth reflects a transition from being funded as a community-run organisation to an event that receives grants that aims to develop cultural organisations to be self-sufficient. MQFF is a model example in an art organisation's road to increased professionalism.

The third case study in this chapter looks at the Hong Kong Lesbian and Gay Film Festival (HKLGFF). The festival's history has two distinct periods. The festival was originally held in 1989 in the Hong Kong Arts Centre. These early years saw HKLGFF functioning as a niche cultural event. Programming decisions were independent from the entrepreneurial demands of a commercial organisation. The festival was on a hiatus for much of the 1990s. Raymond Yeung, Shu Kei, and Wouter Barendrecht reignited the festival as a commercial venture, which saw the festival funded through private funding and sponsorship.

These three case studies represent different positions in the queer film festival circuit. Frameline played an influential role in the formation of early queer film festival culture in the 1970s, which according to Loist "started out as places where independent community films could be shown and the negative portrayal of homosexuality in Hollywood films could be countered" (Loist 2013, 109). This was one of my three case studies to have been established during the first of the four phases established in Rhyne's historical analysis (2007). There were, however, numerous screenings and events showcasing queer cinema in major cities with vibrant LGBTI communities, such as Montreal, London, Sydney and Melbourne. Following Frameline's first festival as "Persistence of Vision," festivals began in New York, Chicago, Los Angeles, Pittsburgh and Boston. Loist's analysis of the subsequent global expansion highlights the uneven nature of this circuit. Festivals did not occur in Europe until 1984 in the former Yugoslavia, now Slovenia. Festivals subsequently began in Central and Western Europe throughout the 1980s. Rhyne's second historical phase sees the beginning of MQFF and the first few years of HKLGFF. Rhyne characterises this period by "newly defined relationships between gay and lesbian film festivals, and the commercial industry" (Rhyne 2007, 4). This second wave of development saw both the professionalisation of existing festivals and the birth of new organisations—mostly in North America and Western Europe. Early Australian film festivals, Melbourne in 1991 and Sydney in 1993, adopted the queer label comparatively earlier than their international counterparts due to the activist nature of the programmers at the helm (Searle 1997). While HKLGFF began in 1989 (temporarily) and Tokyo in 1992, Rhyne notes that the expansion of queer film festivals did not take off in East Asia till the late 1990s/late 2000s, which saw many organisations having issues with local authorities, such as Seoul (1998), Bangkok (1998), and Jakarta (2001). HKLGFF did not reignite this wave until 1999.

Loist (2013) warns against claiming that the global expansion of queer cinemas is a form of Americanisation and homogenisation, arguing:

> Global sexual identities developed in relation to Western models as well as to national forms of capitalism, nation building and local norms of gender and sexuality. There is no linear of progress to be told about global queer identities. Instead, there are several simultaneous activisms and strategies in place (117).

As such, we need to consider each festival in relation to its regional political climate and creative industry structure. This chapter will explore how the festivals in San Francisco, Melbourne, and Hong Kong have matured. Their growth demonstrates the industrial shift in cultural policy to incorporate the logic of the creative industry. This transition will form the conceptual framework for my analysis of the history of these queer film festivals. The creative industries have become an integral mode of analysis in film festival scholarship. As governmental funding becomes increasingly competitive, arts organisations must engage in alternative funding streams. Harnessing the economic potential of creativity has become a strategic imperative for urban planners and policy makers (Caves 2000; Florida 2008; Howkins 2001; Landry 2008). The film festival is an important creative industry that plays a key role in branding cities, where they make the city "cool" and attract tourists (Pederson and Mazza 2011). From this urban planning perspective, festivals can be a "catalyst for urban renewal, attracting tourists and capital investments, enhancing a city's image and creating new jobs" (Crespi-Valbona and Richards 2007, 106). This chapter will establish that the queer film festival now serves multiple constituents, both their respective queer communities and stakeholders that have a financial interest harnessing this creativity. These historical accounts will demonstrate the change in value produced from queer film festivals. This chapter will detail the various stages in the growth from being a grassroots organisation to an institutionalised festival. This structure will aid in contextualising a contemporary analysis of these festivals.

## FRAMELINE'S HISTORY

### 1977–1989: The Growth of a Grassroots Organisation

Frameline has its origins as a grassroots community arts festival. This discussion of its early years sees the formation of the organisation from being underground to becoming a legitimate community event. This growth demonstrates the aesthetic value created by traditional cultural policy. The relationship between cultural policy and cultural value will be a key theme in Frameline's development. Cultural policy is defined as the institutional support that channels "both aesthetic creativity and collective ways of life – a bridge between the two registers" (Miller and Yudice 2002, 1). This changing nature of aesthetic value is characterised in three significant factors during this early period of the festival. First was the political climate within which the festival was born; second was the state of queer cinema and the various groups of films that Frameline programmed; finally, the festival's increased professionalism was aided by both the creation of a proper organisational structure and funding by the National Endowment for the Arts (NEA).

Cultural policy is a means of which the value of this aesthetic creativity is regulated and defined. These regulations of culture are "related to the etymological connection between 'policy' and policing. 'Cultural policy' has deeply entrenched connotations of 'policing culture', of treating it as though it were a dangerous lawbreaker" (McGuigan 1996, 6). Significant questions regarding cultural and aesthetic values arise when considering cultural policy, such as who determines a cultural object's value. Controversy and tensions arise as questions of taste are called into question. Such controversy in a Gramscian hegemonic social order is indicative of contemporary "pluralist democracies" (Berger 1995, 159). This act of assigning certain value to a creative aesthetic is a key facet of cultural studies today:

> That no object, no text, no cultural practice has an intrinsic or necessary meaning or value or function; and that meaning, value, and function are always the effect of specific (and changing, changeable) social relations and mechanisms of signification (Frow 1995, 145).

The cultural value produced by Frameline in its early years was for the purpose of social inclusion, a key aspect of traditional cultural policy. Cultural policy and access to the arts in turn become a form of social policy. Culture in this sense becomes a strategic tool for governments to assist marginal and socially excluded groups with cultural participation. Cultural policy aids socially disadvantaged groups to gain cultural capital. Devised by Bourdieu (1984) as a theoretical relationship between culture and class, cultural capital was the apparent relationship between educational success and access to the consumption of high culture. As such, cultural capital can be viewed as a means of which to tackle social exclusion (Bennett and Silva 2006; Mulligan et al. 2006). Social inclusion and exclusion have three different streams of thought according to Levitas (1998): in terms of social, economic, and political citizenship; as a result of moral decline in society; and in terms of social integration. Cultural policy is seen as a method to increase cultural capital by emphasising participation with the arts.

Negotiations of taste and value, as dictated by cultural policy, are complex and at times tenuous, especially when we take into account cultural policy as a tool for social inclusion. If we view social inclusion as a means of integration, then social inclusion through cultural policy is a means of hegemonic integration. Hegemony is the relationship between dominant and residual or emergent forms of ideology (Williams 1977).

> Hegemony is secured when the dominant culture uses education, philosophy, religion, advertising and art to make its dominance appear normal and natural to the heterogeneous groups that constitute society (Miller and Yudice 2002, 7).

In order for social inclusion and integration to be successful, these dominant and residual ideologies must be harmonious. Cultural works produced by these marginal groups must not disrupt the hegemonic order too greatly;

otherwise, social inclusion will not be achieved. This tension greatly characterised Frameline's history.

The climate within which Frameline was born was a synthesis of politics and art. The notion of community was at its core. Frameline began as Persistence of Vision, a grassroots collective of experimental film works screened at the Gay Community Centre at 32 Page Street in 1977 with a rented projector and a sheet pinned to the board. This first gay film festival was a direct result of the developments in both politics and film. Homophile organisations, such as Daughters of Bilitis and the Mattachine Society, transformed homosexuality from being a private sensitivity to a public collective identity (Armstrong 2002). The 1970s saw San Francisco's gay and lesbian community become an organised progressive movement following the New York Stonewall Riots of 1969, thus becoming one of the few birthplaces for the gay and lesbian rights movements in America. The status of San Francisco as a gay Mecca was perhaps best summarised by Carl Wittman (1970) in his seminal *Gay Manifesto*:

> San Francisco is a refugee camp for homosexuals. We have fled here from every part of the nation, and like refugees elsewhere, we came not because it is so great here, but because it was so bad there. By the tens of thousands, we fled small towns where to be ourselves would endanger our jobs and any hope of a decent life; we have fled from blackmailing cops, from families who disowned or 'tolerated' us; we have been drummed out of the armed services, thrown out of schools, fired from jobs, beaten by punks and policemen.
>
> And we have formed a ghetto, out of self-protection. It is a ghetto rather than a free territory because it is sill theirs. Straight cops patrol us, straight legislators govern us, straight employers keep us in line, straight money exploits us. We have pretended everything is OK, because we haven't been able to see how to change it – we've been afraid (3).

The political climate leading up to Frameline's first festival was indeed exciting with Harvey Milk rising to the affectionate identity as the mayor of Castro Street and eventually being elected as supervisor in 1977 (Shilts 1988). In her historical account of the early days of Frameline, Susan Stryker (1996) notes that many of the filmmakers at this inaugural event either worked or frequented Milk's camera store, thus resulting in a direct fusion of art and gay liberationist politics.

This fusion directly ties into the films programmed by Frameline. In the early days of Frameline, queer cinema was synonymous with experimental and independent filmmaking. According to historical accounts of the development of queer film (Russo 1987; Dyer 1990; Benshoff and Griffin 2006; Rich 2013; Mennel 2014), films with a queer sensibility were initially seen subtextually in both the Classical Hollywood era[1] and underground experimental short films. Such films included Kenneth Anger's *Fireworks* (1947), Jack Smith's *Flaming Creatures*, and Andy Warhol's *Blowjob* (1964) and *Couch* (1964). This underground scene was influenced by "new movie-going behaviour, the live theatre scene, 'beat culture,' and politics" (Staiger 2004, 168). Dyer states that these experimental films present internal conflicting experiences, which can be seen as a result of the then attitudes towards homosexuality. These films can also be viewed as a challenge to the conformities of mainstream life.

*Fireworks* is perhaps the earliest known experimental queer film to date. Dyer states that in this film, sexual desire is portrayed as a wild transcendent force that convention represses. Intensity conveys gay desire as part of an elemental system of power that defies and disrupts straight-laced conventional views of the world. What we can take from films such as *Fireworks* is that queer cinema was born outside of Hollywood's conventions. Works such as that of Kenneth Anger and Gregory J. Markopoulos led to more gay underground filmmakers in the 1960s such as the Kuchar Brothers, who produced artless representations of sexuality. According to B. Ruby Rich in the documentary *Fabulous! The Story of Queer Cinema* (Ades and Klainberg 2006), the audiences for these films were getting their fantasies fed, but their identities weren't being formed in a contemporary sense. Over the course of the 1980s, Frameline changed this.

The censorship production code in the USA, which was in force from 1930 to 1968, forced American audiences to turn to European film for their desire for sex in the cinema (Rich 2013). In this period leading up to the Stonewall riots, European gay and lesbian filmmakers such as Derek Jarman, Chantelle Akerman, Fassbinder, and Passolini challenged and critiqued the homophobic lens on life, such as Akerman's *Je, tu, il, elle* (1974), Fellini's *Satyricon* (1969), Fassbinder's *The Tears of Petra Von Kant* (1972), and Jarman's *Sebastiane* (1976).[2] Perhaps the most significant of these films was Jean Genet's *Un Chant d'Amour* (1950). These films further offered alternatives to Hollywood filmmaking and hence became highly influential on the development of queer cinema.

A notable category of film before the birth of "new queer cinema" in the early 1990s was that of the "loathsome film." This was a queer hybrid form of film that shocked and disgusted mainstream audiences (Harry M. Benshoff 2004). They can be described as examples of deliberate queer camp: they use deconstructive styles that deliberately critique gender and sexuality. Hollywood could often be seen celebrating films that present tragic homosexuals, comedic pansies, and lesbian vampires. Mainstream audiences could not accept these films that presented outrageous queer inversions of both traditional sexuality and Hollywood form. The critical backlash to these films forced Hollywood's complete avoidance of such queer characters and styles throughout the 1970s. Such films included *Boom* and *Secret Ceremony* (1968; both directed by Joseph Losey and feature Elizabeth Taylor), *Beyond the Valley of the Dolls* (Russ Meyer 1970), and *Myra Breckenridge* (Michael Sarne 1970). Another quintessential filmmaker, who produced films that shocked most with such queer irreverence, was of course John Waters with films such as *Female Trouble* (1974), *Pink Flamingos* (1972), and *Mondo Trasho* (1969).

The 1980s saw a significant rise in gay and lesbian independent filmmaking. Some gay-themed films of this era, such as *Prick Up Your Ears* (Stephen Frears 1987), *Waiting for the Moon* (Jill Godmilow 1987), and *Maurice* (James Ivory 1987), were withheld from gay and lesbian film festivals to avoid being labelled as exclusively gay or lesbian (Benshoff and Griffin 2006). Others were attempts at presenting a new gay sensibility with the full intention of making money from a gay audience, such as *Desert Hearts* (Donna Deitch 1985) and *Abuse* (Arthur J. Bressan 1983). These films presented subjects with affirmed gay identities. Frameline, from its inception in 1977 leading up to the boom of new queer cinema in 1991, programmed this assortment of experimental European films and those with either an affirmed gay sensibility or an outrageous queer content. All of these categories of film heavily influenced the programming decisions of Frameline in its early years. The programmes varied from experimental shorts to European showcases to American feature-length films.

A significant development with Frameline's programming was sparked by the event to which is now referred as the "lesbian riot" at the Roxie on June 25, 1986, following the depiction of gay male sex in Midi Onodera's *Ten Cents a Dance* (1986). This riot was seen as a result of discontentment with the lack of lesbian representation in the programming, which "reflected systemic gender-based economic inequalities in the film industry" (Stryker 1996, 367). Lumpkin and the board of directors responded with a concerted effort to promote diversity within the organisation. Frameline set up a completion fund, which was a premeditated resolution to enable women and people of colour to having access to equipment and finances to finish their project.[3] Guest curators for the festival later included Desi del

Valle and Jenni Olsen, thus providing lesbians of the Bay Area the ability to have a stronger voice in the organisation's planning.

This increasing importance of the festival to the Bay Area LGBT community in the 1980s saw Frameline mature from a grassroots organisation of ragtag political hippies to a professional film festival that was closely tied to its audience, which was a result of the diverse voices on the board and those that curated the programmes. For Rhyne, this period saw the regulation of the non-profit sphere, where "loose and informal organisations, through which queer cultural production was produced, distributed, and exhibited into narrowly defined non-profits" (Rhyne 2007, 73). The festival adopted the name Frameline in its fourth year of operation and became a legally binding corporation.[4] This allowed for the festival to apply for both public and private grants, and receive tax-deductible donations, which allowed gays and lesbians to participate "more fully in the non-profit sector as individual donors" (95).

By not having any direct mention of gays or lesbians, the name Frameline made it easier for charitable donations from those uncomfortable with being associated with such an organisation (Rhyne 2007). The fourth festival also saw the introduction of Michael Lumpkin to the organisation, who would run the festival until 2002. Lumpkin would become an incredibility influential figure that moulded the festival into a professionalised film festival:

> More than any other individual, he was responsible for the festival's remarkable transformation over the next decade. What had been primarily a forum for local film talent became, under his direction, a hip venue for film talent from around the world that drew an international audience, showcased the best work in queer film, and increasingly attracted the attention of the mainstream film industry (Stryker 1996, 365).

This is the third significant factor of this time period. The tenth festival in 1986 saw the festival take on a new level of professionalism by having the financial ability to hire Lumpkin as a full-time employee, which was largely a result of the $3.50 admission fee and its distribution arm founded in 1982 (Rhyne 2007). This is a significant transition in the organisation from being run by volunteers to paid employees. According to Stryker's historical account, the board of directors "began to serve more exclusively as a policy-making body" (366) and introduced the Frameline award for the year's exceptional contribution to queer cinema, which has since been won by Vito Russo, Divine, producers Christine Vachon and Marcus Hu and more recently the Kuchar brothers and the outspoken comedienne Margaret Cho.

The year 1988 saw the festival receive its first grant from the National Endowment of the Arts (NEA) thus establishing Frameline as a legitimate cultural organisation. The NEA is an agent of the US government to fund and support projects and organisations that exhibit "excellence, creativity and innovation."[5] This funding further propelled Frameline in an influential position in the field of queer media. As outlined earlier, the highlighted cultural policy aids in social inclusion. This traditional cultural policy upholds the "government's role as protector and upholder of key community values" (Craik 1996, 178). This act of the NEA supporting Frameline was an illustration of cultural democracy at play, thus increasing a populist participation in culture (DiMaggio and Useem 1979). By providing financial support, the NEA has identified Frameline as having a significant role in the production and maintenance of LGBT film in America.

NEA'S relationship with Frameline was a clear display of this cultural value being used as a tool for social inclusion. By supporting Frameline, a significant player in American LGBT film culture, the NEA was helping to open doors for cultural participation for a significant number of American citizens. As has been established, cultural policy is institutional support that encourages both creativity and cultural participation (Miller and Yudice 2002). This support from the NEA sees a marginalised minority become a legitimate community with its own cultural aesthetic. Multiple sites of power and control are a clear demonstration of governmental power with NEA's support for a queer organisation being in direct contrast to the current conservative government in office at the time. Up until the "Culture Wars" of the early 1990s, this was not seen as a conflict of interest.

### 1989–1995: Defiance amidst Crisis

For Frameline and the San Franciscan LGBT community at large, the early 1990s was a time of crisis and community defiance. By 1990, the festival had a significant number of paid full-time staff and temporary festival staff. This second period in Frameline's history was dominated by the so-called Culture Wars, which arose over significant differences of the aesthetic of taste. This defiance translated into queer cinema, which would transform LGBT film for the better. Two key aspects typify this period. First was the birth of "new queer cinema," a wave of queer films that were successful on the mainstream international film festival circuit; second was the conservative backlash from republican politicians over the NEA's support of Frameline. This support began to blur the lines between community amateur art and professional work. Ultimately, this debate highlights the fact that judgement of art that adheres to public decency is determined by a heterosexual society. This period for Frameline was a time for communal defiance.

The birth of queer theory and its radical adoption as a unifying term in the LGBTI community was directly related to AIDs activism during this period of cultural turbulence. The AIDS crisis, and the anger and homophobia that arose, brought about a "renewal of radical activism" (Seidman 1994, 172). AIDS activism fell under the modus operandi of queer due to the homophobic public response to AIDS (Creed 1994), rethinking of sexual practices and identities (Dowsett 1991), and the collective affinity of various minority groups coming together in the struggle. Queer and AIDS became interconnected, both through their anger and a "collapse of identity and difference" (Edelman 1994: 96).

In her now famous article "New Queer Cinema," B. Ruby Rich (1992) describes the new wave of queer film as a phenomenon:

> All through winter, spring, summer, and now autumn, the message has been loud and clear: queer is hot. Check out the international circuit, from Park City to Berlin to London. Awards have been won, parties held. At Sundance, in the heart of Mormon country, there was even a panel dedicated to the queer subject, hosted by yours truly (15).

Indeed, this new phenomenon of independent queer films was received well not just by queer film festivals but also by large-scale film festivals such as Cannes and Sundance. According to producer of films such as *Poison* and *Swoon,* Christine Vachon in *Fabulous!* (2006) stated that in the early 1990s, queer filmmaking and independent filmmaking were one and the same. According to Michele Aaron in her *New Queer Cinema* reader (2004), queer films from this period were united by their sense of defiance. They represent the marginalised *within* the contemporary queer communities. *Tongues Untied* (1989) and *Young Soul Rebels* (1991) both give insight into the black gay male reality; *My own private Idaho* (1991) has two male hustlers as its lead protagonists; and perhaps the most notable example is *Paris Is Burning* (1991), which explores the drag ball culture of black and Latino, gay, and transsexual communities of New York. These films were unapologetic of the lives these characters lead, as seen in both *Swoon* and *The Living End*, where at the centre of both narratives are murderous gay couples. According to Aaron's discussion of these films' defiance, these films defy the sanctity of the past in their narrative, they defy death, and ultimately these films defy cinematic convention. All the films of the new queer cinema era were experimental in some form or another. As Vachon notes in *Fabulous!* individuals that went to see *Poison* at Sundance would never have seen such an experimental film before.

This insurgence of new queer cinema grew exponentially and serviced a community that was in need of respite and queer intellectual stimulation. Writes Rich:

> New Queer Cinema was a more successful term for a moment than a movement. It was meant to catch the beat of a new kind of film and video-making that was fresh, edgy, low-budget, inventive, unapologetic, sexy and stylistically daring (22).

This escalation in queer independent cinema led to a dramatic growth in queer film festivals worldwide, which took their curatorial cue from festivals such as Frameline, Berlin, and NewFest in New York. The early 1990s saw an explosion of queer film festivals, including festivals in Hong Kong and Melbourne.[6]

In terms of Frameline's organisational growth, queer film and politics came to a head during this period when the NEA was put under pressure from Republicans to cease funding the festival. The NEA was established by the US congress in 1965 as an independent agency of the US government aiming to support artistic quality. The festival had been receiving money from the NEA since 1988 and was initially put into serious doubt in 1992 (Haithman 1992). Accordingly, in the same year B. Ruby Rich championed new queer cinema, the NEA defunded Frameline and two other queer film festivals. The festival had been attacked before with Sen. Jesse Helms in 1990 requesting a review of the grant and in 1991 with Rev. Donald Wildman's American Family Association attacking the grant stating federal money should not go to homosexuals. The 1992 defunding of Frameline followed a very bitter dispute between the NEA and the American Family Association in regard to a grant given to an exhibition featuring works by Robert Mapplethorpe and Andre Serrano's *Piss Christ*, with Sen. Jesse Helms stating:

The American people . . . are disgusted with the idea of giving the taxpayers' money to artists who promote homosexuality insidiously and deliberately, who desecrate crucifixes by immersing them in urine, and others who will engage in whatever perversion it takes to win acclaim as an artist on the 'offending edge' and therefore entitled to taxpayer funding (Helms quoted in Quigley 2010, np).

In 1989, Congress amended statutory rules that preside over the awarding of NEA grants to reject funding to obscene art (Adler 1996). In 1992, the NEA rejected Frameline's grant application for $20,000 in a move that was seen to be politically conservative. Tom DiMaria, former executive director for Frameline, believed that Frameline and other so-called controversial organisations were used as fodder to score points with the current conservative government, stating that "there's a lot of political consideration being given to this grant" (DiMaria quoted in Haithman 1992, np). Conservative public figures took specific issue with Frameline's distribution of *Tongues Untied* (Marlon Riggs 1992), a semi-documentary that details the prejudice black gay men feel from both heterosexual society and white gay men. The film had also previously received $5000 from the NEA. Frameline made the film available for purchase both institutionally and individually. This saw both Frameline and Riggs's film attacked by Jesse Helms's homophobic campaign on art that was deemed pornographic or homosexual (Gerstner 2007). Pat Buchanan used the film in his campaign against President George Bush arguing that taxpayers' money was funding pornographic material that glorified homosexuality. The film now holds a level of importance to both the queer film movement and Frameline, with a large poster of the film appropriately hung in the entrance to Frameline's office.

A key thematic concern of cultural policy is that of aesthetic and taste. This incident of NEA rejecting Frameline's grant application raises questions for a more general debate about public money going to art that is either "elitist" or "populist" (O'Neill 1997). Should public arts funding emphasise aesthetic quality or just increase access, thus blurring the boundaries between professional and amateur artists?

These conservative attacks on Frameline bring into questions of taste and decency, the boundaries of which are determined by a heteronormative society, a heteronormative society that the very essence of which organisations, such as Frameline, are trying to battle against. This is ultimately an essential example of what Raymond Williams (1976) refers to as the dominant hegemony in culture dictating to the residual and emergent formations. Yudice and Miller (2002) remind us "national cultural policies are, then, a privileged terrain of hegemony" (8). This conservative judgement of taste from the NEA is a clear display of the tension created when attempts at social inclusion fail to be a harmonious hegemonic negotiation.

In the 1992 festival programme, Thomas DiMaria released a statement about the loss of NEA's funding being a substantial financial loss. It is important to note that homophobic criticisms never originated from the NEA but from "organisations and individuals who have long opposed lesbian and gay visibility of any form" (DiMaria 1992, 7). This statement reminds the audience and readers of the importance the queer film festival plays in the community due to the very power LGBT visibility has:

> This festival is but a small part of centuries of work created by artists whom we would now call lesbian and gay. We must continue to see ourselves as part of that history … not only to prepare for the real struggles ahead, but to pay tribute to so many who have created their art in isolation … We owe it to ourselves, to those who have preceded us and to those who will follow to keep our culture alive, protected and prosperous. No one else will do this for us. For the foreseeable future we must continue to serve as or own critics, historians, artists and audiences. And that's an obligation we must all take seriously (7).

This public statement was a call to arms for the San Francisco community to support Frameline. It is a clear message of defiance that was typical of the queer cinema of the time. For Rhyne (2007), this is not only a discursive move but also indicative of "material strategies for making do in the face of the neoliberalisation of the third sector" (118). This forces these festivals to self-govern. This acknowledgement of the importance of queer cinema sets the trend for the festival's social mission for the coming years.

A brief mention of 1994 is required in any account of Frameline, as it was a significant year for the queer film festival's growth. Following the 18th festival, the festival's debts had risen steeply to the six-figure range (Stryker 1996). For Stryker, this was a result of a paradoxical explosive growth and a mixture of "structural problems and overhead costs that had sky-rocketed" (369). This crisis came to a head when the then festival director Mark Finch committed suicide on January 14, 1995. This tragedy galvanised only the queer community of San Francisco, with Boone Nguyen and Jennifer Morris rising to the challenge of running the festival, the latter of which has only recently resigned from her position. The 19th festival was an immense success, being only a few thousand tickets short of their record of 55,000 in 1994. The level of financial sponsorship had also reached an all-time high, which signalled a new period for Frameline as a significant niche market was established through this success. With the NEA rejecting Frameline's grant application, Frameline was forced to rely on alternative income sources for survival. Securing significant ticket sales and corporate sponsorship became imperative for the organisation's survival.

### 1995–2008: Queer Cinema Goes to Market

The late 1990s saw queer film ride the wave of gay and lesbian consumerism that was beginning to emerge. This "pink dollar" (as it so often referred to) was a result of an increasingly visible gay and lesbian community becoming a marketable niche. Gay and lesbian identities began to be increasingly visible in mainstream media. Although much later in the rise of gay and lesbian visibility, I personally remember watching *Will & Grace* (1998–2006), gay contestants on the Australian *Big Brother* (2001–2008), the American version of *Queer as Folk* (2000–2005), and the lesbian relationship of Willow and Tara on *Buffy the Vampire Slayer* (1997–2003). These were the first images I had personally seen that didn't paint queerness as a joke, and the effects it had on my personal psyche were momentous. Films, print media, and other commodities began to be marketed directly for a gay and lesbian market. Numerous investigations into this "gay dollar" found positive economic outcomes by targeting this niche community.[7] This noticeable economic value produced by the gay community influenced queer cinema becoming increasingly successful and a niche market. For a brief period in the history of queer cinema, numerous light romantic comedies could be marketed towards the gay community, theatrically released, *and* make a small profit. This is indicative of the mainstreaming of gay and lesbian culture during this period. The affiliation between these changes and the marketplace is indicative of neoliberal developments of cultural policy. This is the second key feature during this time period. This shift in cultural policy is driven by the economisation of creativity. This period sees contemporary cultural policy be driven by the creative industry, where culture and economy coalesce for the purpose of organisational development. This has implications for the role Frameline has within the definition of San Francisco as a creative city. Frameline is no longer a tool for social inclusion, but it creates newer forms of consumer value. As a capitalisation of an identity-based political movement, this consumption in turn "mediates the production of social identities" (Chasin 2000, 12). Chasin states:

Of course, people engaged in same-sex sexual behaviour have consumed commodities for as long as there have been commodities; what is new is constitution and consolidation of a social identity in the marketplace. Advertising is one of the central agents of the constitution and consolidation. Indeed, gay and lesbian identity and community were effectively consolidated through the market; in the 1990s, market mechanisms became perhaps the most accessible and the most effective means of individual identity formation and of entrance into identity-group affiliation for many gay people (24).

What remains to be seen is if this consumption legitimises the increased LGBT visibility and, furthermore, if this visibility and equality is distributed evenly to all members of this identity-based community.

During this period, Indiewood offered the opportunity for new methods of distribution for queer films. Indiewood, or the semi-independent film, is a term coined to describe the growth of studio-owned "specialty divisions" that distribute technically independent films. Frameline attempted to capitalise on this, and, in 1994, the festival held a film market to "offer buyers a place where they can scout for films to license in a variety of media" (Toumarkine 1994, cited in Rhyne 2007). A specific example of queer Indiewood in this period is the 1999 film *Trick*, produced by the production company Good Machine and bought by New Line Cinema, which is a subdivision of Warner Bros. Entertainment Inc. The film's synopsis is a simple one. It follows a 20-something musical-theatre writer one night as he and a go-go dancer try to find somewhere to have sex. According to Benshoff and Griffin (2006), the film was marketed heavily through queer film festivals and magazines directed to younger gay males leading up to its release date. For a budget of only $450,000, the film ended up grossing $2.08 million through selected distribution. As Vachon noted at a 2008 Sundance panel on how this film sums up this niche marketing: "No matter what you think of the movie, that movie was really made for exactly the right amount of money and it came out and everybody did well out of it" (Vachon 2008; cited in Knegt 2008, 35). This heralds a new period of queer cinema.

Frameline grew considerably and capitalised on this boom in the pink dollar economy. In speaking with Frances Wallace when she was sponsorship coordinator for Frameline,[8] there was initial hostility towards the concept of corporate sponsorship:

When I first started this job (and I had never experienced this in Australia, which has a more laissez-faire attitude towards sponsorship) there was a sort of backlash. I think that because San Francisco was so political, even some of my co-workers didn't like the fact that I did this job. They were anti-sponsorship; they started to see the festival change. It's a perspective of the 'queer radical left' that you're selling out to a corporation by taking their money. I see that in a culture like this, you are taking from the rich and giving to the queer arts and developing it. If that is the way to develop queer arts in this country, take as much money as you can possibly get (Interview with Frances Wallace 2011).

Gradually as I was in there the program built up quite significantly. That (negative feedback) has not been the case over the last 5 or 6 years. I have not had any negative feedback from either colleagues or externally at all. So I think that mentality has shifted as they see that's what's paying salaries and helping organisations (Interview with Frances Wallace 2011).

Frameline began to take on significant sponsorship deals. Their 17th San Francisco International Lesbian & Gay Festival in 1993 saw financial relationships with big names such as Skyy Vodka and Miller Brewing Company and with local gay businesses such as the Castro Village Pharmacy and their long-time partner Steamworks. The 19th festival in 1995 saw Charles Swab, Absolut Vodka (replacing Skyy), Virgin Atlantic, and the Guardian featured as significant sponsors. The gay and lesbian community provided a significant marketing opportunity for these companies, and Frameline was an avenue for these brand names to be positioned in a positive light for the gay and lesbian community. This was a significant portion of the LGBT community that Frameline has access to, considering the 50,000-plus attendees, the 300-plus festival volunteers, and the growing number of paid and unpaid office staff.

This complex relationship between LGBT culture and the marketplace is an indicative of the neoliberal development of cultural policy. At a higher level, neoliberalism paradigmatically promises material prosperity for all by casting aside a welfare mentality to cater for corporate and economic interests of a select few, to upwardly distribute power, money, and status (Duggan 2003). In terms of cultural policy, neoliberalism is perhaps best summarised by Schiller (1999) in that it is a "pairing (of) unwanted state oversight and regulation of the economy to gain more unfettered freedom of action for private firms" (1). Frameline became increasingly more financially reliant on sponsorship, donors, grants, and ticket sales, and less reliant on public funding. The consequences of this commodification of gay and lesbian culture are far-reaching. For McGuigan (2010), neoliberal cultural policy "is a truly hegemonic phenomenon of our time concerning both political economy and ideological process in the broadest sense" (117). This is ultimately capitalism in a new phase, where it is "no longer puritanical but hedonistic" (121) and, for McGuigan, it is "cool," in that it "invokes the seductive and apparently rebellious features of capitalism today" (122).

This is ultimately a shift of cultural policy being driven by economic concerns and referred to as the creative industries. The creative industries paradigm was first signalled by Britain's New Labour government's Department for Culture, Media and Sport's *The Creative Industries: Mapping Study* (DCMS 1998), where advertising, design, fashion, film, music, television, radio, and publishing amongst many other fields were said to generate a revenue of £60 billion annually and employee over 1.5 million people. This thematic intermingling of culture and the economy has seen the rise of the creative economy (Florida 2002), with industries of "science and engineering, architecture, and design, education, arts, music and entertainment, whose function is to create new ideas, new technology and/or new creative content" (8). Frameline's growth is very much a part of this creative industrial development. The ideological implications of the creative industry create a cultural capitalism, as this is a commercialisation of culture and experience itself (Rifkin 2000), where:

> Marketing is the means by which the whole of the cultural commons is mined for valuable potential cultural meanings that can be transformed by the arts into commodifiable experiences, purchasable in the economy (171).

As such, Frameline's role as a community queer arts organisation plays an imperative role in branding San Francisco as a creative city. A city's distinctiveness is fast becoming an organisational global objective in this branding exercise (Kavaratzis and Ashworth 2005). From the perspective of local authorities and city branding officials, film festivals are popular. They attract film businesses to the city, portray the city as a cultural place, and conduct film businesses (Ooi and Pederson 2010, 319). Frameline is such an example in branding San Francisco as a creative city through constructing the city as the central hub for queer cinema. San Franciscan films will always be played alongside International features. A key example would be the musical *Fruit Fly* (Mendoza 2009), where Filipino performance artist Bethesda moves into a share house in San Francisco as she searches for her biological mother. The film acts as a tribute to San Francisco, shot on locations in the Castro, Mission District, Dolores Park, and so on. There is even a song dedicated to their Muni public transport system. In both situating San Francisco as a place to conduct industry networking and supporting films that portray the city in a positive light, Frameline is actively playing a role in San Francisco as a creative city.

Frameline is often promoted alongside many other Pride events to position San Francisco as a gay tourist Mecca. Other key Pride events are the Pride parade, the Pink Saturday party in the Castro, the Dyke and Trans March, and the Castro Street Fair. Frameline and in turn other Pride festivities are integral to San Francisco's identity as a queer tourist destination. The Castro District especially "has become a vital aspect of San Francisco's tourist economy" (Boyd 2011, 246). The promotion of San Francisco's Pride festivities and gay marketing hooks reveal this spectrum. Sites such as sanfrancisco.travel, thegazstation.com, sanfrancisco.gaycities.com, or gaytravel.com all promote the city as a gay utopia for the traveller, ultimately promoting a citizenship unavailable at home. Even the commodification of gay marriage was used as a pull factor (Boyd 2008), where ultimately "queer tourism underpins and fuels a gay and lesbian rights agenda that assumes the attainment of 'modern queer sexuality' as its ultimate goal" (Puar 2002, 125).

We can see Frameline and other Pride events as key pull factors in promoting San Francisco as a gay utopia. Florida uses his "Creative Index" to measure the rate in which members of the creative class are attracted to such cities. The "Gay Index" is employed as a "reasonable proxy to an area's openness" (Florida 2002, 244–245). This is not to suggest a direct correlation between a city's gay population and a city's status as a creative city; the Gay Index is used to determine how open a city is to culturally alternative individuals. Likewise, Florida's "Bohemian Index" is used to chart the concentration of artists, musicians, and writers and so forth in particular cities. Florida contends that cities with high Bohemian and Gay Indexes create alluring environments for creative workers. Considering that the Bay Area is such a significant area for queer film (no doubt supported by Frameline), San Francisco rates notably high on both indexes. Community arts programmes can alter "broader social perceptions of a region" (Ho 2012, 35). A revision of Florida's Creativity Index saw San Francisco listed in second position narrowly being beaten by Boulder, Colorado.[9] San Francisco is indeed a creative city as "regions in which artists and gays have migrated and settled are more likely than others to place high premiums on innovation, entrepreneurship, and new firm formation" (Florida 2008, 139). Arguably, a vibrant queer arts scene is integral to this identity.

While Florida has been criticised for his reasoning (Montgomery 2005), others fear that the logic of the creative city can water down the radical nature of San Francisco. Brabanzo (2011) argues that Florida's "argument flattens, homogenizes and commercializes the radicalism, resistance and activism of the cities validated through his criteria" (43). Florida's key concern is how urban renewal spurs on economic development and queer community arts organisations are an aspect to boosting a city's Bohemian-Gay Index. This is where the notion of the creative city becomes more complex. While we can identify the importance community art organisations have on a city's creative status, Florida's definition of bohemia is restricted to those employed in artistic and creative fields, while "politics, dissent and activism were not incorporated into the definition" (46). As such, bohemia becomes a marketable brand. Suddenly, the market becomes an influential player into what is deemed valuable, where "today's market has a new twist in the way it benefits some gay people more than others" (Gluckman and Reed 1997, xiii) with the investments into the creative city landscape privileging the elite (Donald and Morrow 2003; Peck 2005). This creative city logic accentuates the "priorities of elite classes and neighbourhoods" (Leslie and Catungal 2012, 114). The creative city heavily influenced by the market does not treat all members of the LGBT community equally.

For both Sender (2004) and Chasin (2000), the apparent enfranchisement of gay and lesbian segmented marketing is merely superficial, stating that these advertisements evoke the impression of an all-white predominately gay male community, while hyper-sexualising the few images of racial minorities. Chasin is ultimately fearful that this gay visibility is at the disbursement of queer political confrontations, which is particularly evident in the identity being perpetuated by this marketing being overwhelmingly gay oriented and not LGBT. It would be imprudent to assume that this is all far removed from politics as this "division of business from politics disavows the extent to which all economic activity has political effect" (3). This gay community is not a pre-existing construction but one imagined by professionals far removed from the LGBT community. I recall a conversation I had during my internship with the programming editor. As I flipped through the festival programme, I remarked on how the majority of the advertisements were directed to gay men. She simply replied that that's just the way it was. Lesbians have less disposable income than gay men, and the programming advertisement simply reflected that. We must not simplify this situation, by reading the queers as being oppressed by the capitalist marketplace as Sender (2004) concludes that the relationship between both mass and subcultures is interdependent and complex in that this "assimilationist critique cannot accommodate the myriad ways in which LGBT-identified people negotiate the specificities of their desires, incomes, and habitus in part through their consumption" (235). The queer film festival's growth lies in this intersection of visibility, market economy, and cultural exchange (Rich 2002).

The 1990s and the turn of the century saw a rapid increase in queer media organisations. The global rise of the queer film festival was a result of the "political motivations of gay and lesbian film communities [coinciding] with the economic motivations of one of the largest export industries in the United States" (Rhyne 2006, 617–618). This growth would continue steadily until the financial hardships of the global financial crisis (GFC), which only added to the importance of multiple income streams for such community non-profit organisations.

## 2008 and Beyond: Frameline and the Future

The Frameline Film Festival and other queer non-profits grew healthily into the new millennium until the GFC hit in 2008. It resulted in the collapse of large financial institutions, the bailout of banks by national governments, and downturns in stock markets around the world. It contributed to the failure of key businesses and a significant decline in economic activity, leading to a severe global economic recession (Baily and Elliot 2009). For non-profit organisations, this economic instability resulted in uncertainty and instability (Anheier 2009). The recent recession hit arts non-profits hard. The New York based Alliance for the Arts carried a survey of over 100 art non-profits organisations and learnt that 67 % of organisations with budgets under $100,000 have had to cut back their budget; 81 % of organisations earning between $100,000 and $1 million cut back their expenditure; and finally 79 % and 80 % of organisations with budgets between $1 million and $10 million and over $10 million, respectively, had to cut back their budgets (2009). The recent recession has also hit San Francisco based non-profits hard with well-known LGBT non-profits going under (or going dangerously close) such as New Leaf: Services for Our Community, Lyon-Martin Health Services, Academy of Friends, and San

Francisco Pride (Doughty 2011).[10] The Frameline Film Festival, so far, has successfully weathered the economic storm of the recent recession. Recent festival programmes have successfully maintained a strong programme, and ticket sales have remained steady. For Frances Wallace, strong financial leadership is of the utmost importance:

> They (queer non-profits) have really suffered in terms of the fall of the American economy and losing money through sponsors and foundations. Unlike Australia, there isn't a lot of city and government support. That is the number one crucial difference between the countries and structure of festivals and the arts. In Australia people complain "oh we don't get enough money from the state or the government" but in the US that money does not come to the arts and the festival. Frameline does get money from the NEA but it's minimal. It would be a $20–$30 000 grant associated with one program, whereas the sponsorship brings in $300 000. American arts culture is really reliant on corporations or on individual wealth (Interview with Frances Wallace 2011).

Frameline, since its grassroots inception in 1977, has always grown steadily through both political and economic instability. It has remained at the very centre of San Francisco's innovative fusion of art and politics. As result of this growth, Frameline now receives significant attention from mainstream press, from general news sites such as *Huffington Post* and *San Francisco Mercury News,* and film-related news sites such as *IndieWire* regularly positioning Frameline as a leading festival for American and International LGBT cinema (Knegt 2013). Festival reviews and news of key films being picked up for distribution highlight the professional nature of Frameline, such as Wolfe Releasing acquiring four films at Frameline 37 (Selinger 2013). Mainstream media coverage of Frameline demonstrates its vital role in the business of queer cinema.

Frameline is situated within a primary position within the North American queer film festival circuit. As Rhyne (2006) notes in her contribution to the Gay and Lesbian Film and Video Forum, the festival is "certainly not representative of the vast majority of festivals, particularly in terms of its institutional size and structure" (619). Frameline had an annual revenue exceeding $1.84 million in 2013.[11] The festival is only rivalled by LA Outfest, which had a revenue of $3 million in the same year. Both festivals are indicative of strategies North American film festivals employ to be sustainable—strong membership support, corporate sponsorship, and commercially oriented ticket sales. The festival is now a media organisation that is at the forefront of a globalised push of Western queer film, which coincides with "local adaptation, national film cultures and basic struggles for LGBT rights and community building" (Loist 2013, 121). In a North American context, Frameline is an institutional leader providing an environment for institutional development through various events for attending programmers, distributors, and filmmakers. Wong (2011a) identifies that this form of structural development relies on "webs of communication and face-to-face contact" (130). Frameline is undoubtedly a regional leader in the North American queer film festival circuit.

## MQFF's History

### The Early Years before MQFF

As has been established earlier with my analysis of Frameline's history, the increased professionalism of the queer film festival is a clear result of the transformation from the rationality of traditional cultural policy to an adoption of creative industry logic. This development of the creative industry mentality will continue to be the conceptual framework in my analysis of the MQFF. This shift to the creative industry mindset is an acknowledgement of the economic benefit derived from nourishing creativity in a wide variety of industries and creates a knowledge economy based concept. This rationality moves cultural value and organisation from a position of state support to an economic agenda (Galloway and Dunlop 2007). This shift establishes a regime of culture (Frow 1995), which involves "mechanisms that permit the construction and regulation of value-equivalence, and indeed permit cross-cultural mediation" (144). Discourses of value are attributed to "high culture" that reinforces the "discrepancy between aesthetic and economic discourses of value as a way of designating aesthetic – that is, non-economic – value as marker of status" (146). As such, the early years of MQFF outlined in this section will be contrasted greatly with that of the increasingly professional organisation seen in later years. This historic account will see the value produced by MQFF change over time. Through an interlocking network of institutions and stakeholders, the non-economic value of the queer film festival will be transformed into a marker of status and, ultimately, provide an economically beneficial output for the stakeholders involved. This is the rationality of the creative industry.

While the traditional cultural industry was primarily concerned with delivering other forms of value, such as social and cultural capital as opposed to monetary value, the creative industry identifies the potential for this value and status to be translated into a position of economic sustainability for the cultural organisation involved. The cultural policy that supported organisations had an objective of social inclusion and cultural participation for its end goal. The creative industry identifies the cultural status of such successful organisations and professionalises these organisations from, just say, a community art festival to an art festival that plays a significant and influential role in its particular field. The logic behind this mindset, for potential investors, is not necessarily social altruism but a new innovative means for exposure and financial profits. This pushes partial responsibility of funding of arts and cultural pursuits to the market and is ultimately a product of neoliberalism:

> The neoliberal bequest of creativity has succeeded the old school patrimony of culture, because economic transformations have comprehensively challenged the idea of the humanities as removed from industry. Rather than working with the progressive goals of social democracy that uses the state in a leftist march of the institutions, this new development favours neo-liberalism (Miller 2009, 94).

Thus, the creative industry identifies the financial importance of the creative individual who belongs to the new generation of workers in the creative class. Contemporary wealth and job creation occurs through the exploitation and nourishment of intellectual property and creative products. We no longer exist in a cultural economy but in an individualistic knowledge economy. The responsibility of creativity is no longer up to cultural institutions (Miller 2009). This recalls my earlier discussion of Richard Florida (2002), where attracting the creative class has been identified as a driving force in the economic development in major cities. The creative worker uses innovation to create meaningful new forms, which places new monetary values on traditional products of culture. The key rationality that Florida's work indicates is the importance of creativity to a city's economic growth. This is a clearer indication of the status given to individual creative capital in the creative industry. This transition to the rationality of the creative industry will form the conceptual framework of my analysis of the MQFF. The previous chapter highlighted the value of such organisations to Florida's conception of the creative class. MQFF has moved beyond the role of merely providing an avenue for social inclusion for a marginalised community.

This marginalisation is clearly demonstrated in the queer film exhibition prior to the festival's first event. Community film screenings had begun in Melbourne many years earlier. The Melbourne Gay Liberation Film Society held film screenings in 1974 and 1975. In 1974, the organisation ran a collection of films pertaining to oppression and liberation held at the Gay Liberation Film Centre at 259 Brunswick Street, Fitzroy. Films screened included *Fortune and Men's Eyes* (Harvey Hart 1971), which depicted homosexuality in the prison system, and films by directors Bunnuel, Cocteau, and Wilderberg. In September 1975, the film collective held screenings of films over a weekend including *The Mad King of Bavaria* (Luchino Visconti 1972) and Curtis Harrington shorts, such as *Picnic* (1948) and *Children of Hiroshima* (Kaneto Shindo 1952). In 1977, the collective Melbourne University GaySoc presented an array of gay films, including *Sunday, Bloody Sunday* (John Schlesinger 1971) and *Les Biches* (Claude Chabrol 1968). By having film events organised by gay liberation groups, we have the early examples of queer community film screenings being intertwined with politics and activism.

In 1986, the Gay Film Week was co-sponsored by the Sydney Gay Mardi Gras and the Victorian AIDs council providing gay and lesbian film festival events with increased legitimacy. In 1986, Gay Film Week was able to bring Vito Russo, author of *The Celluloid Closet* (1981), to Australia to deliver lectures during the festival. Later that decade, The Sydney Gay Mardi Gras co-sponsored the Gay Film Festival with the Australian Film Institute,[12] holding screenings at the State Film Theatre in East Melbourne, which was to be the home of MQFF in the early years. These festivals, with AFI's involvement, added a level of legitimacy to queer film itself, that they were a community art event worthy of the AFI's involvement. In 1990, the Gay and Lesbian Film Week was presented by the Australian Film Institute in conjunction with Mardi Gras and Melbourne Midsumma festival. The week was held at both the State Theatre in Melbourne and at AFI in Sydney. This 1990 festival heralded a new level of consistency that was to support MQFF for its early years. AFI's funding during these early years is a clear use of MQFF as a tool for the social inclusion of a marginalised community. To return to the chapter's conceptual framework of the creative industry, the value produced from these early events exclusively benefited Melbourne's LGBT community and not the wider urban creative economy. This innovative transition gradually occurred in the festival's early years.

## *1991–1994: Management in the Back of a Bookstore*

The inaugural festival began in 1991 as part of the much larger Midsumma, an LGBT arts and cultural festival. The festival began under the name the Melbourne International Lesbian and Gay Film Festival. The initial directors were Pat Longmore and Lawrence Johnston, the former continuing to direct the festival in 1992 alongside Helen Eisler and Crusader Hillis. The first programme consisted of retrospective screenings, such as a "The Physique Films of Dick Fontaine" including *Day of Greek* (1949) and "The Films of Andy Warhol" including *Blowjob* (1963) and *Lonesome Cowboy* (1967), and more contemporary films such as opening night films *Long Time Companion* (Norman Rene 1990) and *Wallflowers* (Robert Smith 1989).[13]

With Midsumma's prior networking's assistance, the initial festival managed to secure numerous sponsorship deals, which is significant considering it was their first year of operation. They received state government support through Film Victoria,[14] support from the gay community in the form of sponsorship from the gay nightclub the Xchange Hotel, the Victorian AIDs Council, and the Gay Men's Health Centre. They also received sponsorship from other organisations like STA travel. Under Film Victoria, MQFF received between $3000 and $5000 from 1990 through to 1995 annually under their screen community engagement/events programme. By being classified as "community engagement," there was an acknowledgement that MQFF in its early days was grassroots community art, instead of the contemporary cultural event it is today.

This funding from Film Victoria is an example of cultural policy supporting an arts organisation enhancing quality of life and community engagement. If we recall that cultural policies are "a privileged terrain of hegemony" and that they are a means of "reconciling contending cultural identities" (Yudice and Miller 2002, 8), then we can identify MQFF as being positioned as a minority *community* arts event. Community arts play an important role in the cultural terrain of a city (Khan 2011; Mulligan and Smith 2011; Ho 2012; Gibson et al. 2012). As such, this support allows MQFF the ability to further engage LGBT Melbournians and develop the diverse vibrancy of Melbourne's cultural industry. At this stage of development, state support was MQFF's primary source of income.

In their second year, the festival changed its name to The Melbourne Gay and Lesbian Film and Video Festival, thus signalling that the festival was to keep aligned with the changing identity politics of the time. By including the term "video," the festival identified the importance video had with gay and lesbian consumers being able to access such films. The festival programme also increased to 120 films and the festival was able to host two international guests, both experimental filmmaker Sadie Benning[15] and performer Georgette Dee, who appeared in the film *All of Me* (Bettina Wilhelm 1991). There was a dramatic transition from 1992 to 1993 as the festival was in major financial deficit. Running prominent queer book-store Hares & Hyenas with his partner Rowland Thomson, Crusader Hillis was a driving force behind the early years of the festival, ensuring its survival:

> 1992 lost a lot of money for the festival. It was a very ambitious festival. It was very good in terms of programming and it was a departure from the previous year, which was all based on male films at 9:00 and lesbian films at 6:30, which even at the time I thought was anti-diluvion and weird to be doing that. Whereas in 1992 we had a lot more, we played around with genre and had more trans films. By 1993 we really decided to absolutely mix it up (Interview with Crusader Hillis 2011)

The year 1993 was the first year Madeline Swain directed the festival. In late 1994, she was employed on a part-time basis (Searle 1997). She would continue to do so until 1995, when Tamara Jungworth became MQFF president until 1997. The 1993 festival began to take shape as a professional organisation with Swain's role being paid part-time for a few months leading up to the festival. According to Swain, there was also the formation of an advisory board, made up of "queer elders" to assist in shaping the festival:

> Crusader also decided to put together an advisory board, to give us some legitimacy but also some queer elders in the business world and the academic world and the film world to help steer us and to bounce ideas off (Interview with Swain 2011).

A significant change to the festival in 1993 was altering the name from the Melbourne Gay and Lesbian Film and Video Festival to The Melbourne Queer Film and Video Festival. This was the first festival of its kind in the world to adopt queer into its title. This change, initiated by Hillis, was a move to make MQFF more representative of the diverse community it sought to represent:

> We wanted it to be more spread out and we wanted it to be more encouraging
> for people to get involved.... With the festival, there was very little reaction to
> the change because the people that were most upset about it generally read
> the street mags, went to clubs and bars but were not at all involved in cultural
> pursuits; whereas people that were interested in arts and culture came from a
> much more of a cultured background and history, where queer things have
> been more mainstream (Interview with Hillis 2011).

This was an innovative approach to the identity politics of the festival. By simultaneously considering the community/audience of the festival and strategic approaches for garnering more economic viability, Hillis was positioning himself as a social entrepreneurial leader. For Swain, the change was a positive move, emblematic of Hillis's support of the wide spectrum of the queer community. In an interview from 1994, former vice-president Chris Berry cited some older members involved with the festival being uncomfortable with the change (Berry 1994, cited in Searle 1997). Minor negative responses to the name change did not translate into a decline in ticket sales. The organisational changes of the festival in 1993, and slight change in structure, helped build MQFF from being a struggling community event to a more professionalised organisation. Attempts at sustainability were made through established connections with *The Melbourne Star Observer,* Midsumma, and Film Victoria. In comparison to Queer Screen in Sydney, however, the festival received very little funding. While Queer Screen received $100,000 from Mardi Gras in 1993, MQFF received less than $10,000 from ALSO foundation and Film Victoria in 1994 (Searle 1997).

### 1994–1997: MQFF and a Creative Nation

As MQFF grew into the 1990s, two key elements mirrored the growth of Frameline during this time period. First, the content of the festival maintained the purpose of the queer film festival during its early years. The festival provided access to films otherwise unavailable and held forums on contentious issues of the time. Second, MQFF's development paralleled the development of Australia's cultural industry as the nation's first cultural policy, *Creative Nation,* redefined cultural value for the purpose of industrial growth.

Following the 1993 edition, the festival had consolidated a loyal audience base. The only other major queer community event in Melbourne was Midsumma, which has always been a geographically spread-out community event, with the obvious exception of the carnival day and Pride march.[16] With the exception of a few significant gay and lesbian films such as *Philadelphia* (Jonathan Demme 1993) and *Torch Song Trilogy* (Paul Bogart 1988), very few LGBT-related films were receiving theatrical releases. (Albeit if any Australian LGBT films were given the opportunity of exhibition other than *Priscilla Queen of the Desert* [Stephen Elliot 1994]). Indeed, it appeared that MQFF had comfortably filled a void for the Melbourne queer community. In her welcoming statement in the 1994 programme, Swain expressed her dismay in not being able to include any of the current major gay-themed films, such as the above-mentioned *Philadelphia* and *Torch Song Trilogy* in the programme:

> And then I cheered up. The films in question either have already been or should be released theatrically. The whole ethos of a film festival is to give people a chance to see things which they would otherwise have no access. This is what this year's festival is all about with over 40 Australian premieres and several Melbourne premieres (Swain 1994, 5).

MQFF's success was directly tied to this logic, by providing the community with content otherwise inaccessible or experiences that would otherwise be unattainable. For instance, the 1994 programme featured a forum on the pink dollar called "Do they only want us for our money? Mainstreaming of marketing to queer culture," featuring panellists Danny Vadasz, Judith Sherwood, Brigitte Haire, and Chris Berry. Also included was a tribute screening for Derek Jarman, the "godfather of queer cinema," who had recently passed away due to AIDs-related causes.

MQFF's growth coincided with the Australian government's concerted effort to nourish the cultural industry. In October 1994, the Australian commonwealth government released the country's first Australian cultural policy under the name *Creative Nation* in order to nurture and protect Australian culture amidst a technological revolution whilst also fostering the economic potential of cultural activity. *Creative Nation* demonstrated that "the government was not indulging in altruism, but rather was trying to redefine and broaden the meaning of art—first, by transforming it into the larger category of 'culture,' and then by changing it entirely into a 'commodity,' an element of industry, as a link in the manufacturing chain, a creator of employment, and a vehicle of trade" (Bereson 2005, 53). *Creative Nation* was a time for redefinition, according to Stevenson:

> *Creative Nation* proved to be a catalyst for re-evaluating the role of the arts in Australian society, the connections between different forms of arts and cultural practice, and the relationship between the arts and government (Stevenson 2000, 16).

The policy aimed to discover new avenues for communication and artistic growth. Citing multiculturalism and diversity as a national achievement, *Creative Nation* cites the recent reinvention of a national identity as an exotic hybrid. In the charter of cultural rights, the policy lists the importance of one's "right of access to our intellectual and cultural heritage, the right to new intellectual and artistic works" and perhaps most importantly "the right to community participation in cultural and intellectual life" (4–5).

The Australia Council, the official Arts funding body for the federal government, acknowledged that government cannot and should not maintain or create a national identity; rather, it stems organically from a grassroots level, from the everyday. The Australia Council policy stated that one of many important areas for research was for audience development and sponsorship development. It seems this is the direction *Creative Nation* wanted cultural bodies to grow in, for a sustainable existence with a healthy balance between public and corporate funding. One significant issue the Australia Council highlighted in the policy was that corporate sponsorship generally flows in the direction of sporting organisations. When arts organisations do receive funding from the private sector, successful recipients are larger cultural bodies. The policy statement was seen as a "preferred future, not a direction to be followed" (276), and it was ultimately up to creative managers to take the lead. *Creative Nation's* objective was to create conditions for sustainable cultural industries, one condition being tax incentives for private sector support:

> Creative Nation provides a rationale for what is actually happening ... (organisations) are already investing human and financial resources in audience development, promotion, marketing, revenue generation activities, and international marketing strategies and are participating with other government departments and sponsors in partnership and investment agreements to produce a sustainable cultural industry (Radbourne 1996, 275).

*Creative Nation* created a cultural environment within which MQFF had to adapt. As a non-profit organisation, the festival was exempt from income tax. Sponsorship arrangements with businesses were also tax deductible. In this period, MQFF received support from both the federal level in the form of funding from the Australian Film Institute (an organisation that receives federal governmental support) and at the state level in the form of sponsorship from Film Victoria, albeit only for a few years. MQFF's income during this period was sourced from a combination of sponsorship, ticket sales, and government support. *Creative Nation* propelled "the link between arts and industry ... 'creative industries' came to be the new programmatic preoccupation of policymakers and bureaucrats" (Bereson 2005, 55). This cultural change moved the festival healthily into the age of the creative industry.

MQFF offered four levels of sponsorship at this stage, which propelled these links between arts and industry. First, there was the opportunity of being MQFF's principal sponsor for the rate of $5000, which was the ALSO foundation for several years. Second, there were multiple principal sponsors who paid $1500; in 1997, these were a mixture of community organisations, such as Three Triple R (RRR)[17] and *The Melbourne Star Observer*[18] and commercial businesses STA Travel and Efbee Hair and Design. Following this were major sponsors who paid $800. Over the years, these sponsors included Global Escorts, Mark Carey Funerals, Frederick Owen & Associates, and PBS 106.7 FM. MQFF also had a wide variety of session sponsors, which allowed for strategic niche marketing such as in 1997 *Outrage* magazine sponsoring "Eye Candy," a collection of gay male shorts, or Palm Court Bed and Breakfast sponsoring the "Real Canadian Women" shorts session. This welcoming influx of sponsorship money allowed for Jungwirth to have a paid position, which was an important step in the professional status of the organisation.

This was not, however, comfortably in sync with the organisation's resource growth. By the mid-1990s, the festival did not receive any financial support from the state government. The 1997 festival ran for over 17 days with over 80 titles exhibited, which was not fiscally responsible; as a result, the festival saw the departure of director Jungwirth, board president Suzie Goodman, and a considerable portion of the board. When comparing MQFF to Frameline, the differences in flows of capital are clear. For many years, Frameline has had a budget that comfortably allows for numerous staff members, while smaller queer film festivals, such as MQFF, have a more tenuous existence.[19]

## 1998–2000: MQFF's Restructure

With the landscape of cultural organisations moving into the contemporary creative industry, MQFF's development was stagnant, and dramatic changes were made. This period saw MQFF undergo a restructure while maintaining its social legitimacy. The year 1998 saw not only Claire Jackson replace Suzie Goodman as board president, a position that she would hold until 2011, but also Deb Fryers direct the festival with Lisa Daniel taking over the following year. Daniel outlines the trouble the festival was in:

> The organisation was in trouble financially. The then festival director (Jungwirth) had left after a couple of years. There had been a couple of ill-advised attempts to make the festival bigger. A year before I started the festival went for three weeks. It was the mid-nineties, there weren't the films to justify that length or the resources to run it and there wasn't the audience to justify it so they lost a lot of money. I think there was also a little bit of ill will about the festival in terms of punters and a few sponsors. Because of that I feel the board got a bit burnt out; because they were so hands on, they were virtually running the organisation in their spare time from full time employment. So the festival was burnt out, financially not in a happy place and it was challenging when I first started (Interview with Lisa Daniel 2011).

This period saw a major restructure of the board. What was once an advisory board of "queer elders" was now a board of professionals from various industries that would *professionally* steer the festival, with individuals from the publishing sector, web design, finances and accounting, legal, public relations, and human relations, and so forth. The board now comprised of both business and community leaders highlighting the "professionalisation" of the grassroots organisation.

The City of Melbourne began supporting MQFF in 1998, and it continues today. The year 2006 saw MQFF receive multi-year funding from the Triennial's Arts Grant. While the city's Triennial *Sponsorship* Program is part of the Events Portfolio and emphasises the strategic economic objective of Melbourne's brand as a destination city, The Triennial *Arts Grant* supports organisations that advance Melbourne as a creative city. City of Melbourne councillor Rohan Leppert explained how the lack of state government support led to the need for a more business-oriented approach:

> We started funding MQFF in 1998 and we only started with a small grant of less than $7,000. We now provide $80,000 and while that is not directly

commensurate to the growth of the festival, it's roughly parallel. The state government has known since 1998 that its funding has not naturally supported MQFF and it's done nothing to overcome that. They have not developed the funding policies to determine whether or not they value these sorts of festivals. MQFF is one of two premier queer festivals in the state[20] and the state government for decades has knowingly not found a way to support them in an ongoing manner (Interview with Rohan Leppert 2015).[21]

According to Jane Crawley, the manager of the City of Melbourne's Arts and Culture portfolio, prior to the Triennial Program, there was very little funding available to organisations like MQFF in the small-to-medium sector:

In the 1990s and early 2000s there was no competitive, public Triennial funding program. There were six large organisations and they were colloquially known as the 'big 6' and they were literally written into the budget. They were organisations like the Melbourne Festival, Melbourne Symphony Orchestra, Fringe Festival, Melbourne International Film Festival and Comedy Festival. So that meant that those organisations did not have to compete for funding. In fact, those organisations didn't even have to *apply* for funding. Their financial allocation was literally embedded in the budget. My predecessor was the person who advocated for there to be a Triennial Program and for it to be competitive and public, much to the consternation of those established organisations.

The first public Triennial process happened in 2006 and that was the first time it had been competitive. Prior to that, organisations like the Melbourne Queer Film Festival could not get multi-year funding from the city. They also couldn't get funding from the Victorian government because the then Arts Victoria didn't support screen and they were unsuccessful from Film Victoria because they literally only funded Melbourne International Film Festival and the St Kilda Film Festival.

That was it. They couldn't actually get any money anywhere else. The only public entity that supported them was Melbourne City Council. It did it on an annual project basis and it was quite modest. That shift to a publically competitive multi-year funding program was really significant. It cut funds from those 'big 6' in order to create enough pool for the other organisations (Interview with Jane Crawley 2016).

MQFF continued to push the social aspects of the festival with the introduction of the "Film Buff-et" in the Cinemedia foyer, where audience members could socialise and have dinner before or after film sessions.

Stocked by food and alcohol sponsors, this bar environment was to become an integral part to the development of MQFF's community. The wide publicity of opening and closing night parties further emphasised the social aspect of MQFF, which acted as a key driver of the City of Melbourne's support. The quintessential force behind MQFF's maturation from this period onwards was the professional partnership of board president Jackson and festival director Daniel. With the commencement of their roles came a restructuring of the festival, as outlined by Daniel:

> The main thing I wanted to do when I started was to repair some relationships. I wanted to make the festival the best festival it could be while still being a queer film festival and that meant saying no to some films that were queer which I just didn't think cut it in terms of what you would want an audience to pay for. I don't feel that just because we cater for a queer audience that we should lessen the quality. What I did in the early days was I made it a smaller festival but a better festival. It took a while for the audiences to come back and realise it was pretty good. I changed the artwork of the festival. It was all rainbow flags. I just wanted good artwork that wasn't necessarily about being queer but about being a great festival (Interview with Daniel 2011).

The 1999 festival ran for only nine days and 2000 festival ran for ten. The overall look of the programme layout had changed considerably as well. Full-page spreads were still given to sponsors, but more room was given to film sessions, with two sessions taking up a whole page. Festival programmes are considered to be film festival ephemera and indicate how film festivals present themselves to audiences and constitute publics (Zielinski 2016). This allowed more film stills to tempt the reader and a higher word count in the write-up on each film.

During this period in MQFF's development, the Victorian state government was part of a wider trend in government cultural policy that moved towards an industry-development approach to arts funding with their *Arts 21* policy. Such governmental state support was tied to the arts-as-industry approach, where "advocates of arts funding were forced to find a way to justify funding for activities that were previously seen as forming an intangible public good. They did so by identifying the arts' tangible benefits – in particular their service to tourism and entertainment industries – and began to characterise the arts as an industry in itself" (Glow and Johanson 2004, 129–130). Such support was not necessarily aimed at immediate financial profits with altruistic objectives for cultural organisations during this time, but to foster self-sufficiency. This was the spirit of *Arts 21*, released by the conservative Kennett liberal Victorian government in 1994, which was a policy that aimed at providing a "strategy for the arts industry into the twenty-first century" (State Government of Victoria 1994). The significant emphasis on this agenda was "development" and "future" (Stevenson 2000). Kennett's ambitious aim was to position Victoria as the cultural capital of Australia (Hallett 1992). Stevenson's analysis of Kennett's policy highlights the focus on excellence, which obscures any concern for access and equity (82). Artistic success is coupled with prosperity, "two goals that may not only not be complementary, but indeed may well be incompatible" (83). The Kennett government's *Arts 21* had an ambition for artistic excellence and an improved cultural identity for the state. This was arguably a key influence in the City of Melbourne Council's evolving arts funding. MQFF's Triennial Arts Grant saw the role of the local government assisting small-to-medium cultural organisations develop sustainability so as to further increase community engagement. This is indicative of their funding description:

> The City of Melbourne is committed to investing in the arts to foster the vibrant creative life of the city. Our triennial program provides three-yearly funding for arts organisations and festivals enhancing Melbourne's cultural identity and reflecting Council's objectives for the City of Melbourne (The City of Melbourne).

This acknowledgement of MQFF's contribution to the city's creative status can be seen as a key conceptual influence in the City of Melbourne Council's Triennial funding programme. In the 2015 funding round, the festival secured $80,000 per annum (Leppert 2015). This government assistance has been critical to the organisational sustainability of MQFF and also meets with the City of Melbourne's objective of 'investing in the arts to foster the vibrant creative life of the city' (City of Melbourne). The Triennial funding programme is not necessarily an altruistic funding model but an initiative to contribute to the city's cultural identity, as "council funding is tied to activating the public realm in a free way, late at night, making unsafe spaces safe" (Leppert 2015). Arts grants provided by the City of Melbourne are significantly larger than grants offered by the Tasmanian and Northern Territory state governments (Clayton and Travers 2009). The MQFF currently receives the Triennial funding under the category "arts festivals." Annual expenditure on the Triennial grant is over $2.2 million. According to Lord Mayor Robert Doyle in a media release advising of the recent recipients, the programme aims to shape the city's cultural life:

> Arts and culture brings life to the streets of Melbourne. The triennial program provides support for organisations that contribute to the cultural life of our city and broaden the scope of late night entertainment on offer, ensuring Melbourne continues to be a creative, vibrant and safe 24 hour city (Doyle, quoted in the City of Melbourne press release 2011b).

According to Jane Crawley, arts organisations need to articulate the synergy between their strategic planning and the council's strategic plan:

> My perspective is that it actually isn't the role of government to be even telling an arts organisation about the value thing. The council has already articulated its values and aspirations. It's really up to the arts industry to determine if there is a synergy there or not. If there isn't, don't bother applying for funding. If there is then sure put something in.
>
> Our strategic goals include the reputation of Melbourne; the degree to which it attracts artists to live here and creative industries to base themselves here; that it attracts people to want to live here because of the reputation of Melbourne and its reputation for creativity and innovation; the contribution that it makes toward the night economies, to a driving destination the things that happens when people come in here; how it represents the culture of Melbourne and its diversity and its queer culture; and the way it contributes to how Melbourne is seen as sophisticated, diverse and queer friendly (Interview with Crawley 2016).

This period was a significant turning point for MQFF, as it was now deemed a valuable cultural event. By receiving support from the City of Melbourne local council under the Triennial Program, the festival was no longer considered just a community organisation but now a professional one that brought a noteworthy contribution to the cultural identity of the city. According to Leppert (2015), the City of Melbourne values "audience numbers, free events and activating the public realm." Being categorised as an "arts festival" and not "community engagement through art" further solidifies the festival's professional nature. This is an acknowledgement of the festival's value to the city. The event brings a significant amount of visitors to the CBD. This influx of people engaging in a cultural event translates into a financial boost to nearby cafes, restaurants, and so forth in the CBD and Federation Square area. This value is also indicative of the opening night event now taking place at Australian Centre for the Moving Image (ACMI)[22] after having taken place at the Astor Theatre in St Kilda.[23] By providing funding, the City of Melbourne is recognising the value added to the cultural identity of the city, that MQFF is an innovative service that will add value to another service (Yue 2006).

These policies created an atmosphere where arts organisations were highly valued. By striving for the Melbourne CBD to be a creative conclave, this environmental milieu has enabled MQFF's growth. This urban progress was seen in key development sites such as the Crown Casino, ACMI, and Federation Square. Large festivals also received state governmental support, such as Melbourne International Film Festival (whose principal partner is Film Victoria) or the Melbourne International Comedy Festival. These spaces and festivals helped create a desirable city to attract creative human capital, such as university students, who are playing an important role in contributing to Melbourne's identity (Shaw and Fincher 2010). While many creative industry workers in Melbourne are increasingly living in the suburbs, state cultural policies still primarily focus on the inner city CBD location (Flew 2012). These policies tell us that a "creative city-inflected understanding of economic growth and city development is deeply embedded among policymakers and key personnel working within state, city and other 'upper level' institutions in Australia" (Atkinson and Easthope 2009, 75). This creative industries mindset, however, values culture only in terms of what financial benefits are afforded to the city. Lobato (2006) highlights this in his analysis of the current state of live music in Melbourne:

> Perhaps the most important lesson we can take away from the Live Music Taskforce example concerns the fickle nature of creative industries discourse itself. The creative industries model values culture only for its economic potential, and has little interest in the array of less cosmopolitan cultural activities that do not register on its city-centric radar. While the survival of events with quantifiable economic benefits seems assured (Melbourne Film Festival, Melbourne Food and Wine Festival, and so on), many others will not fare so well (72–73).

These policies emphasised the economic potential of a dynamic arts sector and sought to foster an economy based on innovation, albeit with events whose "quantifiable economic benefits seem assured."

### 2001 and Beyond: MQFF as Part of the Creative Industries

The new millennium saw an MQFF that had the programming formula of a balance between films that would get "bums on seats" (as is the term that is often thrown around at selection meetings) and films that aim to support the community—there are of course films that fall into both of these categories. This was epitomised by the tag line for the 2004 and 2005 festivals "within every community beats a queer heart." With the steady development of a core loyal audience, MQFF moved to numerous locations for screenings during this period until finding a home at the ACMI. In 2001, MQFF opened at the Astor Theatre[24] and held festival screenings at the Cinemedia Treasury Theatre and the RMIT Capitol Theatre. In 2003, MQFF held its first selection of screenings at ACMI, with its festival screenings split with the Capitol Theatre. By 2004, ACMI was its official home.

In the changing environment of LGBT politics, MQFF has remained relevant by creating environments for discussions of contemporary themes. As stated by Daniel in the 2006 programme's director's welcoming statement:

> As the festival comes of age, so too do we hope to see important social and legal changes ahead for our LGBTI communities. Film is often seen as a reflection of the social values of a particular time and in considering that it's pertinent to see how important a social document our festival has become. This year's themes – gay marriage, body image, community, family, isolation, coming out, death, love and relationships – are all significant to us as we head towards changing times (2006, 9).

Daniel continued to expand the panel discussions and centrepiece presentations presented by MQFF. In 2006, for example, two significant panels were held. First, following the documentary *Do I Look Fat?* (Travis Matthews 2005), was a panel co-presented by Gay and Lesbian Health Victoria and the Victorian Gay and Lesbian Rights Lobby on body image in the gay male community. Second was a discussion on the various positive and negative elements of the gay marriage debate following the documentary *Pursuit of Equality* (Geoff Callan and Mike Shaw 2005). Panellists included activist Rodney Croome, Michael Kelly of the Rainbow Sash Gay Catholics Organisation, University of Melbourne Law Lecturer Kris Walker, Alison Thorne from Radical Women, anarchist and queer activist Tallace Bisset, and conservative blogger John Hard. Marriage rights lobby group Equal

Love sponsored the debate. Another significant centrepiece was the *Imagining Queer* lecture series in 2004, curated by Barry McKay and Marilyn Dooley of the Screen and Sound Australia Research and Academic Outreach Program,[25] which detailed the history of queer representation in Australia since 1910.

Further strengthening its significance with the community was its travelling queer film festival first established in 2007. The festival travelled to Bendigo, Cairns, and Rockhampton for two nights each, showing the highlights of the festival to smaller queer communities. While MQFF still continues to coordinate the queer film screenings in Bendigo, Cairns, and Rockhampton are now organising in their own right by the Tropical Alternatives Film Festival. The significance of community was also aided by the introduction of the festival club in 2003 at the RMIT Capitol Theatre, which was later moved to ACMI's Cube Bar in 2006.

The growing number of awards offered further solidified MQFF as a film institution. In 2006, Lifetime member David McCarthy sponsored the prize money for the audience award for best documentary, which awarded the winning director a $1000 cash prize, which was increased to $2000 in 2008. Also in 2006, there was an increase in the audience award prize for best feature film to a $5000 cash prize. A $500 cash prize is currently awarded to the winner of the audience choice award for best short film. The City of Melbourne has sponsored the award for best Australian short film for many years now. Turtle Cove, a beachfront resort hotel in north Queensland, continued to sponsor the audience choice award for best Australian short film up until 2007, when it was supported by Karen Russell of Step Right Up Distribution & Promotion.

Much like Frameline, MQFF's growth coincided with the development of the creative industries. *Creative Capacity Plus* fostered the creative industries paradigm in Melbourne, which was part of a wider Australian shift in cultural policy (Government of Australia 1994; Government of Queensland 2002). The creative industries merge "arts, technology and business as a way of ensuring a nation's competiveness within an integrated global economy" (Yue 2006, 18). Arts policies in this environment aim to encourage and motivate creativity within processes of performativity. *Creative Capacity Plus* aimed to strengthen community engagement with the arts and increase the sustainability of cultural organisations. At the conference on the arts and local government *Expanding Cultures*, Arts Victoria director Penny Hutchinson outlined the rhetoric of the policy:

> The Bracks Government has long recognized the importance of community building and strengthening ... Victorians say they want to live in strong, friendly and creative communities – and because such communities produce benefits in many areas such as health, education, innovation and employment, and community safety. The Government's arts policy – *Creative Capacity Plus* – aims to increase engagement with the arts for all Victorians, and improve access to diverse cultural experiences (Hutchinson 2007, 2).

This is an acknowledgement of the creative industry's economic potential and greater benefits for the wider community. The arts have an instrumental value, in that the arts industry has the ability to achieve other outcomes; "the Victorian Government is interested in the instrumental benefits of the arts, for example, the possible contribution of the arts in areas such as health, education and community development" (3). This rhetoric is similar in the Triennial policies. MQFF contributes to the vibrancy of Melbourne's creative CBD *and* aids in the social inclusion of Melbourne's queer community.

MQFF has established itself as a significant queer media institution in Australia. This balance between social value and economic viability, the latter of which is ultimately achieved by local council support, ticket sales, and sponsorship, is attributed to the development of the creative industry. While the festival perhaps is not a leader internationally, it is a key player in the Australian queer film festival circuit. Queer Screen in Sydney is the other leading queer film festival of Australia. This is largely due to the direction of Paul Struthers, Sydney's Queer Screen's partnership with both St George Bank and the exceptionally large Mardi Gras Festival. MQFF, however, as had a more influential role in the development of the queer film festival circuit in Australia, through Lisa Daniel's assistance with the development of festivals in Brisbane and Bendigo, had "taken quality queer cinema to film starved locations like Far North Queensland, Darwin, Adelaide, Perth and Ballarat" (Daniel quoted in MQFF 2014). Community film festivals ultimately have a more precarious position in Australia than North America due to varying support from governmental grants and inconsistent interest from the corporate sector. Midsumma in Melbourne and Queer Screen in Sydney are distinct exceptions to this rule.

## HKLGFF's History

The queer film festival in Hong Kong has become an integral source for LGBTI images. In October 2014, I travelled to the region to attend the festival, where I met and spoke to the current festival coordinators, Gary Mak and Joe Lam. This historical account was determined from knowledge attained from their interviews, archival research with their old programmes (where available), and my own observations while visiting the city. Historical research on film festivals requires access to such documents as they "intimate how a festival presents itself to the world and attracts festivalgoers to thereby constitute its publics" (Zielinski 2016, 154). The history of the festival can be divided into two key periods. First, its original few years in the Hong Kong Cultural Arts Centre with the coordination of the festival by Walter Lam and Raymond Yeung and, second, the subsequent period from 1999.

### 1989 and 1992: The Early Years at the Hong Kong Arts Centre

HKLGFF's inaugural film festival was in 1989 and held in the Hong Kong Cultural Arts Centre. This was one of the earliest uses of the term "*Tongzhi.*" Originally meaning "comrade" as a term of address for Chinese Communist Party members, the term was appropriated to be a gender-neutral label for sexual minorities. In her global perspective on the growth of the queer film festival, Loist notes that HKLGFF undoubtedly benefited from "Hong Kong's 'freedom' as a British colony" (Loist 2013, 115). Edward Lam, a theatre director and local activist, directed the early festivals. Three years later in 1992, Lam organised the second festival. There is very little information on the early days of the film festival. According to Denise Tse Shang Tang, who would go on to direct the festival many years later, "the history of the festival is incomplete due to the constant changing of festival organizers and the physical absence of a festival office. Documents have been scattered in various organizations with no centralization" (Tang 2009, 175).

HKLGFF has had little, to no, *direct* support from governmental initiatives or grants. Support for arts organisations is contentious, whereby "the local government's top-down approach to arts planning has generated considerable debate among the existing arts community over what kind of 'culture' should be showcased" (*ArtAsiaPacific* 117). This is supported by my interview with Mak, where film events are not considered as arts events:

In the past there wasn't a single dollar from the Hong Kong government because, first of all, that was the mentality of the Hong Kong government. Not just to the lesbian and gay film festival. They have a very distant from the film industry. For them, film is commercial. Film is a business. So they do not want to support commercial activities. That's why in general they didn't support film events (Interview with Gary Mak 2014).

Various accounts of the programming from these early years describe the festival as a niche event. With Edward Lam as director, the festival focused on documentaries and art-house faire (Tang 2009; Rhyne 2011). This perspective on the early days of the film festival was reiterated in an interview with festival co-organiser Gary Mak, who is also the director of Broadway Cinematheque in Yau Ma Tei:

He [Walter Lam] programmed a lot of hard-core art films, a lot of video work, documentaries, films such as *Go Fish*. The problem was that it wasn't the taste of the mainstream audience and it had a bad box office. Every year he had to work a lot to promote the festival. There was always pressure for the box office. For the Hong Kong Arts Centre, however, it was okay because they were subsided by the government and they could still run the program (Interview with Gary Mak 2014).

If we recall de Valck's Bourdieusian analysis of the International Film Festival Rotterdam (2014), the early years of HKLGFF were very much in alignment with an "art for art's sake ideology." Due to the support from the Hong Kong Arts Centre, Lam's curatorial decisions were autonomous from the entrepreneurial demands of a commercial venture. He was free to programme content without the need to consider the financial viability of particular titles.

Similar to frustrations from lesbian audience members of Frameline, LGBT-themed films produced during this era did not capture the desires of the Chinese community. According to Wong:

The film festival featured movies on sexual minorities produced in Western countries, most of which did not contain Chinese subtitles. On the one hand, the reproduction of Western cultural forms marked the appeal of global gayness and the desire for sameness; on the other hand, the organizers of the film festival perceived labels such as gay, lesbian and queer as Western constructs with specific histories, and thus failed to capture the Chinese experience of same-sex desire and relationships (Wong 2011b, 157).

The growth of HKLGFF is very much in alignment with my readings of both Frameline and MQFF. All three festivals were relatively niche cultural community events in their inception. We will see with the following reawakening of the festival how HKLGFF prospered in the creative industry, much like my other two case studies. HKLGFF did not take on as a commercial venture until its second inception.

While HKLGFF did not take place during the 1997 Handover to China, this momentous cultural event did influence Hong Kong film festival culture. Iordanova (2011) claims that what affected the Hong Kong International Film Festival (HKIFF) was what Ackbar Abbas (1997) refers to as the "disappearance" syndrome and riddled with anxieties about the return to China. For Iordanova, this is one of the many reasons why the festival in Pusan became the forerunning power in the East Asian circuit. The 1997 Handover created a unique socio-political landscape for Hong Kong. According to Botz-Bornstein (2012), "before 1997, Hong Kong performed an exotic East for Western tourists but since the opening of China the city has lost this appeal. Now Hong Kong rather performs 'the West' for Chinese tourists from the mainland" (3). This transition created a cultural landscape for HKGLFF to become, according to Tang (2009), a product of the post-colonialist era. This post-colonialist landscape was a transnational negotiation of cosmopolitan politics. According to Rhyne:

> Hong Kong's identity as a cosmopolitan city, before and after the Handover, and the role that English has played in the history of the colony and the city, is negotiated even in the sub-cultural space of the gay and lesbian film festival.

Hong Kong's cosmopolitan identity is a product of Chinese and British cultures. With China, there is a complex mixture of attachment and detachment, devotion and dissidence (Vines 2000). A locally born and educated generation differentiated themselves from their mainland counterparts (Tsang 2007). They were more "modern and cosmopolitan" (Fung 2001, 595). Leonard notes that while expatriates weren't incorporated in the imaginings of "the people of Hong Kong," they weren't explicitly rejected either, "revealing movement from the discourse of separate existence, which marked the early colonial period, to one of parallel existence, with the possibility of some convergence and sense of shared aims between the two communities"(Leonard 2010, 517–518). Leonard concludes that while postcolonial Hong Kong saw a new distinct emergence of the Hong Kong people, there is still evidence of how "threads of old colonialism may continue to weave through the fabric of new cosmopolitanism" (530). This cosmopolitan negotiation of Eastern and Western politics is seen in HKLGFF's next era, with this search for identity continuing in Hong Kong's gay and lesbian community.

### 1999 Onwards: Gay Cinema Becomes Profitable

In my interviews with both Gary Mak and Joe Lam, both spoke about the festival in 1999 as being an inaugural festival. Raymond Yeung, with the assistance from critic Shu Kei and Wouter Barendrecht, reignited the festival into a commercial enterprise.

> They registered the festival as a separate entity outside of the Hong Kong Arts Centre. That's why we say they are the founders of that entity of the Hong Kong Lesbian and Gay Film Festival. In the beginning they still held it at the Hong Kong Arts Centre. They tried to bring in more accessible work than Edward's style (Interview with Gary Mak 2014).

Sociologist Denise Tang, who has written extensively on her time at the festival (2009, 2011), was approached in 2003 and became co-director with Karl Ulrich. After various changes in management later, both Mak and Lam entered into leadership roles with both Yeung as executive director and Tang in a curatorial role alongside Ginger Yang.

The new festival was a decidedly more commercial activity, as stated by Mak earlier. In 2000, Fortissimo Films, an international independent film distributor, became an official sponsor. According to Tang, this significantly changed the face of the festival, where although it "allowed the festival to obtain internationally renowned films, it further constructs the identity of the festival as a foreign import, an expatriate hobby and a middle-class gay male event (Tang 2009, 176). Barendrecht, who passed away in 2009, was co-chairman of Fortissimo Films and was instrumental in "bringing Asian cinema onto the global market" (187). Barendrecht's networking allowed the festival to secure support from local business, including festival parties at gay bar Propaganda and for films to be rented with little to no cost. As Rhyne notes, "in the wake of government defunding of cultural programmes, Barendrecht's own commercial success translated into a solid foundation of private funding for HKLGFF" (Rhyne 2011, 116).

This commercial success, however, resulted in a dominance of gay male programming and a distinct minimisation of local cultures. Tang joined the festival with a commitment to bring "international and local lesbian works to local audiences" (175). This second reiteration of the festival was positioned as an upper middle-class predominantly gay male event. The following point was echoed by fellow curator Yau Ching, who argues that this "global gay" sensibility results in a dominance of white, muscular, and male bodies, as these are more financially viable (an issue I will take up in Chap. 4), where:

> Hong Kong's film festivals and their audiences, including the HKLGFF, have been "programmed" to take the white, mainly gay—with a little bit of lesbian recently—culture as "natural," "desirable," and "progressive," contributing to further suppression and marginalization of a localized and regional queer culture (606).

This is demonstrated further by the festival's move away from the Hong Kong Arts Centre to Broadway Cinematheque in Yau Ma Tei and Palace IFC in Central and (more recently) The One Shopping Centre in Tsim Sha Tsui. This move to The One was to attract a gay male audience. Interviews with both Gary Mak and Joe Lam indicated that the move to The One was to attract the clientele from California Fitness, a popular gym and cruising venue for the gay community.

> The venue The One shows a lot more commercial films so the taste is more commercially driven. Also, there is a gym inside the same building (California Fitness) and the gym is quite famous for gay people to go. So there is a gay crowd coming down from the gym to the cinema (Interview with Gary Mak 2014).

These moves to The One and Palace IFC are significant as we have the festival space changing from The Hong Kong Arts Centre—with both Lam and Mak describing this space as "underground" and "niche"—to cinemas in shopping centres. When talking about Palace IFC, Mak describes the venue as different from Broadway Cinematheque, which he describes as catering to a more local "art-house film buff" crowd willing to accept more difficult films:

> IFC is in Central and is more for the expats and those living in mid-level or who are working in Central in finance and banking. The audience is more affluent and more English speaking. They talk more about consumption, lifestyle, and parties, instead of sharing about film. For BC, people are more

interested in talking about films. For IFC, they don't really give a shit about what the director says. Most of the time, if there were a director they would just leave (Interview with Gary Mak 2014).

While the implications this drive to commercialism has on programming and the geographical space of the festival will be explored in Chaps. 4 and 5 respectively, what is important here are the implications this growth has for HKLGFF in the creative industry. HKLGFF is primarily supported by various corporate and media partners, such as Fortissimo Films, *Dim Sum* and *Fridae* Magazines, Citi Bank. The Red Ribbon Centre, an HIV/AIDS education, resource and research centre established by the Hong Kong Department of Health, is the primary supporter of the festival. As such, the government indirectly supports the festival. Joe Lam was originally approached by Denise Tang to be involved with the festival for a specific purpose:

> The previous director, Denise, asked me to be involved, because I published a gay magazine in Hong Kong called *Dim Sum*. She knows I have the connections with sponsors and clients, so maybe we could generate more money for the film festival. She asked me if I wanted to help as a consultant and to get advertisers for events (Interview with Joe Lam 2014).

As stated earlier, this journey of HKLGFF from being a relatively obscure arts event to a commercial organisation that is funded by a mix of public and private supporters is indicative of the trend for major queer film festivals growing into the creative industry. Where once these images were marginalised to an elite community (queer cinema being synonymous with experimental artwork), these queer images have now obtained an economic status and are attractive to corporate sponsors, such as Citi Bank. By moving a significant amount of their screenings to venues within shopping centres, the queer film festival attendee becomes a consumer.

## East Asian Queer Film Festivals

HKLGFF is part of a growing East Asian queer film festival circuit. At the second Taiwan Queer Film Festival in 2015, a new alliance was formed of queer film festival organisers in the Asian Pacific Region. Included in the alliance were festivals from Taipei, Tokyo, Seoul, Beijing, Shanghai, Quezon City, Yangon, Jakarta, Bangkok, and Sydney. While there were no representatives of HKLGFF at the festival, they are also included in the alliance. The formation of this alliance coincided with the International Lesbian, Gay, Bisexual, Trans and Intersex Association-Asia Regional Conference. The purpose of this alliance is to share resources and provide support for LGBTI events in Asia. As Loist (2013) and Rhyne (2007) have noted, there was a wave of new queer film festivals during the turn of the century. These film festivals were a push to share LGBTI Asian films as non-American film festivals since the 1990s can be seen as a countermovement in responding to the worldwide domination of US cultural products (Ahn 2011, 26). Rhyne identified this phase as the globalisation of the queer film festival circuit. As noted earlier in this chapter, many East Asian festivals had their inaugural festivals during this period, although many were subsequently banned from governmental censors. Berry (1999a, b) notes that Bangkok's Alternative Love Film Festival had issues with authorities, as did the festival in Seoul. The early struggles of the queer film festival in Seoul saw the emergence of heteronormativity being questioned in Korean society (Kim 2007). Both queer film festivals in Beijing, beginning in 2001, and the Q! Film Festival, beginning in 2002, have had contested relationships with local authorities and communities. The film festival in Beijing was held at the Beijing University Library with pirated copies of films at a bar with "only the domestic movies were officially listed. We showed the other ones in secret, which was certainly illegal" (Cui 2010, 421). The university discovered the festival and they were chased off campus and had to complete the festival at 798, a warehouse converted into a café. The Q! Festival is held in Jakarta, a Muslim country where homosexuality is illegal under local *sharia* law. In 2005, there was the first Asian Lesbian Film and Video Festival, where "visual language provided a new form of communication that bridged the gaps in languages and cultures among Asian lesbians" (2006, 531). Finally, as Loist (2013) notes, festivals began in Osaka (2005), Tokyo (2007), and Phnom Penh (2010).

HKLGFF is comparable to HKIFF within their positions in their respective circuits. HKIFF is one of the pre-eminent film festivals in East Asia. Cindy Hing-yuk Wong notes that "the festival's main competitor is Busan" while the festival "competed successfully with Manila, Singapore, Bangkok and other regional festivals for programming and position" (Wong 2015, 186). Iordanova (2011) states that there are three tiers in the East Asian film festival circuit. Pusan and HKIFF exist exclusively on the first tier. The second tier features large commercial festivals, such as the Tokyo International Film Festival, and industry-backed festivals, such as Taipei's Golden

Horse. I would position Busan and HKIFF in Lee and Stringer's analysis of Berlin, Venice, and Cannes as port city film festivals due to their "primary gateway locations exerting considerable influence on global film culture" (Lee and Stringer 2012, 245). They are all glamorous urban trading hubs invested in tourism linked to the commercial networks and creative clusters that drive the international film festival economy. Like Lee and Stringer's port city film festivals, HKIFF has significant influence over regional film culture and audiences. HKLGFF has a similar position within its regional queer film festival circuit. As outlined earlier, it has played a founding role in the dissemination of queer images in Hong Kong. A clear difference, however, is that HKIFF is a film market for films to be publicised and potentially acquired (Cheung 2011). Many films screened at HKLGFF, however, won't receive a commercial release with the minor few already having distributors, such as Fortissimo distributing *Love Is Strange* (Ira Sachs 2014) in the region.

## CONCLUSION

The current incarnations of Frameline, MQFF, and HKLGFF are unquestionably successful organisations. Frameline's growth from being a small collection of experimental queer work being shown in a community centre to arguably the most influential queer film festival today provides smaller queer non-profits a leading example of how to evolve. Throughout every stage of its development, providing quality queer images for the Bay Area community has remained its most important objective. The festival's growth demonstrates the general conceptual shift in how cultural value is determined. Traditional cultural policy utilised Frameline as a tool for the purpose of social inclusion. By obtaining funding from the NEA, Frameline was established as an important community organisation. This early period of increased professionalism allowed for the organisation to change from being a grassroots-based activist collective to creating a corporate-like management in the form of paid festival director Michael Lumpkin and a board of directors.

The Culture Wars and the loss of NEA funding forced Frameline to rely more so on alternative streams of income. Membership fees, ticket sales, and corporate sponsorship allowed for Frameline to remain growing throughout the 1990s. The success of the New Queer Cinema wave and the identification of the gay market allowed Frameline to be a desirable avenue for corporate sponsors. As Frameline grew into the new millennium, it became less and less like the inaugural festival in the gay community centre in 1977. The GFC and current relative success of Frameline highlight the importance of examining the relationship between economic and social values for community non-profit organisations.

I am reminded of various instances where, as a member of the selection panel for MQFF, I am faced with the dilemma of whether or not to programme an Australian film of a questionable standard. Yes, the festival is dedicated to fostering Australian cinema. However, the festival is also dedicated to providing quality cinema to a paying audience. With increased professionalism comes a greater responsibility for providing Melbourne's queer community with *quality* films with LGBT content.

This consideration of financial metrics is a result of MQFF's adoption of creative industry logic. The growth of queer community screenings in Melbourne, from the Melbourne Gay Liberation Film Society in the 1970s to the City of Melbourne funded film festival we see today, demonstrates the changing value of culture. When associated with Midsumma, the festival was mainly a tool for the social inclusion of a marginalised group in Melbourne. Film Victoria's funding demonstrates cultural policy supporting an organisation for the purpose of community engagement. The festival is now more than purely a tool for enhancing the quality of life for marginalised Melbournians. The festival is now considered a significant attribute to the city's status as a creative city.

Perhaps, as a point of difference, HKLGFF's early years are not an example of a traditional approach to cultural policy utilising an arts organisation for the purpose of social inclusion. Due to its intermittent events during the 1990s, the festival didn't solidify its position within the city's LGBTI community until its reincarnation, where it was reborn into the creative industry's logic to arts management.

This chapter's analysis of the history of these film festivals highlights the importance of examining the relationship between economic and social values for community non-profit organisations. Frameline's troubles during the Culture Wars and both MQFF and HKLGFF's restructurings all demonstrate the nature of these festivals having to consider economic variables, which will bring me to evaluating these film festivals as social enterprises in my next chapter.

## NOTES

1. For further information on subtextual representation on homosexuality in Classical Hollywood Cinema, please see Vito Russo's work on *The Celluloid Closet* (1987). Character stereotypes such as the sissy friend of the female lead in *Our Betters* (George Cukor 1933) or the predatory female villain in films such as *Dracula's Daughter* (Lambert Hillyer 1931) or *Rebecca* (Alfred Hitchcock 1940) were often read subtextually by gay and lesbian audiences as queer.

2. It is important to note that these films are only a select few of films from these directors. Their filmographies are extensive across numerous decades. Derek Jarman's other films included *Caravaggio* (1986), *The Angelic Conversation* (1985), *The Garden* (1990), and of course *Edward II*. Fassbinder's queer work includes *Querelle* (1982) and the tragic *Fox and His Friends* (1974). Fellini's other queer work includes the controversial *Salo* (1975). Other notable European queer films include *Teorema* (Pier Paolo Passolini 1968), *The Damned* (Luchino Visconti 1969), and *The Decameron* (Passolini 1971).

3. Stryker notes that Rose Troche's *Go Fish* (1994) benefited from this grant.

4. The festival previously went by the name "Persistence of Vision" (Stryker 1996).

5. Taken from their website: http://www.nea.gov/about/index.html

6. For an extensive list of international queer film festivals, please see: http://www.queerfilmfestivals.org

7. Such an example is Wiltshier and Cardow's "The Impact of the Pink Dollar: Wellington as a Destination for the Gay Market" (2001), which found that gay men had a significant expenditure for their vacations and were a desirable identifiable niche market.

8. Frances Wallace is now the executive director of Frameline.

9. This revision was conducted by the Martin Prosperity Institute in conjunction with the Rotman School of Management of the University of Toronto: http://martinprosperity.org/2012/06/27/insight-rise-revisited-creativity-index/

10. A recent survey conducted by New Horizons has reported that 96 % of Bay Area LGBT non-profits were negatively impacted by the recent recession. The report can be accessed at: http://www.horizonsfoundation.org/pdf/ImpactofEconomicDownturn.pdf

11. Out of the $1.84 million of the festival's support and revenue in 2013, approximately $418 k was from membership donations and contributions, $64 k was from governmental grants, $366 k was from non-cash contributions and $411 k was from foundation and community grants, $497 k was from festival tickets sales, $91 k was from distribution, $4 k was from merchandise sales, and $7 k being miscellaneous.

12. The Australian Film Institute is Australia's leading screen cultural organisation that aims to support the country's film and television industry.

13. Like many other queer film festivals, opening night of MQFF in the early years featured two films, one aimed at a gay male audience and another for a lesbian audience, thus splitting the audience along gender lines.

14. Film Victoria is a state government agency that supports and invests in film, television, and media projects with an aim to develop a stronger cultural identity for Victoria.

15. The session "an evening with Sadie Benning" featured her films *If Every Girl Had a Diary* (1990), *Me and Ruby Fruit* (1989), *Jollies* (1990), *A Place Called Lovely* (1991), *Living Inside* (1989), *A New Year* (1989), and *Welcome to Normal* (1990).

16. Traditionally, Midsumma's carnival day either opens or closes the festival, where there are community and sponsor stalls followed by a dance party.

17. Three Triple R (3RRR) is a Melbourne-based independent community radio station. It is considered a leader in underground/alternative culture.

18. Now called *The Southern Star*, *The Melbourne Star Observer* is a free weekly tabloid (and now online) newspaper aimed at the LGBT community that is distributed to gay and lesbian community outlets such as bars, gay and lesbian friendly stores and community centres, and so forth.

19. The effect this difference in capital has on film festivals is discussed at length in Loist's (2011) comparison of Filmfest Hamburg and Lesbisch Schwule Filmtage Hamburg/International Queer Film Festival. This effort for sustainability and the ability to afford staff members can run the "danger of commodifying their community as a specialized niche audience" (268).

20. In the interview, Leppert cited Midsumma, an annual arts and cultural festival, as the other premier queer event in Victoria.
21. It should be clarified that this interview took place in 2015. In 2016, Film Victoria sponsored the Film Victoria Award for Best Director in the Australian short film session, which was awarded to Dannika Horvat for her film *The Summer of ABC Burns* (2015). Film Victoria is now a sponsor of the festival with the City of Melbourne remaining as the principal partner.
22. The Australian Centre for the Moving Image (ACMI) is located at Federation Square in Melbourne purpose-built for the promotion and exhibition of Melbourne, Australia, and internationally.
23. The Astor Theatre is located on Chapel Street in St Kilda, which is quite near the popular gay male suburb of Prahran.
24. MQFF held its opening night gala at the Astor Theatre until 2012.
25. Now called the National Film and Sound Archive, The Screen and Sound Australia's Research and Academic Outreach Program was an initiative to promote and provide access to the archive's extensive audio-visual collection.

## Works Cited

Abbas, Ackbar. 1997. *Hong Kong: Culture and the Politics of Disappearance*. Minneapolis, MN: University of Minnesota Press.

Adler, Amy. 1996. What's Left?: Hate Speech, Pornography, and the Problem for Artistic Expression. *California Law Review* 84(6): 1499–1572.

Ahn, SooJeong. 2011. *The Pusan International Film Festival, South Korean Cinema and Globalization*. Hong Kong: Hong Kong University Press.

Anheier, Helmut. 2009. The Global Economic Downturn, Philanthropy and Nonprofits: Reflections on What It Means, and What To Do. Centre for Social Investment, University of Heidelberg & Center for Civil Society, UCLA. Accessed online: http://telecentreeurope.ning.com/profiles/blogs/the-global-economic-downturn

Armstrong, Elizabeth. 2002. *Forging Gay Identities: Organizing Gay Identity in San Francisco 1940–1994*. Chicago: The University of Chicago Press.

Atkinson, Rowland, and Hazel Easthope. 2009. The Consequences of the Creative Class: The Pursuit of Creative Strategies in Australia's Cities. *The International Journal of Urban and Regional Research* 33(1): 64–79.

Baily, Martin Neil, and Douglas J. Elliot 2009. The U.S. Financial and Economic Crisis: Where Does It Stand and Where Do We Go From Here? Brookings: Financial Series No. 7. Accessed at: http://www.brookings.edu/papers/2009/0615_economic_crisis_baily_elliott.aspx

Bennett, Tony, and Elizabeth B. Silva. 2006. Introduction Cultural Capital and Inequality: Policy Issues and Contexts. *Cultural Trends* 15(2–3): 87–106.

Benshoff, Henry. 2004. *Queer Cinema: The Film Reader.* New York: Routledge.

Benshoff, Harry M., and Sean Griffin. 2006. *Queer images: A history of gay and lesbian film in America.* Oxford: Rowman & Littlefield Publishers.

Bereson, Ruth. 2005. Advance Australia: Air or Foul? Observing Australian Arts Policies. *Journal of Arts Management, Law and Society* 35(1): 49–59.

Berger, Peter L. 1995. *Modernity, Pluralism and the Crisis of Meaning.* Gütersloh: Bertelsmann Foundation Publishers.

Berry, Chris. 1999a. Bangkok's Alternative Love Film Festival Raided. *Intersections: Gender, History and Culture in the Asian Context,* May 2. http://interscctions. anu.edu.au/issuc2/Sidcbar.html

———. 1999b. My Queer Korea: Identity, Space and the 1998 Seoul Queer Film & Video Festival. *Intersection: Gender, History and Culture in the Asian Context,* May 2. http://intersections.anu.edu.au/issue2/Berry.html

Botz-Bornstein, Thorsten. 2012. A Tale of Two Cities: Hong Kong and Dubai. Celebration of Disappearance and the Pretension of Becoming. *Transcience* 3(2): 1–16.

Bourdieu, Pierre. 1984. *Distinction: A Social Critique of the Judgement of Taste.* Trans. Richard Nice. Cambridge, MA: Harvard University Press.

Boyd, Nan Alamilla. 2008. Sex and Tourism: The Economic Implications of the Gay Marriage Movement. *Radical History Review* 100: 222–223.

———. 2011. San Francisco's Castro District: From Gay Liberation to Tourist Destination. *Journal of Tourism and Cultural Change* 9(3): 237–248.

Brabanzo, Tara. 2011. When Bohemia becomes a Business: City Lights, Columbus Avenue and a Future for San Francisco. *Journal of Studies and Research in Human Geography* 5(1): 43–59.

Cave, Richard E. 2000. *Creative Industries: Contracts between Arts and Commerce.* London: Harvard University Press.

Chasin, Alexandra. 2000. *Selling Out: The Gay and Lesbian Movement Goes to Market.* New York: Palgrave.

Cheung, Ruby. 2011. East Asian film festivals: Film markets. In *Film festival yearbook 3: Film festivals and East Asia,* ed. Dina Iordanova and Ruby Cheung, 40–61. St Andrews: St Andrews Film Studies.

City of Melbourne. 2011b. Council Renews Support for the Arts. Press Released for the City of Melbourne released 11 August, 2011, available online at: http:// www.melbourne.vic.gov.au/AboutCouncil/MediaReleases/Pages/ Councilrenewssupportforthearts.aspx

Clayton, Janet, and Mary Travers. 2009. *Arts Plus: New Models New Money: Australian Survey.* Kensington: Centre for Social Impact & Arts Queensland.

Craik, Jennifer. 1996. The Potential and Limits of Cultural Policy Strategies. *Culture and Policy* 7(1): 117–204.

Creed, Barbara. 1994. Queer Theory and Its Discontents: Queer Desires, Queer Cinema. In *Australian Women: Contemporary Feminist Thought*, ed. Norma Grieve, and Ailsa Burns, 151–164. Melbourne: Oxford University Press.

Crespi-Valbonna, Monstrerrat, and Greg Richards. 2007. The Meaning of Cultural Festivals: Stakeholder Perspectives in Catalunya. *International Journal of Cultural Policy* 13(1): 103–122.

Cui, Zi'en. 2010. The Communist International of Queer Film. Trans. Petrus Liu. *Positions: East Asia Cultures Critique* 18(2), 417–423.

Daniel, Margaret R. 2006. Camps and Shifts. *GLQ: A Journal of Lesbian and Gay Studies* 12(4): 607–611.

De Valck, Marijke. 2014. Supporting Art Cinema at a Time of Commercialization: Principles and Practices, the Case of the International Film Festival Rotterdam. *Poetics* 42: 40–59.

Department of Culture, Media and Sport. 1998. Creative industries mapping document 1998, DCMS, London, <http://www.culture.gov.uk/Reference_library/Publications/archive_1998/Creative_Industries_Mappin g_Document_1998.htm> last accessed 15/11/2016.

Di Maggio, Paul, and Michael Useem. 1979. Cultural Democracy in a Period of Cultural Expansion: The Social Composition of Arts Audiences in the United States. *Social Problems* 26(2): 179.

Di Maria, Thomas. 1992. Frameline and the NEA. *Sixteenth San Francisco International Lesbian & Gay Film Festival* (Program).

Donald, Betsy, and Douglas Morrow. 2003. Competing for Talent: Implications for Social and Cultural Policy in Canadian Cityregions. A Report prepared for the Strategic Planning and Policy Coordination Department of Canadian Heritage. Hull, QC: Department of Canadian Heritage.

Doughty, Roger. 2011. The Future of LGBT Nonprofits. *The Bay Reporter*, April 14. Accessed at: http://ebar.com/openforum/opforum.php?sec=guest_op&id=319

Dowsett, Gary. 1991. *Men Who Have Sex with Men: National HIV/AIDS Education*. Canberra: Australia Government Publishing Service.

Duggan, Lisa. 2003. *The Twilight of Equality: Neoliberalism, Cultural Politics, and the Attack on the Democracy*. Boston, MA: Beacon Press.

Dyer, Richard. 1990. *Now You See It: Studies on Lesbian and Gay Film*. London: Routledge.

Edelman, Lee. 1994. *Homographesis: Essays in Gay Literary and Cultural Theory*. New York: Routledge.

Flew, Terry. 2012. Creative Suburbia: Rethinking Urban Cultural Policy—The Australian Case. *International Journal of Cultural Studies* 15(3): 231–246.

Florida, Richard. 2002. *The Rise of the Creative Class. And How It's Transforming Work, Leisure and Everyday Life*. New York: Basic Books.

———. 2008. *Who's Your City? How the Creative Economy is Making Where to Live the Most Important Decision of Your Life.* New York: Basic Books.

Frow, John. 1995. *Cultural Studies and Cultural Value.* Oxford: Clarendon Press.

Fung, Anthony. 2001. What makes the local? A brief consideration of the rejuvenation of Hong Kong identity. *Cultural Studies* 15(3-4): 591–601.

Galloway, Susan, and Stewart Dunlop. 2007. A Critique of Definitions of the Cultural and Creative Industries in Public Policy. *International Journal of Cultural Policy* 13(1): 17–31.

Gerstner, Adrian. 2007. Tongues United (1989) Review. *Cineaste* 32(4). Accessed at: http://www.cineaste.com/articles/dvd-review-tongues-untied.htm

Gibson, Chris, Ben Gallan, and Andrew Warran. 2012. Engaging Creative Communities in an Industrial City Setting. *International Journal of Community Research and Engagement* 5(1): 1–15.

Glow, Hilary, and Katya Johanson. 2004. The Politics of Exclusion: Political Censorship and the Arts -as-Industry Program. *Asia Pacific Journal of Arts & Cultural Management* 2(2): 128–141.

Gluckman, Amy and Betsy Reed. 1997. Introduction. In *Homo Economics: Capitalism, Communtiy, and Lesbian and Gay Life*, xi–xxix. New York: Routledge.

Government of Australia. 1994. Creative nation: Commonwealth cultural policy. October 1994, Office for the Arts, viewed 15 November 2016, <http://apo.org.au/node/29704>.

Government of Queensland. 2002. *Creative Queensland: Queensland government cultural policy.* Brisbane: Arts Queensland.

Haithman, Diane. 1992. Judge Rules Against NEA Decency Policy. *Chicago Sun Times*, June 10.

Hallett, B. 1992. More Opportunities, That's the Story Line. *The Australian*, September 4, 8.

Ho, Christina. 2012. Western Sydney Is Hot! Community Arts Is Changing Perceptions of the West. *Gateways: International Journal of Community Research and Engagement* 5: 35–55.

Howkins, John. 2001. *The Creative Economy: How People Make Money from Ideas.* London: Penguin Books.

Hutchinson, Penny. 2007. Arts Victoria and the State Government's Relationship with Local Government. Presented at *Expanding Cultures: Arts and Local Government Conferences*, Prahran, Victoria, July 26–27.

Iordanova, Dina. 2011. East Asia and Film Festivals: Transnational Clusters and Commerce. In *Film Festival Yearbook 3: Film Fesitvals and East Asia*, ed. Dina Iordanova, and Ruby Cheung, 1–33. St Andrews: St Andrews Film Studies.

Kavaratzis, Mihalis, and Gregory J. Ashworth. 2005. City Branding: An Effective Assertion of Identity or a Transitory Marketing Trick? *Tijdschrift voor Economische en Social Geografie* 96(5): 506–514.

Khan, Rimi. 2011. *Reconstructing Community Based Arts: Cultural Value and the Neoliberal Citizen*. PhD Dissertation. Melbourne: The University of Melbourne.

Kim, Jeongmin. 2007. Queer Cultural Movements and Local Counterpublics of Sexuality: A Case of Seoul Queer Films and Videos Festival. Trans. Sunghee Hong. *Inter-Asia Cultural Studies* 8(4): 617–633.

Knegt, Peter. 2008. *Forging a Gay Mainstream: Negotiating Gay Cinema in the American hegemony*. Master's Thesis. Montreal, QC: Concordia University.

Knegt, Peter. 2013. Qu(e)eries: Why don't LGBT movies make money at the box office anymore? *Indiewire*. August 12. http://www.indiewire.com/2013/08/queeries-why-dont-lgbt-movies-make-money-at-the-box-office-anymore-35858/.

Lam, Joe. 2014. Interview by Stuart Richards, personal interview, Hong Kong. 22nd September.

Landry, Charles. 2008. *The Creative City: A Toolkit for Urban Innovators*. London: Earthscan.

Lee, Nikki J.Y., and Julian Stringer. 2012. Ports of entry: Mapping Chinese cinema's multiple trajectories at International Film Festivals. In *A companion to Chinese cinema*, ed. Zhang Yingjin, 239–262. West Sussex: Wiley-Blackwell.

Leonard, Pauline. 2010. Old Colonial or New Cosmopolitan? Changing White Identities in the Hong Kong Police. *Social Politics* 17(4): 507–535.

Leslie, Deborah, and John Paul Catungal. 2012. Social Justice and the Creative Class: Class, Gender and Racial Inequalities. *Geography Compass* 6(3): 111–122.

Levitas, Ruth. 1998. The concept and measurement of social inclusion. In *Poverty and social exclusion in Britain*, ed. Christina Pantazis, David Gordon, and Ruth Levitas, 123–160. Bristol: The Policy Press.

Lobato, Ramon. 2006. Cultural Policy and Live Music in Melbourne. *Media International Australia Incorporating Culture & Policy* 120: 63–75.

Loist, Skadi. 2011. Precarious Cultural Work: About the Organization of (Queer) Film Festivals. *Screen* 52(2): 268–273.

———. 2013. The Queer Film Festival Phenomenon in a Global Historical Perspective. In *Une histoire des festivals: XX<sup>e</sup>-XXI<sup>e</sup> siècle*, ed. Anaïs Fléchet, Pascale Goetschel, Patricia Hidiroglou, Sophie Jacotot, Caroline Moine, and Julie Verlaine, 109–121. Paris: Publications de la Sorbonne.

Mak, Gary. 2014. Interviewed by Stuart Richards, personal interview, Hong Kong. 21st September.

McGuigan, Jim. 1996. *Culture and the Public Sphere*. New York: Routledge.

———. 2010. *Cultural Analysis*. Los Angeles, CA: SAGE.

Melbourne Queer Film Festival. 2014. Farewell to long time Festival Director Lisa Daniel in 2015. *Melbourne Queer Film Festival Blog*. September 11. http://www.mqff.com.au/blog/2014/09/farewell-to-long-time-festival-director-lisa-daniel-in-2015/

Mennel, Barbara. 2014. *Queer Cinema: Schoolgilrls, Vampires, and Gay Cowboys*. New York: Wallflower Press.

Miller, Toby. 2009. From Creative to Cultural Industries. *Cultural Studies* 23(1): 88–99.

Miller, Toby, and George Yudice. 2002. *Cultural policy*. London: Sage Publications.

Montgomery, John. 2005. Beware of the Creative Class. *Local Economy* 20(4): 337–343.

Mulligan, Martin, and Pia Smith. 2011. Art, Governance and the Turn to Community: Lessons from National Action Research Project on Community Art and Local Government in Australia. *Journal of Arts and Communities* 2(1): 27–40.

Mulligan, Martin, K. Humphery, and P. James. 2006. Creating Community: Celebrations. In *Arts and Wellbeing Within and across Local Communities*. Melbourne: Globalism Institute, RMIT University.

O'Neill, Brian. 1997. The Arts Show Audience: Cultural Confidence and Middlebrow Arts Consumption. In *Media Audiences in Ireland: Power and Cultural Identity*, eds. Kelly, Mary J. and O'Connor, Barbara. Dublin: UCD Press.

Ooi, Can-Seng, and Jesper Strandgaard Pederson. 2010. City Branding and Film Festivals: Revaluating Stakeholder's Relationships. *Place Branding and Public Diplomacy* 6(4): 316–332.

Peck, Jamie. 2005. Struggling with the Creative Class. *International Journal of Urban and Regional Research* 29(4): 740–770.

Pederson, Jasper Strandgaard, and Carmelo Mazza. 2011. International Film Festivals: For the Benefit of Whom. *Culture Unbound* 3: 139–165.

Puar, Jasbir. 2002. Circuits of Queer Mobility: Tourism, Travel and Globalization. *LQ: A Journal of Lesbian and Gay Studies* 8(1–2): 101–137.

Quigley, Margaret. 2010. The Robert Mapplethorpe Censorship Controversy. *Public Eye*. Accessed at: http://www384.pair.com/pra/theocrat/Mapplethorpe_Chrono.html

Radbourne, Jennifer. 1996. Creative Nation: A Policy for Leaders or Followers? An Evaluation of Australia's 1994 Cultural Policy Statement. *Journal of Arts, Management Law & Society* 26(4): 271–283.

Rhyne, Raghan. 2006. The Industry and the Ecstasy: Gay and Lesbian Film Festivals and the Economy of Community. eds. Straayer, Chris and Thomas Waugh, "Queer Film and Video Festival Forum, Take Two. Critics Speak Out" *GLQ: A Journal of Lesbian and Gay Studies* 12(4): 617–619.

———. 2007. *Pink Dollars: Gay and Lesbian Film Festivals and the Economy of Visibility*. PhD Dissertation. New York: New York University.

———. 2011. Comrades and Citizens: Gay and Lesbian Film Festivals in China. In *The Film Festival Yearbook 3: Film Festivals and East Asia*, ed. Dina Iordanova, and Ruby Cheung, 110–124. St Andrews: St Andrews Film Studies.

Rich, B. Ruby. 1992. New Queer Cinema. *Sight and Sound* 80: 31–34.

———. 2002. Vision quest. Village Voice. March 26.

———. 2013. *New Queer Cinema: The Director's Cut*. Durham, NC: Duke University Press.

Rifkin, Jeremy. 2000. *The Age of Access: How the Shift from Ownership to Access Is Transforming Modern Life*. London: Penguin.

Russo, Vito. 1987. *The Celluloid Closet: Homosexuality in the Movies*. New York: Harper & Row.

Schiller, Dan. 1999. *Digital Capitalism: Networking the Global Market System*. New York: MIT Press.

Searle, Samantha. 1997. *Queer-ing the Screen: Sexuality and Australian Film and Television*. St. Kilda, VIC: Australian Teachers of Media in association with Australian Film Institute Research and Information Centre and Deakin University of Visual, Peforming and Media Arts.

Seidman, Steven. 1994. Queer-ing sociology, sociologizing queer theory: An introduction. *Sociological Theory* 12(2): 166–177.

Selinger, Julie. 2013. Wolfe releasing acquires four films at Frameline 37, Including Pit Stop and Reaching for the Moon. Indiewire. July 2. http://www.indiewire.com/2013/07/wolfe-releasing-acquires-four-films-at-frameline-37-including-pit-stop-and-reaching-for-the-moon-37171

Sender, Katherine. 2004. *Business, Not Politics*. New York: Columbia University Press.

Shaw, Kate, and Ruth Fincher. 2010. University Students in the Creative City. *Journal of Policy Research in Tourism Leisure & Events* 2(3): 199–220.

Shilts, Randy. 1998. *The mayor of castro street: The life and times of Harvey Milk*. New York: St. Martin's Press.

Staiger, Janet. 2004. Finding Community in the Early 1960s: Underground Cinema and Sexual Politics. In *Queer Cinema, The Film Reader*, ed. Harry Benshoff, and Sean Griffin, 167–189. New York: Routledge.

Stevenson, Deborah. 2000. *Art and Organisation: Making Australian Cultural Policy*. Nathan, QLD: University of Queensland Press.

Stryker, Susan. 1996. San Francisco International Lesbian and Gay Film Festival. In *The Ultimate Guide to Lesbian and Gay Film and Video*, ed. Jenni Olson, 364–370. San Francisco, CA: Serpent's Tail.

Swain, Madeleine. 1994. President's message. *Melbourne Queer Film Festival Program* 5.

Tang, Denise Tse Shang. 2009. Demand for Cultural Representation: Emerging Independent Film and Video on Lesbian Desires. In *Future of Chinese Cinema: Technologies and Temporalities in Contemporary Chinese Screen Cultures*, ed. Olivia Khoo, and Sean Metzger, 169–190. Bristol: Intellect.

———. 2011. *Conditional Desires: Honk Kong Lesbian Desires and Everyday Life*. Hong Kong: Hong Kong University Press.

Tsang, Steve. 2007. *A Modern History of Hong Kong*. London: L B Tauris and co..

Vines, Stephen. 2000. *Hong Kong: China's New Colony*. London: Orion Publishers.

Williams, Raymond. 1976. *Keywords: A vocabulary of culture & society*. New York: Oxford University Press.

Williams, Raymond. 1977. *Marxist and Literature, Marxist Introductions*. London: Oxford University Press.

Wiltishier, P., and A. Cardow. 2001. The Impact of the Pink Dollar: Wellington as a Destination for the Gay Market. *Pacific Tourism Review* 5(3-4): 121–130.

Wittman, Carl. 1970. *Gay Manifesto*. New York: A Red Butterfly Publication.

Wong, Cindy Hing-Yuk. 2011a. *Film Festivals: Culture, People and Power on the Global Screen*. New Brunswick, NJ: Rutgers University Press.

Wong, Day. 2011b. *Visual Anthropology* 24: 152–170.

Wong, Cindy Hing-Yuk. 2015. Creative Cinematic Geographies Through the Hong Kong International Film Festival. In *A Companion to Hong Kong Cinema*, ed. Esther M.K. Cheung, Gina Marchetti, and Ching-Mei Esther Yau, 185–206. Chichester: Wiley.

Yue, Audrey. 2006. The Regional Culture of New Asia: Cultural Governance and Creative Industries in Singapore. *International Journal of Cultural Policy* 12(1): 17–33.

Zielinski, Gerald J.Z. 2016. On Studying Film Festival Ephemera: The Case of Queer Film Festivals and Archives of Feelings. In *Film Festivals: History, Theory, Method, Practice*, ed. Marijke de Valck, Brendan Kredell, and Skadi Loist, 138–158. London: Routledge.

## INTERVIEWS

Crawley, Jane. Interviewed by Stuart Richards, personal interview, Melbourne, 30 May 2016.

Daniel, Lisa. Interviewed by Stuart Richards, personal interview, Melbourne, 5 August 2011.

Hillis, Crusader. Interviewed by Stuart Richards, personal interview, Melbourne, 8 December 2011.

Leppert, Rohan. 2015. Interviewed by Stuart Richards, personal interview, Melbourne, 25 September 2015.

Swain, Madeline. Interviewed by Stuart Richards, personal interview, Melbourne, 12 December 2011.

Wallace, Frances. Interviewed by Stuart Richards, personal interview, New York, 18 July 2011.

## CHAPTER 3

# The Queer Film Festival as a Social Enterprise

The queer film festival has developed into an occasion that exists on cultural calendars alongside other major arts events. Queer cinema is now a mainstay in the independent film scene with queer film festivals now competing against major international film festivals for titles such as *Weekend* (Andrew Haigh 2011), *Blue Is the Warmest Colour* (Abdellatif Kechiche 2013), and *Stranger by the Lake* (Alain Guiraudie 2013). The three case studies in this book have all experienced this growth. While Frameline and HKLGFF began as small experimental film screenings, MQFF was a subset of the larger arts and cultural festival Midsumma. All three are now larger events with considerable audiences every year. In the previous chapter, we established how this evolution coincided with the development of the creative industries, where, ultimately, the social value produced from these events is economically viable. They produce value for their respective cities.

This finding leads me to define queer film festivals as social enterprises, as they are organisations that are more than just commercial entities. The social enterprise sees profitable activities serving a social goal (Doherty et al. 2009). There has always been a social purpose to these events. This direction of film festival studies is an organisational analysis. The organisers of a social enterprise will pursue funding mechanisms beyond traditional governmental and philanthropic avenues which allow for "innovative and effective activities that focus strategically on resolving social market failures and creating new opportunities to add social value systemically by using a range of resources and organizational formats to maximise social impact and bring about change" (Nicholls 2006, 23). The film festival is a part of a

© The Author(s) 2016
S.J. Richards, *The Queer Film Festival*,
DOI 10.1057/978-1-137-58438-0_3

larger cultural industry that sees multiple stakeholders influencing structural decisions (Rhyne 2009). A key challenge for the queer film festival is the management of the double bind, where they must programme for both the community and potential stakeholders (Gamson 1996). Indeed, there are numerous, sometimes conflicting, considerations when managing a queer film festival.

The purpose of this chapter is to provide a definitional framework for defining arts organisations as social enterprises. It is my hope that this analysis of the queer film festival will be applicable to the non-profit arts industry at a more general level. When reviewing the relevant literature for this research project, six key themes arose. First, all social enterprises have an individual that oversees the management of the organisation and is often described as having the personality traits of a uniquely skilled leader; second, the organisation's social mission must identify and address a market failure; third, the organisation must employ *innovative* marketing strategies that differ from their competitors; fourth, the ultimate aim of the social enterprise is to provide a sense of empowerment for its targeted community; fifth, there is often a grave fear that this corporate need to "maximise profits" may force a "mission drift" and that the social enterprise framework could distract the organisations from their original goal; finally, how do these organisations evaluate the success of their ventures? When held against the six criteria, each case study did not always meet its social entrepreneurial status in a likewise fashion. Fieldwork research for this project will be presented at length in this chapter with excerpts from interviews of staff members presented to enrich my analysis of each festival.

## The Social Entrepreneur as a "Business Hero"

The social entrepreneur combines the key business managerial skills of the civic entrepreneur with a unique social ethic. They are the "change promoters in society" (Perrini and Vurro 2006, 69). Henton et al. (1997) assign four major duties and responsibilities to the *civic* entrepreneur. First, they are motivators and networkers, in that they motivate others to look at their community in a different manner thus gaining new levels of responsibility. They endeavour to move beyond their trusted circles to network with other community leaders to begin this process of change. Sarah Deragon, the head of Frameline Distribution, says:

You have to network. You have to be willing to know your bottom line and not be shy because you have to be able to go up to other people and "schmooz" and get their films (Interview with Sarah Deragon 2011).

Second, the entrepreneur is both a teacher and a convener. They assist in educating their community in a "collaborative process of change" (153). A successful *civic* entrepreneur ensures that all participants are aware of the implications of change and that this collaborative change happens within a succinct framework. Third, entrepreneurs are integrators and drivers in that they play a critical role in "supporting their communities as they move from the collaborative process of determining what to do about their situation to the collaborative actions that will actually change their communities" (153). It is the entrepreneur's driving force that ensures that the measurable objectives are achieved. These attributes are emphasised by Frameline executive director, K.C. Price:

The festival needs strong leadership that has the will and the desire and knowledge to raise money to run the festival. That is huge (Interview with K.C. Price 2011).

The final trope suggested by Henton, Melville, and Walesh is the entrepreneur being a mentor and agitator. This trope is twofold. First, they help establish the enterprise from being a temporary change to a "sustainable, continuous capacity" (153). Lumpkin perhaps best exemplified this mentor quality in his fostering of the growth of Frameline to its position today. The agitator characteristic of the entrepreneur sees the fight against contentment in that the need for change is a continuous process.

The social entrepreneur shares these four characteristics. The mission statement behind the social enterprise is what differentiates the social entrepreneur, who engages in "morally motivated behaviour". This is the "why" factor behind their ventures. The social entrepreneur is the driving force behind community organisation, "finding innovative solutions to problems which face the most impoverished and marginalised communities" (Catford 1998, 96). While it would be imprudent to generalise all queer communities as culturally impoverished, they are all to some degree marginalised in wider societies.

The leading figures of the three queer film festivals under analysis embody these characteristics of being at the centre of a community organisation. It is this social role that the social entrepreneur embodies that we must prioritise in our discussion. The social entrepreneur *creates* organisations and uses innovation to *create* change. This creativity is a central aspect to entrepreneurship (Vesper 1982).

> *Entrepreneurship is the creation of new organizations...* If we are to understand the phenomenon of entrepreneurship in order to encourage its growth, then we need to focus on the process by which new organisations are created (Gartner 2002, 62, original emphasis).

If we focus on the creation and development of Frameline, we can see Michael Lumpkin and his associates as innovators at the heart of their community. The key social entrepreneurs in Frameline for our discussion are Lumpkin, former executive director K.C. Price (2003–2014), former festival director Jennifer Morris (1994–2011), and executive director Frances Wallace, who was appointed in 2014. These figures can be read as subcultural celebrities in that their "stardom" is contained to a specific subcultural audience as opposed to the omnipresence associated with more general definitions of stardom (Hills 2003). The subcultural celebrity has status within a niche field. Their celebrity is restricted and specific as opposed to being "culturally ubiquitous and mass-mediated figures" (Hills 2006, 101). Other key Frameline staff members can also be read as subcultural celebrities. Interviews with local press and their introductions to all of the larger screenings aid them in being subcultural figures. Former staff member Harris Kornstein performs as drag queen Lil Miss Hot Mess at various venues in San Francisco; Sarah Deragon is now an established photographer specialising in LGBT weddings, "not-so-corporate headshots," and the popular Identity Project.[1]

Frameline's success lies in its close engagement with the Bay Area community. This can be attributed to the staff members' subcultural celebrity statuses *within* that community. The development of social media and online news sites allow for a newer engagement with Frameline audiences. Writing about subcultural stardom and online media convergence, Ellcessor (2012) argues that this subcultural figure is "an *agent* of media convergence that functions through *connection*" (48, her emphasis). They form "textual, industrial, and personal connections through the use of online social media...(and) smooth the convergences of aesthetics, audiences, and industries that complicate the contemporary media landscape" (48). Frameline staff members traverse various methods of engagement with audiences. For example, Kornstein has used the Facebook account of Lil

Miss Hot Mess to promote festival highlights. Free film tickets would also be given away at various drag shows. In reviews of the festival, Morris and Price would often be featured in a photograph with a high-profile guest of the festival (see Brooks 2011).

By actively engaging in interviews (with both the media and guests at screenings), being active on social media sites as demonstrated in Fig. 3.1, and personally interacting with audience members, Frameline staff members facilitate "connections between various media platforms, texts, audiences and industries" (Ellcessor 2012, 53). Each staff member would also engage different members of the Bay Area LGBT community. The audience members Lares Feliciano, former volunteer coordinator and filmmaker, and Korsten (and Lil Miss Hot Mess) would promote the festival to differ greatly to Price and Morris. Their subcultural celebrity status stems from their direct engagement to the community. While they may remain relatively unknown to the general public, they are recognisable to regular Frameline attendees.

When discussing this trope in interviews, I asked all subjects what it takes to run a successful queer film festival. For Des Burford, Frameline operations manager, part of being at the centre of your community is an

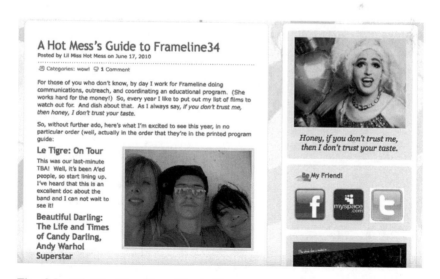

**Fig. 3.1** Lil Miss Hot Mess (Harris Kornstein) uses social media to promote Frameline

understanding and knowing how to tailor the festival programming to its audience's needs and desires. A good social entrepreneur knows what will work and what won't. As Buford states:

> I wouldn't necessarily program the exact same festival here in San Francisco than in Fresno or Denver or in Alabama because a lot of our stuff is beyond queer 101. I don't mean to say that a lot of those places are in a queer 101 place but I think that part of putting a successful program together is knowing your audience and knowing the baseline, what is the current understanding or what is the current framework that your audience has for content. What makes a successful festival is to know the program for your audience (Interview with Des Burford 2011).

In order for the social entrepreneur to be a "business hero," it is imperative for them to couple the skills and traits of a civic entrepreneur with both the creativity and knowledge of their audience. Michael Lumpkin's history with Frameline has established the passion and drive required of a social entrepreneur at the onset of the organisation creation. Both K.C. Price and Jennifer Morris display the imperative elements of strong financial leadership with a sound knowledge of their target market.

Similarly in Hong Kong, the festival director Gary Mak identifies that his knowledge of the changing nature of the Hong Kong LGBT community is imperative in successfully running the festival. While the community was once primarily "aggressive and more liberal," the festival is now a celebration. Mak understands which films are "safe" and which films challenge the audience:

> The festival is more celebratory. We want the films to have that mentality. At the same time as a programmer, I don't want to go all the way in that direction. I want us to think about some of the issues we should be aware of nowadays. I am encouraging the team to program more challenging works. That's why we have some documentary sessions. The HKLGFF audience can really talk about some of the issues in the films that we bring, like gay marriage, seniors, what is happening in Russia. Not just in the *Eating Out* direction, even though we did show all five films and they were very successful (Interview with Gary Mak 2014).

With MQFF, we know that when Daniel came on board in 1999, the festival underwent a total restructure. Daniel wanted to provide the audience with the highest quality product possible. As a result of this, the festival duration was shortened and a minimum standard for quality was enforced. Over the following years, Daniel regained and strengthened the Melbourne queer community's trust in MQFF. The look of the festival programme material also changed, with a more professionalised allocation of sponsorship advertisements and a more strategic placement of the film synopsis, which allowed the programme to be more accessible.

The social entrepreneur is a community leader. With the social entrepreneur as a social-moral motivator, it is imperative for the organisation director to be a "situational and transformational leader that applies innovation and risk taking creativity effectively in highly contingent ways" (Nicholls 2006, 11). Former MQFF director Crusader Hillis sees strong film festival leadership as being about accessibility and one's relationship with the film industry:

> A great awareness of what is happening in the film industry is important, keeping up with technological change and a desire to be accessible in every way; being accessible for all types of interest groups; being well connected in terms of networks. Financial capability, good governance, the list goes on (Interview with Hillis 2011).

Adding to Hillis's points, a key element to leadership is visibility. Daniel has had various profiles in leading publications and websites, as has MQFF's new executive director Dillan Golightly and head of programming Spiro Economopoulos. They have all featured in a variety of media sources when promoting the festival. In 2009, "lifestyle website" *Same Same* selected Daniel as one of the 25 most influential LGBT identities. The website highlights the impact her influence has on the wider community:

> Daniel's careful and dedicated curation of MQFF each year is having a significant impact on our social and cultural landscape as the festival's attendance numbers soar, and more people than ever are witnessing the best in queer film from Australia and the world. She has helped secure the financial and critical status of the festival through times when most community organisations were going under, and her excellent management has secured the festival's survival for a long time to come (*Same Same* 2009).

Further placing Lisa Daniel as a subcultural celebrity, her and Jackson's renovation in Balnarring featured in an episode for the edutainment show *Grand Designs Australia*.[2] This public visibility adds to her subcultural status of being a leader within the Melbourne LGBTI community. This status is acknowledged only within certain segments of this community, as media texts such as *Same Same, The Age,* and the *Lifestyle Channel* carry certain social capital of being engaged and culturally aware.

Much like my interview responses from Frameline, interviews with those involved in MQFF identified that a successful social entrepreneur must combine this subcultural status with certain managerial skills. For Daniel, the key to being in a leadership position for a successful queer community is to have a sound knowledge of how the community works and to be skilful in developing relationships with a variety of people:

> You need to have a good feel as to what the community is. It doesn't really exist anyway... What you and I like are completely different things, we are *only* defined by our sexuality. So you have to have some kind of feel as to what an audience might want. It's about relationships with audiences, relationships with sponsors, and relationships with community organisations. Being good at relationships is crucial (Interview with Daniel 2011).

Daniel touches on a significant point in her response here. The Melbourne queer community is quite unique in its geographical diversity. Melbourne has no particular "gay ghetto," albeit a high proportion of MQFF attendees hail from both the Prahran/South Yarra, Brunswick, and Collingwood areas of Melbourne. Knowing how to cater for and communicate with a diverse community with only one aspect of their identity in common is an imperative aspect to successful film festival management. Likewise, Joe Lam of HKLGFF had a similar influence on the festival in Hong Kong. He redesigned the look of the festival when he became involved:

> I re-designed the guidebook. Wouter, before I was involved, passed me a flyer in the club and it looked horrible. I didn't want to watch the films because the flyer was quite bad. Since I have taken over, people will pick it up and want to know what it is. We changed the guidebook, made it more professional, we designed the logo, and we put it in bigger cinemas. Palace IFC and the One are in shopping malls now, not the small Hong Kong Art Centre. Before it was underground. Now you have big posters outside the cinema. I want people to know about this cinema, for tourists to know about the film festival. That's how it will become more mainstream (Interview with Joe Lam 2014).

We can thus draw the conclusion that for queer film festival directors to be deemed successful social entrepreneurs, they need to firstly possess sound business managerial skills in managing their staff and contacts and knowing how to deliver a product their audience will want to see and relate to. The social mission is integral to their organisation's identity creation process. Failure for the social entrepreneur manager to continuously adhere to this can result in an organisation that resembles that of a for-profit organisation (Borzaga and Solari 2004). Furthermore, they need to combine this civic entrepreneurial skill with the moral ethic of the social entrepreneur and combine a quality programme that stays true to their social mission, which will ultimately generate a socially empowering environment for the festival.

## THE SOCIAL ENTERPRISE TARGETS A GAP IN THE MARKET

The need for any particular social enterprise stems from the needs of any disadvantaged or marginalised community not being met. This is usually due to these desires not being financially beneficial. For Haugh (2005), these gaps are untapped marketing opportunities thus allowing the social enterprise to meet the needs of a particular community that were previously going unmet. It is clear that the queer film festival's success lies in the feeding of these unmet desires. At the 2014 patron launch of the MQFF, festival director Lisa Daniel joked that she often gets asked "why do you need a queer film festival when we have *Modern Family?*" Ultimately, ignorant questions such as these prove the sheer importance of queer media organisations in the arts community. When interviewing subjects, I simply asked them what needs the queer film festival meets that would otherwise go unmet. The responses highlighted three key desires of the queer community.

The first significant desire the queer film festival provides was highlighted in the introduction of this book. The very purpose of the film festival is to assist in the promotion and distribution of independent film outside of the hegemony of Hollywood. The film festival is the "best system we have for giving movies an opportunity to be seen when commercial concerns are not the first priority" (Pickard 1998, 11). The festival offers access to queer media outside of the narrow identities presented on television and widely released feature films. According to Wallace, without the queer film festival, this broad array of films would not reach their intended market:

> The program celebrates international and American independent queer programming and if Frameline didn't exist there just wouldn't be that avenue to see that depth of programming (Interview with Frances Wallace 2011).

Simply put, without the queer film festival, there would not be this avenue to nourish and support queer independent film. There appears to be a misconception that advanced media dissemination online and digital connectivity allow these films to be available outside of the festival. Ultimately, according to K.C. Price, this just isn't that case:

> I think the importance that the queer film festival has is that it really offers to the LGBT community a wide variety of queer cinema that they aren't going to have access to otherwise. I often hear people say 'oh I could just catch it on Netflix' or 'I will download it online' and I don't think that that is necessarily true. Any year when you go through the program guide there are just so many films that just aren't getting distribution opportunities and therefore just aren't accessible (Interview with K.C. Price 2011).

MQFF director, Lisa Daniel, confirms the findings from my San Francisco interviews. The first, and most obvious, need MQFF meets is access to queer films that would have otherwise been inaccessible to the Melbourne community. For Daniel, this factor demonstrates the crucial role MQFF plays in Melbourne's cultural landscape:

> Certainly a depiction of queer characters and themes which you don't normally see, we screen 150 films, maybe 5 of those would get a commercial screening or maybe an ABC, SBS or Foxtel release. That says to me that it's absolutely crucial still; just the main point of queers being able to see some aspect of their lives on screen (Interview with Daniel 2011).

MQFF screenings provide an atmosphere unattainable in a general film festival environment. In 2009, I recall attending the documentary *Prodigal Sons* (Kimberly Pierce 2009) both at Frameline and later at a much smaller screening for MIFF. The film later screened as part of MQFF's programme the next year in 2010. Likewise, in Hong Kong, both Joe Lam and Gary Mak stated in their interviews that queer films are available outside of the queer film festival, namely at the HKIFF and at Broadway Cinematheque, the latter of which was screening *Concussion* (Stacie Passon 2013) at the venue while the festival was happening:

> The international film festival is very annoying (laughs)! They get all the best films. They stole quite a few this year: *Lilting* was their opening film. Hong Khou (director) came to Hong Kong for the opening. Their office is not giving us the film this year. Another film was *Tom at the Farm*.[3] We screened

that as well because it's such a good film and not many people saw it. They had two screenings and they didn't sell out (Interview with Joe Lam 2014).

These viewing experiences have led me to conclude that a queer film screening in a more mainstream film festival is decidedly less queer as the social dynamics at play are entirely different. The communal viewing experience of watching a queer film with like-minded spectators is thus entirely put under the microscope. This leads us into the second and third needs the queer film festival meet. Second, an identity-affirming experience, and, third, interaction with one's community. By providing access to a diverse array or queer stories, attending queer film festival screenings acts as an identity-affirming experience, where "the centrality of media culture... illuminates the recursive trajectory of identity formation" (Linne 2003, 669). Media is important in contemporary identity formation, and this provides an alternative space for media to flourish outside of the hegemony of Hollywood. Compulsory heterosexuality is not as dominant in society and not as "monolithic as what is once was" (Baker 2008, 116). Queer film aids in this transformation. Des Burford shares this position:

> Affirmation and validation; yes we have pride, yes we have Dyke March, yes we have Trans March but there is something so special about coming together in one room and watching a queer story unfold and know that everyone in that room is rooting for that character... we have come a long way since the code era of Hollywood. It's like "oh wow there are nuances, and subtleties of queer desire and it's just kinda out there". I think that's a really beautiful thing and being able to watch that with your lovers, your friends and your partners is fantastic. So I think that ultimately it gets back to validation and affirmation (Interview with Des Buford 2011).

Buford's response highlights the importance of community engagement to the queer film festival's social mission. This engagement with the community distinguishes a niche film festival from general international film festivals. An interview of particular interest is that of festival intern and filmmaker Sam Berliner.[4] Berliner had his film *The Genderbusters* in Frameline's 2011 programme. His interview thus offers unique insight into experiencing the film festival as an audience member, festival staff member, *and* a filmmaker:

> My ideal audience was the Transtastic screening. Where else am I going to find a big group of people who the film will speak personally too, or there is

something in the film that they can relate to as part of their life? The really great thing about film is not what happens during the film but what comes after the film.... Raising awareness about an issue and doing something to actually help something (Interview with Sam Berliner 2011).

Of particular note in Berliner's response is his acknowledgement that this communal experience would not be possible without the experience the queer film festival sanctions. It is not just the act of watching the film that queer film festival offers either; it is the social interaction that occurs before and after the screening amongst one's community. This transformational experience that the festival provides leads me to the next desire that Frameline provides for its audience: *interaction* with one's community. Philip Walker believes that the queer film festival provides the possibility of a collective identity:

You can consume media at home but it's not the same. There is something about watching it with others at the festival; it's a way for people to be exposed to other kinds of people. So if you are a muscly white guy, going to a trans doco could be an eye opening experience, like opening night[5] or *Becoming Chaz* (Interview with Philip Walker 2011).

There are various forms of interaction that occurs at the queer film festival. Walker points out that there is connection *between* different subcategories of the queer community. I personally recall one friend in San Francisco telling me there are gay male friends she ever sees only at Frameline due to most LGBTI-related events in the city being strictly divided between sexual identities. Frameline offers opportunities for these mixed interactions at parties or key screenings, such as opening night's *Gun Hill Road* (Rashaad Ernesto Green 2011) or *Becoming Chaz* (Fenton Baily and Randy Barbato 2011).

The key difference between queer representation in a queer film festival context and queer characters appearing in a mainstream television show or film is that the former is free from stereotypes or clichés, which are usually designed to make the conservative audience more comfortable. This is a factor that is usually brought up in selection panel meetings for MQFF, where we can make the obvious observation that a particular film is aiming at having a crossover appeal to a straight audience. This factor was raised in my interview with fellow selection panel member Paul Tonta, who is also festivals and special events manager for distributor Madman Cinema, when discussing the film *Different from Whom?* (*Diverso Da Chi?* Umberto Carteni 2009):

> I found the two Italian films in the festival this year, *Loose Cannons* (*Mine Vaganti* Ferzan Ozpetek 2010) and this one [*Different from Whom*] were films that are made for straight audiences, where they are mainstream but have queer characters and it's as if they are made for a mainstream audience so they have to pander to those who are a little uncomfortable [with queer characters]. I thought both *Different from Whom* and *Loose Cannons* were like that. That's the negative side of having a commercial cinema with queer content; that they are afraid they are going to alienate a straight audience (Interview with Tonta 2011).

Tonta's response recalls that a term I have often heard at queer film festivals is "by, for and about," whereby the film's content is solely aimed at a queer audience and doesn't need to compromise any aspect of their queerness for a straight and possibly uncomfortable audience.

The screenings themselves act as an opportunity to experience film in a safe environment. Feliciano raised this notion of a collective identity in a safe environment:

> Queer films play at larger festivals but not as much, it's a small percentage. Just because a queer film is playing at a large festival, doesn't necessarily mean that it's going to feel like a safe space to watch it. It doesn't necessarily mean it will be a hostile place but I think part of what is so valuable about a queer film festival is that it provides both space for exhibition of queer work and a safe space for queer audience experience. I have the same film that played at Frameline also play at the SF International Women's film festival and that was a very different audience and a very different experience.[6] It was just a very different vibe. When you make a film that is queer and is intended for a queer audience, that feeling when you are watching is going to be a lot warmer and fuzzier when it's with a queer audience. You are going to feel a lot less alienated, a lot less alone, which is what being queer in a heteronormative patriarchal world feels like (Interview with Feliciano 2011).

MQFF's Rowena Doo's response to this took into account the possible consequences of there no longer being a queer film festival in Melbourne. How would the cultural landscape change?

> I think a very big hole would be left in the community if there weren't a festival; it comes down to that social connection. Film is an incredible leveller,

we all like film, and it's very hard to find someone who doesn't like film. From that point of view, it's a great way of bringing people together from the community who might not always do that, or maybe they don't even identify as gay yet. So if there was no queer film festival I feel the community would be a lot more marginalised, more disenfranchised and a lot more people who would be in danger of not reaching their potential as people because they wouldn't feel comfortable as themselves. I saw instances after instances over the last 13 years of people, as captain Von Trapp would say, 'blooming grew' because of their connection with the festival, which is why you work in a festival, it's not for the pay, you are never going to get rich (Interview with Doo 2011).

Doo's response encapsulates the need for social connection that the queer film festival provides. MQFF provides a space in which a variety of identities on the queer spectrum can meet in a self-affirming activity. These responses recall Anderson's (1983) idea of the imagined community, where although each audience member will not necessarily meet face-to-face, however, they may share similar interests or have a shared interest. By imagining all other audience members as having a similar sexual and gender identity, the individual feels as those the space is safer, as opposed to seeing *Brokeback Mountain* (Ang Lee 2005) at the cinema multiplex with homophobic patrons. Here we see the imagined community being mediated through queer media escaping the heteronormative patriarchal world, which Feliciano talks of. In applying Anderson's concept of the imagined community to film festivals, Iordanova (2010) argues that they "suspend the 'imagined' element of the community by substituting it with a very real one that is, nonetheless, configured around the same axis of imagination that drives the ideas of nation and nationalism" (13). In *From Nimbin to Mardi Gras: Constructing Community Arts* (1993), Gay Hawkins discusses the construction of a community art aesthetic and how activities such as Mardi Gras create the possibility for the imagining of a queer community. When such community events are positioned alongside "high art," their status as non-art makes their eligibility for state support problematic. However, when these practices "are put into the context of cultural rights, of people representing themselves, their progressive potential is revealed" (131). This social aesthetic displays a direct participation in community-minded culture. Much like my analysis of Frameline, we are seeing an imagined community being mediated through queer spectatorship. The queer film festival fills a social need quite similar to Pride parades in that they are an opportunity for various subcategories of the queer community to come together and experience an imagined collective identity.

Another level of interconnectivity provided by the queer film festival is of a globalised queer community, as outlined by Alexis Whitham:

> You get to see so much more of the queer community at large through the festival, such as in China, Guatemala or any other country that is represented in the festival, or what it looks like to be queer in Kansas versus San Francisco. I think in particular in San Francisco, people can get really into the fact that it is a place that you can feel accepted all the time and nobody looks at you weirdly for your weird haircut or your style of dress being genderqueer. *You can* get away with that here. I think it serves as a really nice reminder for San Franciscans that other people are still going through things that maybe we aren't going through every day because we live in a bubble of acceptance for most of the time (Interview with Whitham 2011).

Whitham argues here that being queer in San Francisco can be like living in a queer bubble. When I undertook my internship in 2009, I vividly recall my supervisor asking me about my life back in Melbourne. I mentioned that the majority of my friends back in Australia identified as straight. Baffled, she simply replied "why?" She couldn't understand why I would choose to associate with a majority of heterosexuals stating that in San Francisco you just didn't really "need them." I came to realise this even further when during my three-month stay, I associated with few straight-identified people either. I had never lived in a "gay ghetto," and it was truly a remarkable experience. What the queer film festival serves these members of the queer bubble in the Bay Area is what life is like in other regions of the world, whether it be in other American states or in countries where it is illegal to practice homosexual relations. What this creates for the audience in San Francisco is the feeling of a global community. States Rhyne:

> If queer identity, culture, and communities are in fact being internationalized, then they are inexorably linked to globalization. These economic channels of cultural exchange are key modes through which gay and lesbian organizations imagine "community" beyond geographic boundaries and give it a primary function in gay and lesbian political life (Rhyne 2006, 619).

This feeling of being associated with something bigger is a result of both having access to this material and the affirmation of identity that takes place. For HKLGFF's Gary Mak, this global connectivity is connected to education. For Mak, without the festival, other NGOs would attempt to fill the void; however, they "can't replace the impact of cinema, because society needs this education and activism through cinema in regards to coming out and safe sex" (Interview with Gary Mak 2014). The queer film festival provides a self-affirming social activity that is important to any community.

HKLGFF does not meet this social enterprise criterion to the same extent as MQFF and Frameline due to the nature of their programming being considerably more male dominated. This is a factor that has seen HKLGFF received criticism for in the past. As stated in my previous chapter, Denise Tang joined the festival "with a commitment to bring international and local lesbian works to local audiences" (2011, 117). Tang also notes, however, that the festival "has often been perceived as a primarily upper middle-class gay male event" (117). A challenge for the festival is their minimal programming of lesbian and local content and works without Chinese subtitles. Yau Ching supports this point, who argues that this dominance of predominantly white, gay, and male content further marginalises local content (2006). While this is an issue that will be explored further in Chap. 4 when I look at the films programmed, this is an issue worth noting here as it an issue that impacts the social value produced by HKLGFF. The issue of Chinese subtitles is, in particular, a challenge for the festival, as Joe Lam notes:

> It is very expensive to provide subtitles for gay and lesbian films. The cost to subtitle is about HK$8000–HK$10,000, including translation and projection; the screening fee is around HK$5000, there are about 100 seats in a theatre so a sold out screening would get us HK$10,0000; then you have to pay back the money to the cinema. We would be losing money. We can only have subtitles when some companies pay for it when it's distributed in Hong Kong. *Love is Strange* had subtitles because Fortissimo have the film and are going to distribute it (Interview with Joe Lam 2014).

This is an example of social and economic values coming into conflict. Providing Chinese subtitles would allow for more local audiences to participate in the festival. There is a distinct lack of international gay and lesbian films with Chinese subtitles available in Hong Kong. This is an avenue HKLGFF is unable to meet due to financial restraints.

## INNOVATION

The core aim of any social enterprise is to be financially independent from *just* philanthropy and governmental grants. This infers that the organisation must develop new strategies in order to address previously unmet needs of the targeted community. Innovation for social enterprise is about careful management of resources with an understanding of the importance of pursuing revenue outside of philanthropy, where non-profits are "shifting from a traditional philanthropic dependency... to a focus on the measurability of results and the identification of all potential commercial sources of revenue" (Perrini and Vurro 2006, 60). Ultimately, innovation can occur on three separate levels. First, innovation is the development through which something new and valuable is created and made available to the community that had previously been unavailable (Drucker 1985). This refers back to the previous trope of the social enterprise, where the organisation delivers needs and desires of a community that had previously been unmet. Furthermore, innovation is employed to apply new ideas or the "reapplication of old ideas in new ways... to devise better solutions to our needs" (Leadbeater 2007, 2). This second level of innovation analyses *how* these unmet desires are delivered to the community. Third and finally, innovation is employed so that the organisation can function competitively in the market and to ultimately show that businesses can be economically sustainable and deliver social benefits (2). I asked all interview subjects if they found their respective festivals innovative and the responses corresponded to the three levels of innovation mentioned earlier. This is an important addition as "social enterprise innovation can additionally address how economic and social innovatory practices, outcomes, and principles come together for empowerment as well as effective implementation" (Westall 2007, 2). Perrini and Vurro (2006) state that entrepreneurial innovation is all about the identification of opportunities, as social enterprises "stand out for focusing their attention on a different set of possibilities: innovative ways to create or sustain social change by bringing two different cultures – business and non-profit – together under one innovative and hybrid organization" (72).

At the very basic level, Frameline meets the needs of the San Francisco Bay Area's queer community that were previously going unmet as outlined by development coordinator Jennifer Kim:

To feel included and to see others like themselves is still important. We talk a lot about when we write grants that the slice of LGBT programming that you see on mainstream television is still such a narrow slice. So to have a film festival that brings in all these different voices and people and lifestyles and sexualities, *that's* super innovative (Interview with Jennifer Kim 2011).

Frameline maintains its success by employing innovative strategies to meet these needs of the community, which is to provide access to quality queer cinema and a communal experience. For MQFF's Lisa Daniel, a significant aspect of innovation comes down to the films at the levels of both filmmaking and programming. In her interview, we discussed the careful consideration that is put into short film packages:

The filmmaking is the most innovative part of it. Definitely, because you have to be innovative in terms of how you select the films and how you put them together. You could just put together a girl's shorts package and throw girls shorts in that mean nothing. That's the whole curatorial aspect, putting those shorts together. ACMI once screened a shorts package, about 6 years ago, out of order because they didn't want to have to go from 35 mm to digi-beta to some other beta so they put the three 35 mm together on a loop and then I found out half way through and I cracked the shits with them massively and they never did it again. The shorts have to have some kind of relationship with each other (Interview with Daniel 2011).

Innovative curatorial consideration is the key to a successful film festival programme, as outlined earlier by Daniel. Paul Tonta concurs that innovation lies in the programming, particularly with the highlighting of films in the programme:

In terms of programming, at times it certainly is. One good thing about having a festival that is quite successful is having an audience go on a journey with and take chances; you can be innovative in your programming. There are some particularly innovative choices in the program.[7] The innovation in say having a centrepiece session and programming *Last Summer of Lay Boyita* (Julia Solomonoff 2009); that's a really gutsy innovative move because it's highlighting a film that a lot of people wouldn't see. So an Argentinean film about 12 year olds, one of whom is intersex, it's not a big-ticket item, it's a hard sell. You are pushing that which is innovative (Interview with Tonta 2011).

Innovative programming was highlighted by programming and hospitality associate Alexis Whitham:

> I think that Frameline does a good job because we would give a good time or venue slot to a film that isn't on paper going to be a financial hit... Not to say that it's a great slot but there is a film called *Bob's New Suit* (Alan R. Howard 2009) that is a likable film. It's a film that the festival director liked. I saw it and I liked it, it's not really breaking down any barriers in certain ways but in some ways it is. It is a simple *Lifetime* movie with a trans character... The important part of the story is the family. This director started making the film in 2009 and submitted through the regular channels. Sure it played at 1:15 on Tuesday, but it was a Castro screening so 600 or so people ended up seeing it. Now if you played that film at the Roxie you would have had 180 maximum. By putting it at the Castro, you get the people with the Castro passes, the weekday matinee passes, and you get most of the programmers as they stay at the Castro for the week. You get the people seeing a 1:15 film but it would be more than a screening at the Roxie at any other time in the week. I think that director got more responses from programmers than he normally would have because it was a Tuesday afternoon and nothing was up against it like *Tomboy* (Celine Sciamma 2011) which *Gone* (John and Gretchen Morning 2011) was. That's a tough slot for *Gone* being up against *Tomboy*. By going up against nothing it (*Bob's New Suit*) was great. I think those are important decisions. I think Jennifer, KC and Des's knowledge of venues, times and who goes to what is really interesting. Sometimes I would like at the program and go whaaa? But it usually works out! (Interview with Whitham 2011).

Whitham's discussion of the programming strategy employed for *Bob's New Suit* demonstrates how these innovative strategies are employed in order for the festival to remain competitive and attract wider audiences.

When asked about the role innovation plays with the festival in Hong Kong, Joe Lam highlighted the desire to programme more challenging and experimental work in the future. The accompanying photographic exhibition "Kiss Me" at XXX in San Wan, an upcoming hip neighbourhood, was also raised as an effort to extend the festival's activities beyond the film screenings. The gallery was designed to challenge the increasing instance of homophobia in Hong Kong (Chan 2008). This homophobia was seen as a reaction to increased visibility (Fig. 3.2).

Strategic development of a queer film festival is important. MQFF's innovation lies in its new strategies to remain financially viable in the form of its new "Sweethearts" patron drive. MQFF's non-profit status allows for

**Fig. 3.2** Kiss Me Exhibition, curated by The Gaunts and Joe Lam, was part of HKLGFF 2014

donations to the festival to be tax deductible. The newly created Sweethearts programme allows for a new income stream for the festival. The Sweethearts programme is the primary means for the festival to acknowledge Melbourne's philanthropic community. Aside from the symbolic privileged status philanthropic patronage brings you, the Sweethearts patronage drive allows a personalised priority ticketing and seating service; voting rights to the Sweethearts award; acknowledgements on the website and in the programme; opportunities to mingle with the filmmakers, board management, and staff; and of course tax deductibility for their donation. The core aim for any social enterprise is to be financially viable and independent from a reliance on governmental grants, which this new patronage programme allows. This is an avenue Frameline has mastered in terms of the significant membership number and signifies MQFF's growth and maturation. HKLGFF has recently employed similar methods to court high-paying members:

> For the past four or five years, Joe has worked with Kee Club, which is more for celebs and rich people because they run with membership, which is expensive. The common audience would not be able to pay. Joe has ties with the club and has a membership. We have done events there and screened films that are more avant-garde. They would bring in artists. This helps the festival to bring in more 'upper class' people. That is innovative (Interview with Gary Mak 2014).

Finally, an example of digital innovation is Frameline's initiative "Frameline Voices," which aims to provide a broader access to films by and about queers of colour, transgender people, youth, and elders. It provides streaming LGBT video content for free on YouTube and Vimeo. Hits have been received from all over the globe including Saudi Arabia, China, India, Russia, Indonesia, Taiwan, Mexico, and Egypt. Social networking websites have become increasingly important to LGBT youth hoping to find identity and belonging. LGBT youth are more likely to search for community online rather than sex (Paridis 2008). The Internet is now a primary venue for LGBT youth for the formation of identity, autonomy, and sexuality (Subrahmanyam and David 2008). Frameline Voices is a quintessential example of a social enterprise's innovation assisting in this identity formation.

## SOCIAL EMPOWERMENT

The desired outcome for any social enterprise's targeted community is social empowerment, which occurs through social change, being both sustainable development and the movement of social groups. The empowering capacity of any social enterprise occurs through the organisation's relationship with their targeted community. The social enterprise is an empowering "catalyst for social transformation" (Alvord et al. 2004, 262) aiming to "transform larger systems in which they are embedded" (263). This scaling up is in relation to expanding the impact an organisation can have on a community, not necessarily about becoming a larger organisation (Uvin et al. 2000). They can achieve this with three separate strategies. First, expand the size of the organisation and cover a "larger number of beneficiaries" (1411);

second, increase the diversification of activities provided by the organisation; the final strategy occurs in two folds, to both directly impact the lives of the beneficiaries and (perhaps most importantly) to indirectly affect other actors who work with the same target group.

The first strategy, in regard to increasing the size of the organisation, has been discussed in depth in my previous chapter. Frameline began as a small grassroots organisation of volunteers screening their own experimental work. Now the organisation is a multimillion dollar enterprise that employs seven full-time staff and about a dozen staff during the festival season, plus offering numerous internships. Furthermore, over 400 volunteers participate in the day-to-day running of the festival. The festival programme now screens over 200 films, consisting of features, documentaries, and shorts from across America and internationally. Frameline has indeed increased in size so as to now be considered an influential power player in queer cinema internationally. As such, Frameline has developed a significant influence over the queer community of San Francisco. For Gamson's (1996) discussion on the two New York based queer film festivals, "collective identities... are continually filtered and reproduced through organizational bodies" in that "identity boundaries are shaped by and shift through organizational activity" (235). In producing this socially constructed collective identity, Frameline has had to remain adaptive and publicly legitimate to the community. With its growth in size, Frameline has increased its services it provides the queer community of the Bay Area. Perhaps most obviously, according to Whitham, Frameline has created close ties for many community sponsors with their community sponsorships:

> We are always willing to do trade and promote smaller queer organisations. Frameline is willing to promote any small queer organisation (Interview with Whitham 2011).

A community sponsor is usually attached to many of the screenings during the festival. For instance, *Becoming Chaz* was co-presented by the Transgender Law Centre and Original Plumbing; *Leading Ladies* (Daniel Beahm 2010) was co-presented by queerballroom.com and the North American Same-Sex Partnered Dance Association; *Gen Silent* (Stu Maddox 2011) was co-presented by Openhouse, LGBT Community Partnership, and Institute on Aging. This ensures that Frameline is supporting the local community and that the social messages behind these films transcend the theatre and into the community.

Second, Frameline is more than just a film festival. Frameline acts as a distributor of over 250 titles, selling titles to academic institutions and rentals to small community groups. According to former distribution coordinator Sarah Deragon, the pricing fee for renting films works on a sliding scale, so as to allow access for groups with a tighter budget. Frameline offers filmmaker support in numerous ways. Firstly, there is the Frameline Completion Fund, which provides grants to emerging and established filmmakers:

> The program seeks to provide a much-needed source of financial contributions to artists who often struggle to secure funding to complete their works. Grants ranging from $1,500 to $5,000 are available for films that represent and reflect LGBT life in all its complexity and richness. For two decades Frameline has provided over 100 grants totalling $343,000 to help ensure that LGBT films are completed and viewed by wider audiences (Frameline).

All grants range from $1500 to $5000. Films that have benefited from the Frameline Completion Fund include *Go Fish* (Rose Troche 1994), *Watermelon Woman* (Cheryl Dunye 1996), *By Hook or By Crook* (Harry Dodge and Silas Howard 2001), *We Were Here: Voices from the AIDS Years in San Francisco* (David Weissman 2010), Frameline 35 opening night feature *Gun Hill Road* (Rashaad Ernesto Green 2011), and *Pariah* (Dee Rees 2011), with the two latter films playing at Sundance. Frameline aims for this grant to support the "under-served audience" in the queer community and encourages applications by "women, people of colour and transgender persons."

Frameline also runs the Generations Film Workshop, where they run 12-week filmmaking course for both young and elderly LGBTQ-identifying individuals living in the Bay Area. Participants collaborate on all stages of producing a film, which is to premiere at Frameline. Furthermore, every month there is a free screening at the LGBT community centre, followed by discussions on issues of particular importance to the LGBT community. Previous films have included *Diagnosing Difference* (Annalise Ophelian 2009), *Training Rules* (Des Mosbacher and Fawn Yacker 2009), and *Screaming Queens: the Riot at Compton's Cafeteria* (Victor Silverman and Susan Stryker 2005). Perhaps the most socially empowering initiative on offer from Frameline is the Frameline Voices programme, which allows Frameline titles to be freely accessible over video-sharing websites YouTube and Vimeo.

Finally, a social enterprise's empowerment can be seen in how it directly affects its beneficiaries and, more importantly, *indirectly* affects other actors in touch with these beneficiaries. This is no more apparent for Frameline considering its influential status in the queer film festival circuit. In 2009, I undertook an internship with Frameline as its hospitality assistant, where I dealt with all the accredited guests attending the festival. Stakeholders invested in the festival range from distributors such as Strand Releasing and MTV's Logo network, journalists, filmmakers, and actors and most importantly other queer film festival programmers. On my fieldwork research trip to Frameline in 2011, I mingled with Lisa Daniel from MQFF, programmers from North American queer film festivals such as Image and Nation in Montreal, the Pikes Peak Lavender Queer Film Festival in Colorado Springs, and the Savannah Gay and Lesbian Film Festival in Georgia. European queer film festival programmers included Brian Robinson from the now titled BFI Flare Film Festival and Mel Pritchard from the Hamburg Queer Film Festival. Frameline is now a leading player in the queer film festival circuit considering that the majority of travelling queer film festival programmers choose to attend Frameline and not Outfest in Los Angeles.[8] This places it in a position to indirectly affect other LGBT communities worldwide through the stakeholders travelling to its film festival.

MQFF fulfils these three requirements, albeit in a different fashion to Frameline. First, while the film festival programme size has remained steady over the last two decades of its existence, the size of the audience has progressively strengthened over the last 12 years of Lisa Daniel's involvement with the festival. As discussed previously in Daniel's first few years of involvement, a relationship of trust was gradually established with the audience and a higher retention rate with attendance increased. The strength in audience numbers was due to the increased professionalism of the festival, which is a significant factor of social empowerment according to Swain:

> It's seen as a really established event. It's such a long way from a backyard or amateur little something. When I first came out back in the Trojan War, I wrote off into *Spare Rib* and this thing came in a brown paper back to a made up name. I was in college. It was this hand written pamphlet with some poems and drawings. It was excruciating but I remember riding off on my bike and reading it in the forest somewhere in Surrey. But we are so far away from that. There is nothing furtive about it, there is nothing amateur about it, and there

is nothing backdoor about it. It's out and proud and an incredibly well run event. You got the Spanish film festival, you got the queer film festival, you got the main film festival, there is no difference perceived by the community, which is really valid. In that way it's really socially empowering (Interview with Swain 2011).

Second, scaling up is possible due to the organisation's number of activities, which have increased dramatically over the last several years. In 2010, the festival ran its first annual screenings in Yarraville[9] at the Sun Theatre, an event sponsored by the Maribyrnong City Council. The festival also has its annual screenings in Bendigo.[10] Up until 2013, MQFF hosted several screenings for Midsumma in the Fairfield amphitheatre.[11] Usually, the films are the highlights from the previous year's programme; however, in 2012, the film *D.E.B.S.* (Angela Robinson 2004) was included. This extends MQFF's activities beyond the strict festival period. For panel selection member Mark Pace, this notion of the travelling film festival is a significant aspect to the organisation's social empowering possibilities as there is an acknowledgement to the decentralised and scattered nature of Melbourne's (and Victoria's) queer community:

> I think number one, it gives people an opportunity to see themselves in cinema, which I think is really important for young people, but also rural queer people as well. I think a great part of the festival is that it goes to rural parts of the community (Interview with Mark Pace 2011).

The final key factor to social empowerment for MQFF is the impact on other beneficiaries. While this occurs on a smaller scale for MQFF than what it does for Frameline, we still see an influence on other similar organisations. While Frameline's effect is international, MQFF's impact is felt on the cultural landscape of Melbourne. For Daniel, this can occur when dealing with sponsors:

> Being in the community, it exposes a lot of companies to that business as well, which is really positive. We had Volkswagen as a sponsor for five years, and it really changed the way that company saw queer people and queer organisations and that's fantastic (Interview with Daniel 2011).

For Mark Pace, this can occur when dealing with filmmakers:

> I think any film festival has a responsibility to not only screen films but also to assist filmmakers making their next projects, to perpetuate queer film making and the festival does that with cash prizes that are made available throughout the festival that are awarded by audience voting (Interview with Pace 2011)

Unlike Frameline, MQFF does not have programmers attending to discover new trends in queer cinema. Nevertheless, MQFF's change into a professional organisation has allowed the organisation to have a profound impact on the cultural landscape of Melbourne. MQFF is a strong supporter of local short filmmakers via its short film awards. Since its inception, the number of niche community-based film festivals has grown, not to mention socially minded film festivals such as Tilde: the Trans and Gender Diverse Film Festival, Girls on Film Festival, the Human Rights Arts and Film Festival, and the Melbourne Environmental Film Festival. MQFF has paved the way for community film festivals to grow and be viable and successful.

Ultimately, this comparison of the social empowerment generated from both Frameline and MQFF solidifies Ulvin et al.'s "scaling up" model (2000). As MQFF became increasingly professional, as outlined in Swain's response, more beneficiaries are affected. In turn, this growth increases the variety of activities undertaken. This is demonstrated through the festival's events outside of the traditional festival period. Finally, this growth positions MQFF in an influential position. While it is by no means on the scale of Frameline, MQFF is a leading player in Australian queer cinema.

HKLGFF fulfils these requirements in a similar vain to MQFF. We know that once Raymond Yeung began the festival's second entity with Shu Kei and Wouter Barendrecht in 1999, the festival grew considerably beyond the screenings at the Hong Kong Arts Centre. Likewise, with Gary Mak and Joe Lam, the festival now occurs at the three main film theatres Palace IFC, Broadway Cinematheque, and The One. By screening more commercial faire, the festival is able to reach more patrons. The festival is beginning to meet the second criterion for scaling up by increasing the variety of activities provided. While there are the promotions of free drinks or entries to gay night clubs—for instance, the ticket stub for *Frangipani* (Chandrasekaram Visakesa 2014) received a free drink at Propaganda—the festival also offers a minor amount of other activities. The festival invites directors to speak after their films, and they held the "Kiss Me" exhibition at XXX in San Wan. When compared to both MQFF and Frameline, however, HKLGFF meets these criteria only minimally.

The final criterion of scaling up, impacting on the lives of beneficiaries and other actors who work with the same target group, is an important factor when considering HKLGFF as a social enterprise. First, the festival has occasionally worked with other LGBT-based Hong Kong organisations, such as briefly being involved with the arts and cultural festival Pink Season Hong Kong. Specifically, however, the festival was influential in queer cinema's increase in exhibition in both Hong Kong and Mainland China. In her account of gay and lesbian film festivals in East Asia, specifically in terms of negotiating a global LGBT movement with local culture, Rhyne argues that the Beijing Queer Film Festival owes a considerable amount to HKLGFF in that "both have deployed this discourse of cosmopolitan citizenship as part of the ethos of the festival, and this global perspective has framed the significance of the festivals within China and beyond it" (2011, 122). For Rhyne, HKLGFF has been a leading player in the region when dealing with both the governance of national cultural policy and transnational corporate attention. In this sense, the festival in Hong Kong can be seen as offering impact to like-minded organisations, thus allowing the festival to meet this criterion.

## CORPORATISATION

There is fear that queer organisations may compromise their social mission by taking on sponsorship agreements. In his manual on queer social enterprises, *End of the Rainbow: Increasing the Sustainability of LGBT Organizations through Social Enterprise*, Lee Davis (2008) discusses possible fears for queer non-profits turning to the marketplace for improving their sustainability. There are concerns that social entrepreneurship and queer social change are incompatible, as many believe the market itself to be the cause, not the solution, to LGBT inequality. Is resource generation and achieving one's mission irreconcilable?

Frameline is currently in a good financial condition and attracts many sponsors who wish to market to the Bay Area LGBTI community. Interestingly however, there are few requirements in order to be a sponsor for Frameline according to sponsorship coordinator Frances Wallace and associate Philip Walker respectively:

> We are a neutral organisation politically so we don't take political sponsorships; we don't take tobacco money or online gambling. Anything that goes into a questionable area goes to the board of Frameline and they decided if we

would take their money. It's a case by case basically (Interview with Wallace 2011).

We can't take tobacco money. It really just depends. We pretty much talk to anyone. We aren't going to go after firearms and the NRA or NOM [the National Organisation for Marriage]. We have taken money or traded with groups such as Manhunt, where the guy was found out to be giving money to John McCain, so they owed the gays some goodwill and I don't know if that's why they took it or if they thought it was a good fit but we *would* talk to anybody (Interview with Walker 2011).[12]

According to Wallace, most sponsors receive special screenings, and it is through this process that a clear hierarchy of decency is created with the films screened in the programme:

Most of the sponsors receive sponsored screenings. Of course we understand intimately what the company is and what they would want to be associated with, we work with some big 'all American' companies that wouldn't want to be associated with the S&M doco or the Bruce LaBruce doco. So you keep them happy, you make sure you guide them in the best way possible (Interview with Wallace 2011).

While there was a general consensus amongst all interviewed staff members that Frameline's sponsorship did not compromise or detract from its social mission, Harris Kornstein, a former employee from Frameline, is uneasy about the organisation's lack of minimum requirements for sponsorship:

Corporations can market themselves as gay friendly simply because they have given us money whereas they don't necessarily have to do anything with their internal policies and I thought that that was interesting that Frameline doesn't screen for anything. For instance, Frameline could say that they screen for companies that offer domestic partnership benefits for their employees or that they have a non-discrimination policy that includes gender identity and they don't do that. Probably many of the sponsors have those things but there is no sort of litmus test to make sure they are actually LGBT friendly other than will they give Frameline money. I think in some way it gives them an easy stamp of gay approval (Interview with Kornstein 2011).

During the Pride month of June, there are two major events for the Bay Area's queer community, Frameline and the Pride parade. After personally attending both these community events, it is painfully evident that there is a stark contrast in the relationship between their revenue generation and social mission. While Frameline's sponsorship at face value does not detract from its social mission of providing the queer community with quality queer cinema, the Pride parade is an onslaught of corporate floats and brand names. For Whitham, Frameline is more than just a party event:

> If you are going to Frameline, very few people are buying the party only ticket; they buy the film *and* party ticket.[13] They are there for the experience of something film related. I think film is always at the very centre of everything we do and I think that is the driving force with what we do. We party and have a good time, we have our vodka and beer sponsors but that is not why they come to Frameline, that's the 3rd or 4th reason (Interview with Whitham 2011).

Whitham's response identifies integrity in the management of corporate sponsorship in that everything is secondary to the films programmed. Buford's response supports this finding, as there is an evident distinction between the management of corporate sponsors between the parade and the film festival:

> At the end of the day it is our mission to put queer images out there and create dialogue. I think Dyke March and Trans March are still radical community events but looking at Pride, it does feel like it has jumped ship and gone a little corporate. And not to say that tourism dollars isn't great for the entire bay area community because they are but I fail to see personally how pride is as transformative on a one to one level as Frameline is. What I mean by that is yes it is completely powerful to go down Market Street and march in the parade and see dykes on bikes and see whoever is performing on the main stage and really have a 100% joyous celebration about sexuality and gender and gender identity expression *but* at the same time it's like 'is that all there is?' (Interview with Buford 2011).

The Pride parade (which is commonly referred to as Pride) has lost its political edge in regard to its relationship with the community. Ultimately, it comes down to the management of the exposure the sponsors have to the target market, says Harris Kornstein:

> I do think the Frameline is really elegant in the way that it handles its sponsors. There are a lot of impressions for their brands but it doesn't feel as in your

face. Whereas with Pride … when half their contingents in the parade are the Google group or the AT&T group, it's just boring because there is nothing else. Since Frameline has films, if you watch a two-minute advertisement you have forgotten it by the end. It doesn't feel that intrusive. Pride was originally 'Gay Day' which was a commemoration of the stonewall riots, so that came from a more overtly political place so I think it has more to do with a sense of selling out. Frameline came from a somewhat political place but more from a representation politics kind of way. I think that that is different (Interview with Kornstein 2011).

Frameline's sponsorship agreement with the Israeli consulate has caused controversy. Whenever an Israeli film is programmed into the festival, the consulate pays all transportation costs of the film and for the filmmaker to attend the festival. The lobby group Queers Undermining Israeli Terrorism (QUIT) has repeatedly protested Frameline when this occurs. Frances Wallace is very straightforward in regard to the issue, in that it is showing support merely for the filmmaker and is not taking sides in the Israeli Palestine conflict.

As we are politically neutral we aren't showing support to Israel or Palestine. We are just supporting an international filmmaker from wherever. There does end up being a lot of protest around that and we get a lot of feedback about that (Interview with Frances Wallace 2011).

QUIT claims that by accepting funds from the Israeli consulate, Frameline is assisting in the re-brand Israel campaign and "pink washing its negative image its grave violations of international law, human rights, and crimes against the Palestinian people (Alternative News, np)."[14]

I would support boycotting Israeli films on the boycott principles. I think that it is accepting money from the government, which we know is specifically being targeted to San Francisco and to the LGBT community as part of a very specific campaign to brand Israel as gay friendly and therefore as not a violator of human rights. I just think that that is so obvious… Frameline is clearly taking a side by accepting the money. I think to not accept the money would be seen as a political act or a political statement… I mean, it's only a political statement because the Israeli consulate would make it seem as such because, categorically, it is more objective to not take money then it is to accept it. They are 'damned if they do, damned if they don't.' But which side do you want to be damned by though? I think the fear is a loss of donors, who would paint Frameline as anti-Semitic or anti-Israel, which I think is totally false and shallow. I would like Frameline as an institution to say we are not anti-Semitic, we are taking a principled stance in favour of human rights and to just own it (Interview with Kornstein 2011).

As Kornstein's response indicates, this is a combative issue for Frameline, which highlights the complexity of contemporary politics around identity. Israel's sponsorship of Frameline is part of a larger Pink Washing campaign, according to Schulman:

> In 2005, with help from American marketing executives, the Israeli government began a marketing campaign, "Brand Israel," aimed at men ages 18 to 34. The campaign, as reported by *The Jewish Daily Forward*, sought to depict Israel as "relevant and modern." The government later expanded the marketing plan by harnessing the gay community to reposition its global image (Schulman 2011, np).

The queer movement against Israel brands this as a form of homonationalism, or "pinkwashing," in that by positioning Israel as a gay-friendly vacation destination, human rights violations in Palestine go continuously ignored. Puar (2007) argues that contemporary gay rights are integrated into the logic of a Western imperialist consumerism. Here, gay rights are seemingly used as a public relations strategy (Whitaker 2010). Pinkwashing maintains that gay rights are symbols of modernity and a forward-looking society, and, as such, Israel's current violations of international law no longer matter. The Brand Israel campaign offers a narrow representation of predominantly white gay men aligned within a discourse of nationalism. Does accepting money from the Israeli consulate compromise Frameline's social mission? Is it playing a supportive role in the re-branding of Israel to a queer-friendly destination or is it simply supporting a queer filmmaker travel to the largest queer film festival in the world and further its connections in the industry? Philip Walker states that Frameline often receives money from various international governmental cultural bodies:

> While seemingly controversial, when we had an Italian film we had money from the Italian cultural institute. The Barbara Osher Foundation of Sweden has supported us. It's not uncommon to get money from a consulate. It is just unfortunate that it happens to be Israel. It was basically 'damned if you do, damned if you don't.' It got oddly politicised. We are political in that we are here but we don't take a stance. They were supporting the film the *Queen has*

*No Crown* (Tomer Heymann 2011)[15] that ironically is very critical of Israel (Interview with Walker 2011).

There are two critiques that can be made here. First, this viewpoint of Frameline as only supporting a queer filmmaker is indicative of neoliberalism's depoliticising of contemporary LGBT culture; and that this highlights contemporary directions of cultural policy, which were highlighted in the earlier discussion of the queer film festival entering the creative industry. However, a contrasting perspective of this issue would be that by boycotting Israeli films, Frameline would be issuing its own brand of cultural censorship and would limit the accessibility and diversity of its programme. Ultimately in its aim to increase access to a diverse array of queer images and provide a community event for the Bay Area, it seems that accepting funds from the Israeli government to specifically support the attendance of an Israeli queer filmmaker does not actually hinder and detract from its original mission statement.

When asked if HKLGFF's corporate sponsorship influences any programming decision, Lam said this was not the case:

> No, they have their own private screening. It's very funny, Interbank have been supporting the last few years and they want to book two films: one a comedy and another that is serious about gay issues. This year they decided *Eat with Me* and the other is *10 Year Plan*—neither are serious movies! (Interview with Joe Lam 2014).

While the above interview response does indicate that corporate sponsors have no direct influence over decisions made, the strategic decision to move the screenings from the Hong Kong Arts Centre to more commercial venues (and, in turn, programming more commercial faire) *was* to attract sponsors, Fortissimo in particular, and a larger audience. The festival's current primary sponsor is the Hong Kong Red Ribbon sponsor, which did receive a small backlash from their "Be Negative" campaign.

> People would call me shouting and saying really bad things in Cantonese about the slogan we are using (Be Negative) being discriminating. Then I got two people on FB telling me the slogan was discriminating. I asked him if he looked at the whole website and he was just like "no, I hate the slogan." I asked HIV related NGOs if they had any problem with the slogan and they said no (Interview with Joe Lam 2014).

A significant apprehension of community organisations when taking corporate sponsorship agreements is that it will make concessions with the festival's social mission. Earned income can create a variety of tensions for any non-profit organisation (Smith et al. 2010). With careful management of audience's exposure to corporate sponsors, resource generation need not necessarily get in the way of achieving one's social mission, which in the case of the queer film festival is to provide access to quality and entertaining queer community screen events. This is the same for MQFF. For Mark Pace, revenue generated from sponsorship deals is necessary:

> Sponsors are something that is necessary for every major event, for every festival. So whether or not we have big brands sponsors on board I don't think detracts from the festival and if that helps us bring more films to the patrons then I don't see that as a bad thing (Interview with Pace 2011).

Revenue generation assists in both providing access to queer cinema and supporting queer filmmakers through film festival prizes, such as Shaun Miller Lawyers sponsoring short film awards. MQFF's 2010 annual report demonstrates the festival's reliance on revenue other than governmental support. The festival received governmental support at the amount of AU $51,365 and AU$58,314 in 2009 and 2010 respectively. Finances from other avenues, namely ticket sales and sponsorship, came to the amount of AU$529,986 and AU$571,563 in 2009 and 2010 respectively. It is important to keep in mind that social and commercial entrepreneurships are not necessarily dichotomous but "rather more accurately conceptualised as endpoints on a continuum ranging from purely social to purely economic" (Austen et al. 2006, 3).

This revenue generation creates social capital. I previously established that LGBT-identified audience members are disenfranchised in relation to queer content in mainstream film and television. This revenue generation, in regard to sponsorship and the role the "bums on seats" film play, is imperative in adding social value to this disenfranchisement. In order for the social enterprise to achieve this social capital, the social entrepreneur must "create complex alliances with individual and organisational members.... The challenge for the social entrepreneur is then not only to collaborate effectively with these disparate allies, but to connect with them in the first place" (Myers and Nelson 2010, 272). It is clear that for a queer social enterprise to be the size of MQFF, Frameline, or HKLGFF, careful negotiation of sponsorship is imperative, and dismissing corporate sponsorship as unethical and incompatible with social change is naive.

## The Evaluation of Success

The analysis of a social enterprise's success requires both a qualitative and a quantitative analysis. Two analyses regarding the social enterprise will be required in determining a social enterprise's success, both the Blended Value Proposition (BVP) (Emerson 2003) and the moral legitimacy of the organisation. The BVP ascertains that economic, social, and environmental values operate simultaneously and cannot be separated. As such, the value generated from the organisation is a complex interplay between economic viability and meaningful social change. This meaningful social change emphasises the moral legitimacy of the organisation. Have the activities of the organisation contributed to the social mission? Whether or not the activities of the organisation have benefited those making the evaluation should not be taken into consideration. So how do those interviewed evaluate the success of the organisation both quantitatively and qualitatively? For HKLGFF's Joe Lam, success is ultimately determined by the festival's ticket sales:

> It's really about money. Cinema is so small here we have to make an impact. You have the balance of commercial and art house movies. I think about not losing money every year. Gary [Mak] runs the program but I am about spending money carefully. Last year was the highest box office ever. For me it's about the box office because that is how many people are supporting you and are coming to the film festival (Interview with Lam 2014).

Economic success is determined in regard to ticket sales and membership contributions. Ultimately, if films at the festival moved an attendee, then they may in fact become a member or see more films, which is a possible method of transforming emotional value into financial profit. All of the interview subjects concurred that strong ticket sales alone were not enough to determine success, such as Frameline's Des Buford:

> Ticketing sales and reaching your budget is definitely what makes a festival successful but I think more than that is how the audience is responding to the film (Interview with Buford 2011).

Daniel concurs that you can't measure the festival by ticket sales alone:

> The obvious answer is ticket sales but I don't see it just like that. There are a whole variety of reasons why people don't get to the festival or can't afford it so I take a lot of creed in anecdotal stuff and feedback on the festival website or feedback via Facebook or Twitter, social media and responses to blogs. Ticket sales are obviously the way you would measure it though. Last year's festival was really easy. Everyone was really happy. I felt like there was a lot of love in the room. For those 12 days there was a lot of positive energy. I feel it's all about the relationships, in both the organisation and the board and the punters and how we treat our audience (Interview with Daniel 2011).

HKLGFF's ticket sales have proven the festival to be a success, according to Gary Mak:

> Of course, for the immediate figures it's the box office. So far the festival is doing well, especially for the last three to five years we have actually been sustainable just from the box office we earn. So we are doing okay, unlike in the Arts Centre era. They struggled to survive and sustain themselves because they relied heavily on the box office (Interview with Mak 2014).

Another recurring perspective when it came to tickets sales was that the financial metrics of the festival being bigger isn't necessarily better. Frameline's Whitham and Kim state:

> I don't think the name Frameline will ever get the recognition of say a festival like Sundance but I don't think that is what success is. It's not about being the biggest festival that everyone knows about (Interview with Whitham 2011).

> I have heard them use the term 'right sizing.' In our heyday we had 80, 000 people coming and now we are 60, 000. But is that the right size? What is the right size to be able to be sustainable and successful? I think this year went smashing compared to what could have happened with the whole economy (Interview with Kim 2011).

This "right sizing" takes into account that you cannot judge success purely in terms of economic status. It seems that a festival any larger would detract from its social mission. By remaining at its current size, Frameline is allowed to retain its close ties with the community. For Alexis Whitham, this ensures its success year after year. Ultimately, the audience of Frameline trust the programming:

> There are a lot of ways to evaluate success. I think Frameline is successful because it returns every year... You know those dates and you know it will have a good line up; it will get great submissions from great filmmakers. I think it is successful because people will show up even if they don't know what the film is. They will just trust Frameline. People will buy a Castro Pass before they will know the schedule or what is playing. Because members trust us that there will always be enough good films at the Castro to be worth buying a pass. That's success (Interview with Whitham 2011).

For Harris Kornstein, one method to ensure that these close ties with the community are respected is for the critical reactions to remain objective:

> For better or worse, Frameline has a lot of good relationships with critics. From a marketing perspective, it's great if no one says anything negative but I also think that weakens the festival. I don't think that everything that gets shown or everything that gets good reviews is actually good. I think that when you go to see a movie that got a good review that's in fact bad, it can weaken your trust... A lot of films get written about (positively) and not all are good (Interview with Kornstein 2011).

Constant glowing praises of the festival can be a blessing in disguise as community trust can be damaged if weak films are given stronger reviews than they deserve.

Ticket sales alone can't be the only sign of success for the festival. Anecdotal evidence of personal enjoyment and, ultimately, socially empowering experiences are important in deeming the festival a success. It is important not to limit our assessment of any social enterprise merely to "the economic, managerial, strategic, or decisional nature of the practices" (Hjorth 2010, 315) but to acknowledge the sociality that is being created. Events such as film festival speed dating, panel discussions, the travelling film festival, the festival bar, and so forth are crucial to fostering communal experiences at the festival. This moral legitimacy must be an important determinant to the festival's success. This is supported by Mak's outlook on HKLGFF:

> Rule 1: Sustain ourselves; Rule 2: Influence the growth in an individual. That is more meaningful. In the old days when I was younger, I saw a lot of

screenings at the Hong Kong Arts Centre during Edward Lam's era. I saw a lot of gay films, documentaries; it affected me; that's the power of cinema, how it shapes the personality of an individual. Queer cinema has the power to do that. For that we don't have a scientific measurement (Interview with Mak 2014).

How do they measure their qualitative success? Ultimately, there are the usual methods of audience feedback forms and reviews in local press, but K.C. Price agrees that it is indeed more difficult than measuring ticket sales:

> Well it is certainly harder to measure for evaluation purposes but in terms of getting a sense if something works or not you pretty much know. I could take a lot of screenings throughout the festival and I could tell you if that worked or not (Interview with Price 2011).

For evaluative purposes, Frameline conducts focus groups to determine audience responses, says Wallace:

> Financially, you can read that pretty easily in terms of ticket sales and atten-dance. But in terms of the experience I think it is more through our research or study groups where you find out a lot more in depth information. The research is conducted through the festival. We usually do strategic planning once a year, where a small group of outside constituents are brought in. The development department does small focus groups with members. With dif-ferent groups we usually do it three to four times throughout the year (Interview with Wallace 2011).

A large proportion of interviews determined that the success of the festival lies within the emotional transformative moments, such as the documentary *Wish Me Away*, which documented the coming out of country music star Chely Wright. These subjective personal accounts alone are not enough to prove success. Instead, the queer film festival (and other social enterprises) must endeavour to conduct rigorous audience surveys and focus groups and hope that these emotional transformative moments translate into a financial profit, be it the purchase of a membership or the development of trust and continued attendance.

The qualitative social change generated from the social enterprise is just as important as economic viability, of which prioritising alone can cause a conflict of interest with the social mission. This sustainable social change highlights the possible moral legitimacy of any project. When analysing community organisations, we must "dissociate entrepreneurship from a managerial economy and to intensify its social, cultural and ethical sides" (Hjorth 2010). Ultimately, however, one can assume that the more positive experiences that the festival provides, the stronger the trust is between the queer community and the festival. This would no doubt translate into strong healthy ticket sales, which currently is the primary determination as to whether the festival will be able to continue at its current size.

## CONCLUSION

This chapter has highlighted six key traits of the social enterprise. The purpose of referring to three queer film festivals is to demonstrate that not all festivals meet these criteria equally. For instance, when asked about the roles social empowerment and innovation play with their management of the festival, neither Joe Lam nor Gary Mak from HKLGFF spoke to those themes in much detail. This is not to say that the festival in Hong Kong isn't socially empowering or innovative. The accompanying art installation in San Wan, "Kiss Me," was a creative direct response to growing conservatism in the region. Each of the festivals examined approached themes of empowerment differently.

Furthermore, this is not to say that this social enterprise model is applicable to *all* queer film festivals. The application of this model is particularly complex for festivals in hostile environments. This chapter is a proposition for non-profit queer organisations to consider the management of social empowerment within a neoliberal environment. The Side-by-Side International Film Festival in St Petersburg, Russia, has a diverse array of sponsors. They receive consulate support from the Netherlands, Sweden, Australia, Canada, Switzerland, and Germany alongside support from a variety of media organisations and corporate sponsors. The festival emerged out of a need for a safe cultural space for LGBTI Russians (Schilt 2008). While the social empowerment generated from this festival is more aligned with political activism, as opposed to MQFF, Frameline, or HKLGFF, this is still a demonstration of a queer film festival balancing social value with economic sustainability. The Q! Film Festival in Jakarta, however, finds itself more as a non-profit that is supported through associations with local cultural institutions and foreign embassies. Like Side by Side, the festival is driven an activist mission to "give the public another perspective of queer people" (Badalu cited in Setiawan 2009, np). The festival differs, however, in that volunteers primarily run the festival. It does not meet the professional status as other festivals.

In sum, the drivers of the queer film festival used their subcultural status in their respective communities to promote the events. The social entrepreneurs combine the managerial expertise of a civic entrepreneur with their awareness of the local LGBT community. For obvious reasons, their main objective for making their organisation a success is read not in terms of financial profit but in terms of achieving their social mission.

The organisation's social mission must identify and address a gap in the market. Interview responses emphasised three key desires of the queer community. The first desire, which has been stressed considerably thus far, is for the festival to assist in the promotion and distribution of independent film, which would otherwise be unavailable. Second, access to these films allows for an identity-affirming experience. Third, the queer film festival allows for the occasion to experience a communal coalitional identity in a shared environment. Of note for this criterion, a challenge faced by HKLGFF is the matter of Chinese subtitles for local audiences being too expensive. Likewise, the festival has also been criticised for programming a dominance of gay male content at the expense of lesbian and local content.

Innovative strategies are employed to ensure the success of the festivals in question. From responses, this is implemented through alignment with changing technology and careful programming decisions. There is, however, room for Frameline to be more innovative and boundary pushing when it comes to identity politics and for them to embrace the queer label.

Social empowerment occurs through social change, sustainable development, and social movement. Interview responses coincided Ulvin et al.'s process of "scaling up" (2000), which emphasises the allowance for the possibility for more social empowering activities. First, festival growth allows for recipients to be affected. Second, a wider variety of activities can be undertaken, which is demonstrated through the festival having events outside of festival time. Third, the organisations can empower other likeminded organisations to continue similar work. The social enterprise achieves social empowerment when the cultural environment, in which the organisation's social mission is embedded, begins to transform.

There are the concerns over the incompatibility of social enterprise and LGBT social change. For many that work for traditionally non-profit queer organisations, the core reason for their involvement is to work for "the greater good" and a commitment to furthering LGBT equality. For Frameline, the relationship with the Israeli Consulate has angered many in the Bay Area. This relationship with Israel calls into question the neoliberalist nature of the contemporary creative industry.

Qualitative success with the social empowerment of the community is indeed harder to define but imperative to articulate. Organisational analysis alone is not enough to determine a social enterprise's success, however. In order to do so, examination of the programming is required, in terms of both film content and space. While Frameline, MQFF, and HKLGFF are all indeed successful organisations, a summation on whether they fulfil their social missions cannot be made until the programming is scrutinised, a project which will be undertaken in the following chapter.

## NOTES

1. The Identity Project seeks to explore the labels members of the LGBT community choose to identify with when defining their gender and sexuality.
2. "Balnarring Rammed Earth" first aired on November 1, 2012, on the Lifestyle Channel, Australia.
3. *Tom at the Farm* was popular at the 2014 HKLGFF and received additional screenings.
4. Other interview subject Lares Feliciano is also a Bay Area filmmaker.
5. The opening night film for Frameline in 2011 was *Gun Hill Road.*
6. Lares Feliciano has had her film *Push On* (2010) featured in both Frameline and other Bay Area film festivals.
7. This interview response is in the light of the 2011 MQFF.
8. Discussions with many of the visiting programmers lead me to believe that Frameline is more hospitable to their guests and that the festival is a more enjoyable atmosphere.
9. A suburb in Melbourne's inner Western metropolitan area, Yarraville, has recently had rapid gentrification and an increase in arts and cultural events.
10. Bendigo is a major regional city in Victoria, North West of Melbourne.
11. The Fairfield Amphitheatre is located in Melbourne's inner eastern suburbs.
12. Numerous blogs were in uproar in 2008 when it was revealed that Manhunt, a popular gay online dating site, co-founder Jonathan Crutchley donated $2300 to US presidential campaign of John McCain, such as Open Left (http://www.openleft.com/diary/

7781/), Joe My God (http://joemygod.blogspot.com/2008/08/ manhunt-founder-donates-max-to-mccain.html), and Towleroad (http://www.towleroad.com/2008/08/mccain-takes-23.html). Joe My God's blog has the catchy phrase "Get on, get off, get betrayed."

13. Frameline's opening and closing night offer tickets that are party only or film only as well as film and party tickets.

14. Taken from the alternative news blog: http://www.alternativenews. org/english/index.php/topics/economy-of-the-occupation/3633- boycott-frameline-film-festival-pinkwashing-israeli-apartheid. QUIT's call to action can be viewed here: http://www.quitpalestine.org/ actions/frameline%20phone%20zap.htm

15. This interview took place after the 2011 festival.

## WORKS CITED

Alvord, Sarah H., L. David Brown, and Christine W. Letts. 2004. Social Entrepreneurship and Societal Transformation. *The Journal of Applied Behavioural Sciences* 40(3): 260–282.

Anderson, Benedict. 1983. *Imagined Communities: Reflections on the Origin and Spread of Nationalism.* London: Verso.

Austin, James, Howard Stevenson, and Jane Wei-Skillern. 2006. Social and Commercial Entrepreneurship: Same, Different, or Both? *Entrepreneurship Theory and Practice* 30(1): 1–22.

Baker, Paul. 2008. *Sexed Texts: Language, Gender and Sexuality.* London: Equinox.

Borzaga, Carlo, and Luca Solari. 2004. Management Challenges for Social Enterprises. In *The Emergence of Social Enterprise,* ed. C. Borzaga, and J. Defourny, 333–349. London: Routledge.

Brooks, Brian. 2011. Frameline at 35: Organizers Sound off on LGBT Film, Vocal Audiences and 3½ Decades. *Indiewire.* June 24. Accessed online at: http:// www.indiewire.com/article/frameline_at_35_organizers_sound_off_on_lgbt_ film_vocal_audiences_decades

Catford, J. 1998. *Social Entrepreneurs Are Vital for Health Promotion—But They Need Supportive Environments Too. Health Promotion International* 13: 95–98.

Chan, Phil. 2008. Stonewalling through Schizophrenia: An Anti-Gay Rights Culture in Hong Kong? *Sexuality & Culture* 12(2): 71–87.

Davis, Lee. 2008. *End of the Rainbow: Increasing the Sustainability of LGBT Organizations through Social Enterprise.* London: NESsT.

Doherty, Bob, et al. 2009. *Management for Social Enterprise.* London: Sage Publications.

Drucker, Peter F. 1985. *Innovation and Entrepreneurship: Practices and Principles*. London: Heinemann.

Ellcessor, Elizabeth. 2012. Tweeting @feliciaday: Online social media, convergence and the subcultural stardom of Felicia Day. *Cinema Journal* 51(2): 46–66.

Emerson, Jed. 2003. The Blended Value Proposition: Integrating Social and Financial Results. *California Management Review* 45(4): 35–51.

Gamson, Joshua. 1996. The Organizational Shaping of Collective Identity: The Case of Lesbian and Gay Film Festivals in New York. *Sociological Forum* 11(2): 231–261.

Gartner, William B. 2002. Who is the Entrepreneur? is the wrong question. In *Entrepreneurship: Critical Perspectives on Business and Management*, ed. Norris F. Krueger, vol. 2, 153–177. London: Routledge.

Haugh, Helen. 2005. A Research Agenda for Social Entrepreneurship. *The Social Enterprise Journal* 1(1): 1–12.

Hawkins, Gay. 1993. *From Nimbin to Mardi Gras: Constructing Community Arts*. St. Leonards, NSW: Allen & Unwin.

Henton, Douglas, John Melville, and Kimberly Walesh. 1997. *Grassroots Leaders for a New Economy: How Civic Entrepreneurs Are Building Prosperous Communities*. San Francisco, CA: Jossey-Bass.

Hills, Matt. 2003. Subcultural Celebrity and Cult TV Fan Cultures. *Mediactive* 2: 59–73.

———. 2006. Not Just Another Powerless Elite: When Media Fans become Subcultural Celebrities. In *Framing Celebrity: New Directors in Celebrity Culture*, ed. Su Holmes, and Sean Redmond. London: Routledge.

Hjorth, David. 2010. Ending essay: sociality and economy in social enterpreneurship. In *Handbook of research on social entrepreneurship*, ed. Allain Fayole and Harry Matlay, 306–316. Cheltenham: Edward Elgar Publishing.

Iordanova, Dina. 2010. Mediating Diasora: Film Festivals and 'Imagined Communities'. In *Film Festival Yearbook 2: Film Fesitvals and Imagined Communities*, ed. Dina Iordanova, and Ruby Cheung. St Andrews: St Andrews Film Studies.

Lam, Joe. 2014. Interview by Stuart Richards, personal interview, Hong Kong. 22nd September.

Leadbeater, Charles. 2007. Social enterprise and social innovation: Strategies for the next ten years. A social enterprise think piece for the Cabinet Office of the Third Sector.

Linne, Robert. 2003. Alternative Textualities: Media Culture and the Proto-Queer. *Qualitative Studies in Education* 16(5): 669–689.

Mak, Gary. 2014. Interviewed by Stuart Richards, personal interview, Hong Kong. 21st September.

Myers, Paul, and Teresa Nelson. 2010. Considering Social Capital in the Context of Social Entrepreneurship. In *Handbook of Research on Social Entrepreneurship*, ed. Alain Fayolle, and Harry Matlay, 271–285. Cheltenham: Edward Elgar Publishing.

Nicholls, Alex. 2006. *Social Entrepreneurship: New Models of Sustainable Social Change.* Oxford: Oxford University Press.

Paridis, Elise. 2008. *LGBT Youth and Online Environments: A Mixed Methods Approach.* Presented at: The American Educational Research Association conference, February 19. New York: Stanford University.

Perrini, Francesco, and Vurro, Clodia. 2006. Social Entrepreneurship: Innovation and Social Change Across Theory and Practice. In *Social Entrepreneurship*, eds. Mair, Johanna, Jeffrey Robinson, and Kai Hockerts, 57–86. New York: Palgrave Macmillan.

Pickard, Christopher. 1998. Making and Breaking Films. In *The Variety Guide to Film Festivals*, 11–22. New York: Pedigree.

Puar, Jasbir. 2007. *Terrorist Assemblages: Homonationalism in Queer Times.* Durham, NC: Duke University Press.

Rhyne, Raghan. 2006. The Industry and the Ecstasy: Gay and Lesbian Film Festivals and the Economy of Community. eds. Straayer, Chris and Thomas Waugh, "Queer Film and Video Festival Forum, Take Two. Critics Speak Out" *GLQ: A Journal of Lesbian and Gay Studies* 12(4): 617–619.

———. 2009. Film Festival Circuits and Stakeholders. In *Film Festival Yearbook: The Festival Circuit*, ed. Raghan Rhyne, and Dina Iordanova. St Andrews: St Andrews Film Studies.

———. 2011. Comrades and Citizens: Gay and Lesbian Film Festivals in China. In *The Film Festival Yearbook 3: Film Festivals and East Asia*, ed. Dina Iordanova, and Ruby Cheung, 110–124. St Andrews: St Andrews Film Studies.

Same Same. 2009. Lisa Daniel: Film Festival Director. *Same Same.* Accessed on 11 November 2011 at: http://www.samesame.com.au/25/2009/LisaDaniel

Schilt, Paige. 2008. Russian Officials Attempt (But Fail) to Squelch the Nation's 1st LGBT Film Festival. *The Bilerico Project,* October 6. Accessed 20 August 2015.

Schulman, Sarah. 2011. Israel and 'Pink Washing'. *New York Times,* November 22.

Setiawan, Iwan. 2009. Q! Film Festival: A Never Ending Journey. *The Jakarta Post,* July 19. Accessed 20 August 2015.

Smith, Wendy K., Andy Binns, and Michael L. Tushman. 2010. Complex business models: Managing strategic paradoxes simultaneously. *Long range planning* 43 (2): 448–461.

Subrahmanyam, Kaveri and David Smahel. 2008. *Digital youth: The role of media in development.* New York; London: Springer.

Tang, Denise Tse Shang. 2011. *Conditional Desires: Honk Kong Lesbian Desires and Everyday Life.* Hong Kong: Hong Kong University Press.

Uvin, Peter, Pankaj Jain, and David Brown. 2000. Think Large and Act Small: Toward a New Paradigm for NGO Scaling Up. *World Development* 28(8): 1409–1419.

Vesper, Karl. 1982. Research on Education for Entrepreneurship. In *Encyclopaedia of Entrepreneurship.* Englewood Cliffs, NJ: Prentice-Hall.

Westall, Andrea. 2007. How can innovation in social enterprise be understood, encouraged and enabled? A social enterprise think piece for the Office of the Third Sector.

Whitaker, Brian. 2010. Pinkwashing Israel. *Brian Whitaker's blog*. Accessed at: http://www.al-bab.com/blog/blog1006b.htm

Yau, Ching. 2006. Bridges and Battles. *GLQ: A Journal of Lesbian and Gay Studies* 12(4): 605–607.

## INTERVIEWS

Buford, Des. Interviewed by Stuart Richards, personal interview, San Francisco, 7 July 2011.

Daniel, Lisa. Interviewed by Stuart Richards, personal interview, Melbourne, 5 August 2011.

Deragon, Sarah. Interviewed by Stuart Richards, personal interview, San Francisco, 2 July 2011.

Doo, Rowena. Interviewed by Stuart Richards, personal interview, Melbourne, 21 December 2011.

Feliciano, Lares, Sam Berliner and Nissa Poulson. Interviewed by Stuart Richards, personal interview, San Francisco, 7 July 2011.

Hillis, Crusader. Interviewed by Stuart Richards, personal interview, Melbourne, 8 December 2011.

Kim, Jennifer. Interviewed by Stuart Richards, personal interview, San Francisco, 7 July 2011.

Kornstein, Harris. Interviewed by Stuart Richards, personal interview, San Francisco, 21 July 2011.

Pace, Mark. Interviewed by Stuart Richards, personal interview, Melbourne, 7 May 2011.

Price, K.C. Interviewed by Stuart Richards, personal interview, San Francisco, 7 July 2011.

Sam. Interviewed by Stuart Richards, confidential, San Francisco, 8 July 2011.

Swain, Madeline. Interviewed by Stuart Richards, personal interview, Melbourne, 12 December 2011.

Tonta, Paul. Interviewed by Stuart Richards, personal interview, Melbourne, 5 August 2011.

Walker, Philip. Interviewed by Stuart Richards, personal interview, San Francisco, 10 July 2011.

Wallace, Frances. Interviewed by Stuart Richards, personal interview, New York, 18 July 2011.

Whitham, Alexis. Interviewed by Stuart Richards, personal interview, San Francisco, 8 July 2011.

CHAPTER 4

# Queer Film Festival Programming and Homonormativity

There are currently two spectrums at play in the queer film market. As outlined in Chap. 1, there is the gay Indiewood faire intended for mainstream markets, while there are those films that are solely intended to play on the queer film festival circuit and get distributed within a niche market. These queer films have benefited from the significant growth of the queer film festival circuit, a phenomenon "financed as much by global capital as by philanthropic funding" (Rhyne 2006, 619). Of course, films can traverse from market to market. For example, *Weekend* (Andrew Haigh 2011), like a select few other films each year, played at many queer film festivals such as Frameline and Outfest and international film festivals, such as Sundance. The film went on to receive a limited distribution in theatres. There are also mainstream films that have a distinct queer subtext, such as *Neighbours* (Nicholas Stoller 2014) and *22 Jump Street* (Chris Miller and Phil Lord 2014).

It is how niche films, marketed primarily towards a queer audience, are programmed that bridges the two foremost conceptual research areas of this book. According to the social enterprise logic, queer film festivals need to programme the "bums on seats" films to remain financially viable; it just so happens that a significant proportion of these successful films adhere to homonormative identity politics, which works in the service of dominant contemporary economic and political systems. This social normalisation further marginalises those that challenge conventional kinship structures, the gender binary, and other dominant hegemonic manifestations. Many queer film festivals aim to strike a balance between engaging in

© The Author(s) 2016
S.J. Richards, *The Queer Film Festival*,
DOI 10.1057/978-1-137-58438-0_4

contemporary politics and maintaining their status as an elite cultural event (Stryker 1996). There has been valuable writing on the changing relationships between festivals and communities (Gamson 1996; Rich 1999), as well as the LGBTI audience as a counter-public (Kim 2007; Gorfinkel 2006; Perspex 2006). This chapter aims to highlight the role the films play in this dynamic field. This concept of homonormative identity politics will be scrutinised and developed within this chapter.

Thus far, I have argued that the queer film festival has grown from being a community arts festival to a corporate elite film institution. As an organisation, it has grown and developed in adherence to the creative industry logic. Being economically sustainable and programming marketable films is of the utmost importance. If a film has to adhere to dominant identity practices in order to be palatable to the desired market, which is evident in queer-themed Indiewood films (Richards 2016), do films on the queer film festival circuit have to make similar concessions? Due to the social enterprise's fostering of economic value, do the films on the queer film festival circuit align with homonormative ideologies in a similar manner to the gay Indiewood film? As we shall see, the analysis of the queer film festival as a social enterprise and the identification of homonormative trends in the programming share a common relationship to neoliberalism.

## Heteronormativity

Homonormativity was conceptually born out of both neoliberalism and heteronormativity, which was conceptually developed in 1993 by Michael Warner in *Fear of a Queer Planet*. Heteronormativity reveals the burden and limitations produced when heterosexuality is taken as normative within society (Chambers 2003). A tool of queer critique, heteronormativity identifies the extent to which heterosexual privilege permeates through our everyday life:

> Because the logic of the sexual order is so deeply embedded by now in an indescribably wide range of social institutions, and is embedded in the most standard accounts of the world, queer struggles aim not just at toleration or equal status but at challenging those institutions and accounts. The dawning realisation that themes of homophobia and heterosexism may be read in almost any document of our culture means that we are only beginning to have an idea of how widespread those institutions and accounts are (Warner 1993, 6).

This collection of essays was published at a time of great revision for gay and lesbian studies in social-theoretical traditions. Warner's introduction heralded the moment of a scholarly embrace of queer theory that stemmed from burgeoning realisations about the constraints of gay and lesbian studies. Warner's concept of heteronormativity opens up the dialogue to critique pre-existing work in which a discussion of sexuality is deemed irrelevant.[1] Warner's introduction also outlines what it means to be queer in the everyday:

> In the everyday political terrain, contests over sexuality and its regulation are generally linked to views of social institutions and norms of the most basic sort. Every person who comes to a queer self-understanding knows in one way or another that her stigmatization is connected with gender, the family, notions of individual freedom, the state, public speech, consumption and desire, nature and culture, maturation, reproductive politics, racial and national fantasy, class identity, truth and trust, censorship, intimate life and social display, terror and violence, health care, and deep cultural norms about the bearing of the body, Being queer means fighting about these issues all the time, locally and piecemeal but always with consequence (xiii).

Heteronormativity opened up the limitations of gay and lesbian studies, which were bound by a strict gender binary. Judith Butler's "heterosexual matrix" (1990) identified the social constraints around the cultural intelligibility of sex, gender, and sexuality. Her arguments on the denaturalisation of gender enabled new avenues for the analysis of gay and lesbian politics. This revision of how we thought about sexuality politically followed many feminists, such as Gayle Rubin (1975), Adrienne Rich (1980), and Eve Kosovsky Sedgwick (1985, 1990), who began to rethink the relationship between gender and sexuality. Rich maintains that heterosexuality was an oppressive political institution. Rubin's sex/gender system examines how society alters biological sexuality into products of a Marxist activity and establishes that "sexual terms be restricted to their proper historical and social contexts, and a cautionary scepticism towards sweeping generalisations" (157). Rubin saw sexuality and gender as economic institutions through which society transforms one's biological make-up into products of human activity. Another leading figure in this re-conceptualisation was Sedgwick, for whom gay politics is only a starting position. *Between Men* (1985) and *Epistemology of the Closet* (1990) argue that contemporary structures of power and oppression can be seen adequately only from the homo/hetero binary. Ultimately, what the concept of heteronormativity allowed was the formulation of a queer critique of sexual oppression and power. Heterosexual privilege was put under the microscope:

> So much privilege lies in heterosexual culture's exclusive ability to interpret itself as society. Het culture thinks of itself as the elemental form of human association, as the very model of inter-gender, as the indivisible basis of all community, and as the means of reproduction without which society wouldn't exist (Warner 1993, xxi).

Queer theory denaturalised the inherent power and privilege that identity politics entails. This interrogation of the heteronormative lens is implemented by deconstructive methods, where the critique of contemporary power structures stems from post-constructionist notions of identity (Foucault 1980). Sexuality and gender are not inherently fixed but moulded and produced by societal contexts. Our identities are not pre-existing but are performances of social constructions of our own culture (Butler 1990). This is a departure from biologically essentialist accounts of identity (Phelan 1989; Phelan 1994; Blasius 2001). The adoption of the term "queer" by activists and academics is an "aggressive impulse of generalization; it rejects a minoritising logic of toleration or simple political interest-representation in favour of a more thorough resistance to regimes of the normal" (Warner 1993, xxvi). Thus, identity politics, as a method for organisation, is revealed to be defined as an opposition to otherness:

> An identity is established in relation to a series of differences that have become socially recognized. These differences are essential to its being. If they did not coexist as differences, it would not exist in its distinctness and solidity. Entrenched in this indispensable relation is a second set of tendencies, themselves in need of exploration, to conceal established identities into fixed forms, thought and lived as if their structure expressed the true order of things. When these pressures prevail, the maintenance of one identity (or field of identities) involves the conversion of some differences into otherness, into evil, or one of its numerous surrogates. Identity requires differences in order to be, and it converts difference into otherness in order to secure its own self-certainty (Connolly 2002, 64).

Queer dismantles the privilege and power inherent in this creation of otherness. As a product of queer critical thinking, heteronormativity allows us to interrogate social and sexual norms.

As has been discussed at length in queer academia, queer subjectivity opposes the norm, be it in the form of heteronormativity or homonormative organisations. Norms construct our ideas of the normal, a process of power often referred to as normalisation:

> A norm operates within social practices as the implicit standard of *normalization*... norms may or may not be explicit, and when they operate as the normalizing principle in social practice, they usually remain implicit, difficult to read, discernible most clearly and dramatically in the effects that they produce (Butler 2004, 41).

We must view queer as a verb: through the act of *queering* something, one is opposing and critiquing the norm. This is where the complex contradictory nature of queer comes into play, as "it stands in complicated relation to various norms and to the power structure of normativity" (Jakobson 1998, 513). Resisting the norm in whatever form it may take may have negative consequences due to the ease in which the meaning of queer can be lost in the rising tension between critical theory and actuality. The relationships of normative binaries—man/woman, hetero/homo, gay/lesbian—and so forth with queer are complicated, as Halperin explains:

> It sometimes gives a false impression of inclusiveness, of embracing in equal measure all species of sexual outlaws. It thereby promotes the misleading notion that a queer solidarity has decisively triumphed over historical divisions between lesbians and gay men (or between lesbians and gay men, on the one hand, and [for example] sadomasochists, fetishists, pederasts, and transgender people, on the other) and that differences of race or gender no longer pose political problems for queer unity that require urgently to be addressed (Halperin 1995, 64).

## HOMONORMATIVITY

Homonormativity takes the critical weaponry of heteronormativity and uses it to create a dialogue surrounding assimilationist trends in the LGBT community. Originally developed by Lisa Duggan, homonormativity is defined as not contesting "dominant heteronormative assumptions and institutions, but upholds and sustains them, while promising the possibility of a demobilized gay constituency and a privatized, depoliticized gay culture anchored in domesticity and consumption" (2003, 50). For Duggan, homonormativity is a result of a polarity in neoliberalism between economic and cultural politics:

> The Achilles' heel in progressive-left politics since the 1980s, especially has been a general blindness to the connections and interrelations of the economic, political, and cultural, and a failure to grasp the shifting dimensions of the alliance politics underlying neoliberal success (xvi).

As such, homonormativity essentially stems from neoliberalism in that:

> The *economy* cannot be transparently abstracted from the *state* or the *family*, from practices of racial apartheid, gender segmentation, or sexual regulation (xii).

In a neoliberal-fuelled political economy, one's financial status decides if access to equality is possible. A key element of neoliberalism is the attack on "downwardly redistributive social movements" (xii) in that hegemonic identity boundaries are the "channels through which money, political power, cultural resources, and social organization flow." This leads many in the contemporary LGBT rights movement to be more concerned about assimilationist tactics than disrupting the status quo. This is a superficial distancing from progressive politics that would aim to identify and disrupt heteronormative ideals. Instead of seeking to examine the notion of the family in relation to neoliberalism, homonormativity is a new paradigm that seeks to infiltrate and support this conservative institution. This is a depoliticisation and privatisation of the gay rights movement. As such, assimilationist tactics do not seek to contest pre-existing neoliberal power dynamics in society but enforce a "narrow, formal, non-redistributive form of 'equality' politics" (44). Homonormative politics speaks in a double voice, to both an imagined homogeneous gay public and a "national mainstream constructed by neoliberalism" (50). In the time of homonormativity, we are not in a "culture war" but within a "superficial 'multiculturalism' compatible with the global aspirations of U.S. business interests" (44). This is not challenging the patriarchal preconceptions of sexuality and gender but accepting one's place within the hegemony, where hegemony is that "system of power that has the support of the subordinate" (Artz and Murphy 2000, 2). This normalisation of the gay and lesbian movement is a significant departure from the deconstructionist efforts of queer politics. These assimilationist tactics recall earlier essentialist identity formations of the earlier gay and lesbian liberation movement.

This neoliberal turn is embodied in the increased professionalism of the LGBTI movement. Professionalism may increase the "legitimacy and effectiveness of the LGBT movement" (Stone 2009, 469), but there is the strong possibility of the suppression of dissent and radicalism, and a shift to more corporate styles to increase an organisation's legitimacy in the eyes of the public and to increase the chance of obtaining grant-funding from the wider community (Ward 2008). The "mainstreaming" of the LGBT movement has created top-down decision-making processes for leading LGBT rights organisations, such as the Millennium March on Washington (Ghaziani 2008). There are hints that radicalism has been integrated into this "mainstreaming," albeit in a superficial fashion:

> Thus radicalism has been somewhat integrated into formal LGBT organizations but oftentimes in conventional ways, such as changing a mission statement to reflect bisexual and transgender inclusion rather than embracing multi-issue politics that would include the full range of potential transgender issues such as poverty, homelessness, and health care (Stone 2009, 470).

Corporate representation of diversity can result in only superficially involving visibly diverse identities involved in the decision-making, ignoring "other salient identities such as class, which obscures the class bias of corporate diversity culture" (471).

The tension between normative sexual representation and queer analysis is perhaps articulated best by Michael Warner in *The Trouble with Normal* (1999). The relationship between alternative sexualities and mainstream culture is about sexual shame and the stigma that is attached to it. Leading gay organisations deal with this shame in a manner that deviates their social mission into a process of normalisation.

> The official gay movement. . . has lost its sight of that politics, becoming more and more enthralled by respectability. Instead of broadening its campaign against sexual stigma beyond sexual orientation, as I think it should, it has increasingly narrowed its scope to those issues of sexual orientation that have least to do with sex. Repudiating its best histories of insight and activism, it has turned into an instrument for normalising gay men and lesbians (24–25).

Warner co-opts the terms "stigmaphile" and "stigmaphobe" from sociologist Erving Goffman (1963), whereby a stigmaphile space is where we find commonality with those who suffer from stigma and the stigmaphobe space being the world of the mainstream, where conformity is ensured through fear of stigma:

> Like most stigmatized groups, gays and lesbians were always tempted to believe that the way to overcome stigma was to win acceptance by the dominant culture, rather than to change the self-understanding of that culture (50).

When leading organisations attempt to win such acceptance by the dominant culture, most notably in the USA through the equal marriage movement and the right to serve openly in the military, the parameters of this hierarchy of sexual shame crystallises in the LGBT community, where "gender conformists and monogamous couples in the suburbs are seen as more respectable and worthier pillars of the community than the rest of us" (49). The "lifestyle" of mainstream gays and lesbians is "indistinguishable from the most heterosexual couples in similar professional and economic circumstances" (Bawer 1993, 33–34). This can be viewed as the tolerance of the undesirable by the patriarchal society. This campaign "insists on the importance of the state embodying and upholding certain norms that stand to one side of formal liberal principles, such as those that consecrate and privilege heterosexual marriage" (Brown 2006, 97). This consolidation of the pre-existing dominance sustains the abjection of the tolerated. With this reformulation of the hierarchy of sexual shame, assimilationist leaders of the lesbian and gay community have moved from the stigmaphile position to the stigmaphobe privilege. For Warner, this has never been more apparent when those promoting equal marriage rights are "advocates for lesbian and gay identity rather than for non-normative sexual cultures" (86). New sexual boundaries are established. Ultimately, this tolerance of the normative gay and lesbian is a management of the "demands of marginal groups in ways that incorporate them without disturbing the hegemony of the norms that marginalize them" (Brown 2006, 36).

As outlined by Murphy et al. (2008) in their introduction to *Radical History Review*'s special edition on homonormativity, this realignment of norms is all about shifting just who is marginalised in this new hegemonic order:

As prominent and mainstream lesbian and gay rights organizations strategically embrace agendas that vie for acceptance within contemporary economic and political systems, one could argue that they have abandoned many of the political commitments of their LGBT activist predecessors, especially their foci on the redistribution of economic resources and the protection of sexual freedoms. This shift has made strange bedfellows out of lesbian and gay rights organizations and social conservatives: both endorse normative and family-oriented formations associated with domestic partnership, adoption, military service, and gender-normative social roles; both work to marginalize and disempower those who challenge serial monogamy and those belonging to categories—including transgender, bisexual, pansexual, and intersex constituencies—that are seen as eccentric within a traditional binary gender or sex system (Murphy et al. 2008, 4–5).

Therefore, an area under discussion for queer politics is the intersection of sexual normativity and hegemony. Keeping in mind that the political "does not denote the *sphere* of politics, but the *processes, regimes* or *logics* of language, knowledge and power inherent in doing politics" (Varela et al. 2011, 1, their emphasis). This is an analysis of the manifestation of the hegemonic processes, regimes, and logics in the political rubric of homonormativity. This is in terms of the "political rule or domination, especially in relations between social classes, and especially to definitions of a ruling class" (Raymond Williams 1977, 109).

It is important to note that the concepts of "hegemony" and "sexual normativity" are not mutually exclusive, as Duggan distinguishes:

The cultural and social organization of gender and sexuality is embedded within the institutions and everyday practices of global political economy, and is inextricably imbricated with the organization of race, dis/ability, nation, empire and religion (Duggan 2011, xxv).

It is possible for hegemony to be pushed beyond the Gramscian ideological limitations of class and assist us in new theories regarding heteronormative (and in turn homonormative) power (Ludwig 2011). A homonormative redistribution of hegemonic power can occur through mimicry. In "Normative Dilemmas and the Hegemony of Counter Hegemony," Castro Varela and Dhawan extend the discussion of hegemony to the contemporary issue of same-sex marriage, informed by postcolonial theorist Homi Bhabba's essay "Of Mimicry and Man" (1984). Their arguments are two-fold. First, using Bhabba's idea of mimicry,[2] in same-sex marriage, there is an imitation of normative heterosexual marriage that also destabilises the norm. If heterosexual marriage brings "respectability, social status and marital benefits to those who are permitted to enter this institution, then same-sex marriage can be read as a contestations of hegemonic heteronormativity" (104). However, Castro Varela and Dhawan complicate this by arguing that same-sex marriage reinforces the marginalisation of those that choose not to marry, as "debates surrounding same-sex marriage politics problematize the idea of family, rearticulate care-politics and reinvent partnership, but they also stabilize the idea of monogamous love and exclude non-normative alliances from parity of participation" (116). Homonormative relationship recognition such as gay marriage can be seen as a manifestation of the realignment of hegemonic sexual normativity in patriarchal society. Those that do not adhere to this mimicry are marginalised.

## HOMONORMATIVE CINEMA

It is the intention of this chapter to analyse how these tensions between the stigmaphile and stigmaphobe positions become actualised in the queer film festival programme. How have heteronormativity and homonormativity become actualised in film and television?

Film and television are powerful mediums in which norms are constructed:

> As a constitutive element of culture, television participates in both the fashioning and refashioning of norms. Norms are not static and remain variable... Television must be thought of not merely as a 'representation of reality'—a reality ostensibly 'out there' beyond the screen—but as a cultural practice that produces and reproduces the norms of gender and sexuality that *are* our lived reality (both political and social) (Chambers 2006, 84–85).

Homonormalisation is a result of neoliberalising trends in contemporary identity politics. This normalisation takes on the form of increasingly professional political organisations and an identity-based consumption of gay and lesbian constituents. "Within traditional models of 'normalisation,' this is explained by reducing or eradicating forms of 'difference' that are ascribed to people which render them devalued citizens" (Richardson 2005, 521). This normalisation creates a type of "purification," a sanitisation in which gays and lesbians are reconfigured as desexualised normative citizens situated within domestic settings (Warner 1999). This desexualisation of the gay citizen is evident in Sender's analysis of contemporary marketing in gay media, where gay subcultural capital is determined by "good taste and sexual discretion" (2004, 226). Stigma is attached to the stereotype of the hyper-sexualised gay subject—abject queer sex, the HIV/AIDS epidemic, and so forth. This is a reconfiguration into the ideal neoliberal citizen, a "self-regulating homosexual subject who chooses stable co-habiting relationships" (Richardson 2005, 522). In order to achieve this equality and sameness, it is the responsibility of the sexual other to "adopt disciplined sexual practices through the internalisation of new norms of identity and sexual practices associated with a certain (heteronormative) lifestyle, with various rights granted through demonstrating a specific form of 'domestic' sexual coupledom" (521). In order to achieve happiness, the homosexual neoliberal citizens must take responsibility for themselves, where under neoliberalism, "*symbolic* prohibitive norms are increasingly replaced by imaginary ideals (or social success, of bodily fitness...)" (Žižek 1999, 368). This is a process whereby the left accepts the current neoliberal terrain. The depoliticised (and, I argue, desexualised) left subject epitomises the inability to universalise particular issues above minority levels (Dean 2009). As such, "much of contemporary mainstream lesbian and gay political and cultural activity is based in the neoliberal philosophy of consumer rights rather than that of citizen rights" (Murphy et al. 2008, 5). Homonormativity is thus born out of a post-political neoliberalist rhetoric in that this is an internalisation of societal norms. Homonormativity is absolutely prevalent in contemporary independent gay cinema. Duggan's theory of homonormativity is based on a transition from confrontational political strategies to the "abandonment of progressive-left organizations, and the adoption of a mainstream, neoliberal brand of identity/equality politics" (Duggan 2003, 440).

There is very little scholarly literature on the manifestation of homonormativity in contemporary LGBT cinema. In his analysis of queer-themed Indiewood films, Knegt's argument (2008) is founded on the idea that the "Indiewood" movement was a "hegemonic negotiation" of the American film industry, which saw the dominance and subservience of queer cinema. Hollywood was the established hegemonic order with independent film as the counter-hegemonic reaction. With independent cinema increasingly showing economic possibilities, this Indiewood movement was a modification of this hegemony with an adoption of normative sexual norms. This continues to be an interesting study into the political divide between cinema as a tool for queer social empowerment and product for consumption. Queer cinema's journey has voyaged from the radical new queer cinema to the niche gay market (Rich 2000) and is the "abandonment of progressive-left organisations, and the adoption of a mainstream, neoliberal brand of identity/equality politics" (Duggan 2002, 44). Gay Indiewood cinema is a hegemonic negotiation of the American film industry, which "correlates to formations represented within 'the new homonormativity'" (Knegt 2008, 6–7). Indeed, contemporary queer cinema can be used to interrogate the ever-changing nature of identity politics:

> The contemporary mainstreaming of gay and lesbian identity—as a mass mediated consumer lifestyle and embattled legal category—demands a renewed queer studies ever vigilant to the fact that sexuality is intersectional, not extraneous to other modes of difference, and calibrated to a firm understanding of queer as a political metaphor without a fixed referent (Eng et al. 2005, 1).

When discussing contemporary LGBT-focused cinema and homonormativity, two key films continuously arise, *Brokeback Mountain* and *The Kids Are Alright*. Knegt's aforementioned work (2008) and a collection of essays from journal *GLQ* (2007) discuss the conservative framework within which *Brokeback* is embedded. Likewise, Jack Halberstam (2010) has argued the same for *The Kids Are Alright*,[3] stating that the film is entrenched in a suffocating domesticity. While Cholodenko's "first film played against stereotype by setting its lesbian drama in a drugged out world of high-art,[4] this film loads sexual inertia, domestic dowdiness and bourgeois complacency onto the lesbian couple and leaves the sperm donor dad in the enviable position of being free, cool and casually sexual" (np). While LGBT representation certainly has grown significantly in films, television, and advertising over the last two decades, the nature of representations of same-sex coupling has changed (Becker 2006). There are fears it is growing into a homogeneous banality. *Color Lines* blogger Daisy Hernandez says of Cholodenko's film, "*The Kids Are All Right* is ... a revealing portrait of where the gay movement has been headed for some time now: white suburbia, Mexican gardener included" (np).[5] The whiteness of Cholodenko's film is problematic. By the conclusion of the narrative, the three supporting characters of colour are dismissed in a variety of ways.[6] Hernandez continues:

But it's also a portrait of the white gay movement, which has struggled with its race issues for some time now, most publicly after Prop. 8 passed in California and hysterical white gay boys blamed black voters for keeping them from the joys of registering at Tiffany's. If that happened though it was largely because the movement has failed to build institutions where people of color, like those in *The Kids Are All Right*, play more than minor roles (Hernandez 2010, np).

Here, instead of challenging the ideological dynamics of the dominant norm, like a quintessentially queer film should, we have the gay world mimicking the straight world where economic power creates racial privilege. This act of mimicry, as aforementioned, is the privileged epitome of homonormativity.

It seems a common trend in analyses of homonormative representation of same-sex coupling in cinema and television sees catering to (that is, not alienating) heterosexual audiences as a significant factor. Tricia Jenkins (2005) sees films such as *The Wild Things* (1998), *Cruel Intentions* (1999), *Not Another Teen Movie* (2001), and *American Pie 2* (2001) as texts that "dilute their lesbian portrayals ... (by) heterosexualising these scenes in order to promote the conventional straight male's lesbian fantasy" (492). These films feminise and water down their lesbian portrayals as the butch lesbian character would challenge and confront patriarchal assumptions about female sexuality (Ciasullo 2001) and as such remains near invisible in mainstream media depictions of female homosexuality. A significant aspect of these analyses is that these case studies all deal with *mainstream* depictions of LGBTI characters. This research, however, concerns LGBTI films that specifically cater to LGBTI audiences and as such don't need to worry about alienating a possibly conservative heterosexual audience.

A significant portion of LGBTI films aiming to attract a wider market *within* the LGBTI community undergo a similar hegemonic compromise with regard to the representation of their characters. Similar to Katherine Sender's analysis on gay-oriented advertising (2003), this research begins with the assumption that "markets are shaped, not discovered" (Ohmann 1996, 91). As such, the gay market recreates the boundaries of sexual norms by privileging this "ideal image of the gay consumer as (an) affluent, white, male, thirtysomething, genderconforming and sexually discreet" individual (Sender 2003, 335). The contemporary mediated gay male still exists in hegemonic constructions of masculinity (Emig 2000, 211) and a predominantly white society whereby in "neoliberalism's gay formations, race is 'merely cultural' and therefore a kind of symbolic surplus value" (Munoz 2005, 102). Says McBride of the "universal love story" tag line given to *Brokeback Mountain*:

> Two African American men could not possibly have been viewed as representing universal gay male experience in the way that the whiteness of the characters in *Brokeback* can and does. Even if we could get beyond that hurdle, would the film jive with the white cinematic and televisual image of gay life that mainstream U.S. culture has manufactured, packaged, and produced? (McBride 2007, 96–97).

Intrinsically, we can see that there is room for an examination of the films of the queer film festival. This book will examine *how* these boundaries of sexual norms manifest within the queer film festival. This requires conceptual organisation to structure this analysis.

## THREE CHARACTERISTICS OF HOMONORMATIVE REPRESENTATION

My analysis of the queer film festival's programming emerges from this uneasiness in contemporary LGBTI cinema. To aid my interrogation, I will highlight three key characteristics of homonormativity present in the films. These three characteristics will form the framework of my discussion of Frameline's programming. First, is the film anchored in a depoliticised consumerist ideology? Is the film's main priority to have the largest audience possible? Is there a distinct depoliticisation of the queerness of the characters? This is not to imply that the queerness of characters *must* be a political issue for the films but an absence of engagement with contemporary issues is a key element of Duggan's homonormativity. Second, are the film's characters confined to domestic settings? A distinct element of homonormativity is both privatisation and the preference of heteronormative ideals, namely the attempted recreation of the nuclear family. Anchoring the narratives in a distinctly domestic setting epitomises this. Finally, and perhaps most importantly, is there a hierarchy of sexual identities? Knegt (2008) identifies a privileging of "white gays and lesbians played by attractive and 'gender-appropriate' actors and actresses" (6) in mainstream gay and lesbian cinema. This is an internalisation of patriarchal norms into the political medium of cinema.

These three characteristics of homonormativity will segment the evidence that both affirms and challenges this conservative ideology. The following chapter investigates the manifestation of homonormativity and its effects in queer film festival programming. The aim of these chapters is to find out if both homonormative films and socially empowering films can coexist. In turn, I will interrogate the programming of Frameline and MQFF to see if queer films defy these three characteristics of homonormativity. Five-year periods for each film festival are examined. My closing analysis of HKLGFF 2014 will examine the role a "global gay" sensibility has on local programming. As I introduced in the Introduction, Aaron (2004) identifies the emergence of new queer cinema in the early 1990s as a cinema of defiance. Do any contemporary queer films tap into this counter-hegemonic defiance in a similar way to that of the wave of queer films that preceded them? This chapter undertakes an ideological critique of the narrative features programmed. Films selected for analysis were primarily feature-length narrative films. A significant conclusion drawn from my analysis of both the queer film festivals' social entrepreneurial status was that box office intake or venue locations are not the sole (or even dominant) factor in determining a film's success. As such, a variety of films were chosen for analysis in this chapter. Films range from significant positions in the programme (opening, closing, and centrepiece films) and smaller sessions at theatres such as the Roxie and the Victoria theatres in the Mission District or the studio space at ACMI for MQFF.

## Depoliticisation and Consumerism

All films are political. By applying Comolli and Narboni's (1971) well-known seven categories for ideological categories of film, we can see the possibility for a film to be progressive, in that their *category e* film can:

> seem at first sight to belong firmly within the ideology and to be completely under its sway, but which turn out to be so only in an ambiguous manner.... The films we are talking about throw up obstacles in the way of the ideology, causing it to swerve and get off course. The cinematic framework lets us see it, but also shows it up and denounces it. Looking at the framework one can see two moments in it: one-holding it back within certain limits, one transgressing them (Comolli and Narboni 1971, 32–3).

Comolli and Narboni assert that a film need not be overtly radical or make commentary on dominant political ideologies in order for it to be deemed progressive. Treatment of the realist aesthetic is complex. As structuralists, they see films as being products of their ideological environments. While Bazin (1967) believes film is a reproduction of reality, Comolli and Narboni argue that this "reality" is nothing more than a reproduction on the dominant way of seeing. The realist aesthetic reproduces dominant cultural principles that define the way we *experience* the world. The realist aesthetic appears not to challenge societal relations. According to Klinger (1986), the progressive text appears "supportive of the ideology that conditions its existence, hampers the straightforward expression of it through the production of a formally impelled rupture with the veneer of its own premises" (78). In other words, the film appears to support dominant ideology but uses formal cinematic codes and conventions to critique particular political manifestations.

The concept of the progressive text is being utilised as a disclaimer for my discussion of depoliticised LGBT films. LGBT characters in contemporary queer cinema need not be overtly political in order for the film to be deemed "politicised." Many gay male films exist where the sexuality of the lead male characters existed purely for commercial interests, devoid of any political pursuits. In Sender's analysis on contemporary gay advertising (2003), there is a distinct privileging of the "affluent, white, male, thirtysomething, gender-conforming and sexually discreet" gay individual (335). Two of these films cinematically represent the depoliticised homonormativity that Duggen proposed. *eCupid* (J.C. Calciano 2011) is perhaps the epitome of this contemporary trend of banal American gay cinema, while the film *Leave It on the Floor* (Sheldon Larry 2011) is a politically watered-down musical reminiscent of the drag ball scene of *Paris Is Burning* (Jennie Livingston 1991).

*eCupid* is a standard American gay male romantic comedy. Programmed at the Castro Theatre for Frameline 35 and in the largest ACMI theatre at MQFF, the film was a big drawcard for the gay male community. Every queer film festival usually has a number of romantic comedies in its programme.[7] The film's narrative is fairly conventional in that our lead protagonist is unfulfilled and unhappy at the commencement of the narrative, ventures into "single-dom" only to realise the age-old adage "you don't know what you have until it's gone." Marshall (Houston Rhines) has the seven-year itch with his boyfriend Gabe (Noah Schuffman) and as a result downloads a smart phone application called "eCupid," which

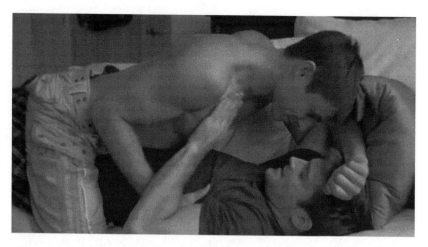

**Fig. 4.1** *eCupid*'s main selling point is this privileged gay male figure

promises him true love. The application then functions independently from Marshall's control forcing him to admit to Gabe that he isn't happy anymore. Now single, the application begins to invite over conventionally attractive men for dates and parties as seen in Fig. 4.1. This gay playboy lifestyle forces Marshall to realise he indeed loved Gabe all along. The cast is all white and gender appropriate with the drawcard for the film being the attractiveness of the lead actors. The film is like a feature-length Abercrombie & Fitch advertisement.[8] This objectification of the masculine, waxed, oiled-up muscled body is the drawcard to this film as exemplified in one of their key film stills to promote the film:

Masculinity, here, is being positioned as a desirable commodified identity (Rahman 2004). Marshall represents the epitome of the privileged gay male image that Sender describes in her book *Business Not Politics* (2004). Gay markets are not pre-existing entities but formulated through both political activism and commercially minded media. Sender's research into LGBT-oriented advertising found a certain level of legitimacy given to a certain "brand" of gayness over other sexual identities. Sender noted that when featured in advertising to be shown to a wider audience outside of the LGBT community, gay and lesbian images go through a process of desexualisation as the "class position in gay men is made precarious in part by public evidence of their sexual culture" (339). In other words, queer people lose authority and status in a wider patriarchal society when they are seen to be sexually active subjects.

This stigma attached to the sexually active gay male character is seen in *eCupid*'s narrative. While, yes, the attractiveness of the male cast is used to sell the film, the dramatic tension of the plot all centres on the possibility of sexual intercourse. Marshall is initially disappointed that Gabe is always either too tired or wanting an early night to have sex thus leading to their separation. But once the application starts dictating his love life, all Marshall's encounters with clichéd gay male characters result in him being pushed out of his comfort zone. The encounters are episodic in nature (it could read as the plot to a porn film). When sporty college boy Dawson randomly arrives at his house for sex, Marshall squirms underneath him and sends him on his way. Marshall constantly denies all of the advances from his co-worker, Keith, whose attempts at flirting with Marshall in the bar comes off as a joke. When Keith invites Marshall to a pool party, Marshall turns him down politely and leaves. The film's narrative promises us that Marshall is to briefly lead this playboy lifestyle, yet the film's narrative doesn't actually have Marshall engage in any sex acts whatsoever. Marshall's discomfort with any sexual connection with men is palpable.

As outlined earlier in my discussion on the queer film festival as a social enterprise, the social enterprise is to target a market failure and deliver. Films such as these fluffy romantic comedies are intended to be romantic stories for a gay community that are free from the stigma associated with the sexual activity identified by Sender. There is no need to desexualise these characters so as to not make any conservative straight audience uncomfortable. Yet clearly, *eCupid* adheres to the trends of the gay media outlined in Sender's analysis. A white, middle-class, gender-appropriate, and sexually conservative gay male is the privileged figure in these films. There is an unnecessary desexualisation occurring here. As mentioned above, Comolli and Narboni outline the possibility for a progressive text occurring within a traditional cinematic framework in their *category e* film. A film such as *eCupid* fails to challenge any dominant ideology at play, which in this case is the stigma attached to the sexually active gay man. As such, the film falls into their *category a* film in that it is "imbued through and through with the dominant ideology in pure and unadulterated form" (Comolli and Narboni 1971, 31). This realist aesthetic presents a skewed representation of gay masculinity. By valuing whiteness, muscularity, and youthfulness, this film supports a dominant ideological allegory of what masculine beauty is. The privileged male figure in *eCupid* is a homonormative one, as it does not challenge any societal relations.

In regard to race, formal cinematic norms are not used to rupture that naturalisation of white dominance. Much like Richard Dyer has argued in his work on whiteness (1997), white culture for *eCupid* (and indeed many films outlined below) is invisible and seen as the norm, where "white people create the dominant images of the world and don't quite see that they thus construct the world in their image" (Dyer 1997, 9). The image of the gay man in *eCupid* positions whiteness as *more* desirable than non-white figures. A culture of whiteness is perpetuated through the circulation of these images (Gross 2005; Yep and Elia 2007; Puar 2005). The only non-white principal cast member is Italian-American party planner Carson (a nod to *Queer Eye for the Straight Guy* perhaps?). Much like Jack from *Will & Grace*, his effeminacy is played for cheap laughs, and he is not situated in any romantic context. If anything, his presence is an intrusion into Marshall's life. The social effects of such inherent racism is littered through the gay community with terms such as "rice queen" and "potato queen" and many dating profiles reading "no chubs, femmes or Asians please."[9] By highlighting the overriding whiteness of these films, their position of power is open to critique "by undercutting the authority with which they/we speak and act in the world" (2). *eCupid* is an example of the many gay male films in both Frameline's and MQFF's programme that use the privileged gay male image in the promotion for the film:

Frameline 31
    *Shelter* (Jonah Markowitz 2007)
    *2 Minutes Later* (Robert Gaston 2006)
    *You Belong to Me* (Sam Zalutsky 2006)
    *A Four Letter Word* (Casper Andreas 2007)
Frameline 32
    *Japan Japan* (Lior Shamriz 2007)
    *Were the World Mine* (Tom Gustafson 2008)
    *Another Gay Sequel: Gays Gone Wild* (Todd Stephens 2008)
Frameline 33
    *Light Gradient* (Ruckenwind, Jan. Kruger 2009)
    *Redwoods* (David Lewis 2009)
    *Mr. Right* (Jacqui and David Morris 2008)
    *Hollywood Je T'aime* (Jason Bushman 2009)

Frameline 34
   *Is It Just Me?* (J.C. Calciano 2010)
   *From Beginning to End* (*Do Comeco Ao Fim*, Aluzio Abranches 2009)
   *Going South* (*Plein Sud*, Sebastian Lifshitz 2009)
   *The String* (*Le Fil*, Medhi Ben Attia 2010)
Frameline 36
   *I Do* (Glenn Gaylord 2012)
   *Joshua Tree, 1951: a Portrait of James Dean* (Matthew Mishory 2012)
   *Love or Whatever* (Rosser Goodman 2012)
   *Naked as We Came* (Richard LeMay 2011)
   *Mixed Kebab* (Guy Lee Thys 2012)
   *Our Paradise* (Gael Morel 2011)
MQFF 2008
   *A Four Letter Word* (Casper Andreas 2007)
   *The Houseboy* (Spencer Schilly 2007)
   *Kiss the Bride* (Jay Cox 2007)
   *Shelter* (Jonah Markowitz 2007)
MQFF 2009
   *Were the World Mine* (Tom Gustafson 2008)
   *Between Love and Goodbye* (Casper Andreas 2008)
   *Dog Tags* (Damion Dietz 2008)
   *I Dreamt Under the Water* (*J'ai Reve Sous L'eau*, Homoz 2008)
   *Mr. Right* (Jacqui and David Morris 2008)
   *Mulligans* (Chip Hale 2008)
   *The New Twenty* (Chris Mason Johnson 2008)
MQFF 2010
   *From Beginning to End* (*Do Comeco Ao Fim*, Aluzio Abranches 2009)
   *The Big Gay Musical* (Casper Andreas and Fred M. Caruso 2009)
   *David's Birthday* (*Il compleanno*, Marco Filiberti 2009)
   *Eating Out 3: All You Can Eat* (Glenn Gaylord 2009)
   *Hollywood Je T'aime* (Jason Bushman 2009)
   *Lucky Bastard* (Everett Lewis 2009)
   *Redwoods* (David Lewis 2009)
MQFF 2011
   *Buffering* (Darren Flaxstone and Christian Martin 2010)
   *Is It Just Me?* (J.C. Calciano 2010)
   *The One* (Caytha Jentis 2010)
   *Strapped* (Joseph Graham 2010)
   *The String* (*Le Fil*, Medhi Ben Attia 2010)
   *Violet Tendencies* (Casper Andreas 2010)

MQFF 2012
*August* (Eldar Rapaport 2010)
*Eating Out 5: The Open Weekend* (Q. Allan Rocka 2011)
*eCupid* (J.C. Calciano 2011)
*Going Down in La-La Land* (Casper Andreas 2011)
*The Green* (Steven Williford 2010)

This is a clear trend in the queer film festival that adheres to patriarchal ideologies of masculinity that fails to embrace any queer notions of playing with gender. While some of these films may seem to challenge a heterosexist view of the world, they "do not effectively criticize the ideological system in which they are embedded because they unquestioningly adopt its language and its imagery" (Comolli and Narboni 1971, 32). Gay male narratives need not necessarily entail cultural resistance against heterosexism. This hyper-masculinity "re-idealizes heterosexual norms *without* calling them into question" (Butler 1993: 231, original emphasis). This idealisation of masculinity is an appropriation and reinforcement of patriarchal discourse. This is a "branded" masculinity wherein "profit can be produced by generating insecurity about one's body and one's consumer choices and then providing consumers with the correct answer or product" (Alexander 2003, 551). As Yep and Elia (2012) argue in relation to television show *Noah's Arc*: "The process of assimilating and blending into the U.S. heteronormative mainstream produces docile and de-politicized gay bodies and identities" (894). This ideological view of male beauty is not natural but a cultural falsehood that has been heavily influenced by a heteronormative preference for a certain type of masculinity.

My first experience of *Leave It on the Floor* was a thoroughly enjoyable one. I was swept up in the explicit raucousness of the screening at the Castro Theatre for Frameline 35. The film received a centrepiece screening and was sold out. There was clapping, singing, dancing in the aisles, and so on. It truly was an active participatory event. I revisited the film a second time as part of my role on the MQFF selection panel, both in the privacy of my home and then at the Closing night screening of the 22nd festival in 2012, and was surprised by the film's lack of engagement with the gender politics of its heavily influential antecedent *Paris Is Burning*. *Paris Is Burning* was a documentary that explored race, gender, class, and sexuality in America through an examination of the drag ball scenes in New York. The ball environment was a carnivalesque space for empowerment, free from the oppressive social hegemonic order of race and sexuality. Says Dorian Corey in the film: "Now the fact that you are not an executive is merely because of the social standing of life . . . Black people have a hard time getting anywhere and those that do are usually straight." The film itself provided a voice for those traditionally marginalised within the gay community.

*Leave It on the Floor* is problematic in that the gender politics are watered down. Yes, we have a variety of gay male characters with varying degrees of masculinity and femininity, but there is no engagement with the issue of the relationship this queer bubble has with the outside world. There is only one key transgender female character, Eppie Durall, whose false pregnancy positions her as a mere walking punchline. In *Paris Is Burning*, the various categories of "realness" are discussed in terms of the inequalities black and Latino queers face in contemporary American society. One struggles in the real world to reach an executive position because of racial and sexual inequalities *so* one attempts to pass as an executive in the ballroom scene. It is social commentary pure and simple. The categories in *Leave It on the Floor* fail to have this social bite. Categories such as "with a Gaga twist"[10] or the body builders in khaki underwear fail to articulate any social commentary. Aside from the song "His Name Is Shawn" played at Eppie Durall's funeral, which deals with the banishment of queer youth from their families, the film has a distinct lack of awareness of any inequalities *within* the gay community. This is further emphasised by an audience member's discomfort during the following Q&A:

> I thought (director) Sheldon Larry's speech at the end of *Leave it on the Floor* was negative. He spoke a lot of the oppression of the African American race while he was a big white Jew talking about it with eight African American stars behind him who didn't get a chance to speak because he wouldn't give up the microphone. He was kind of hypocritical at that point (Interview with "Nick" 2011).

The Q&A rearticulated the racial inequalities already present within the gay community with a Caucasian director speaking for the African American experience. Another programmer asked the question "so what does a white Jew know about African American culture?" only for Philip Evelyn (Princess Eminence) to save the day by responding with that the cast had input on the script. Though the songs are appealing and appear to be protest inciting, such as "Knock the Mother-fuckers Down," the film's gender and racial politics fail to address any actual inequality these characters face in the outside world. Blackness for this film is something to be fetishised, where "whites return again and again to this fetish in order to satisfy a self-created urge to be white" (Farley 1997, 463). Much like Yep and Elia's analysis of *Noah's Ark* (2012), *Leave It on the Floor* takes place "in a complex landscape of pervasive heteronormativity, Whiteness, neoliberal politics, and consumer-driven economy" (897). Here the white consumer both simultaneously eroticises and fears the black male body. This depoliticised film positions the African American characters as something to be objectified, as characters that do not get the privilege to challenge any societal white dominance. Such a lack of political engagement and fetishisation are tied with a homonormative political ideology that promotes white privilege.

The popular gay film *Shelter* is a classic example of this typical gay male figure seen in the gay mainstream press. The film received screenings at 8:15 p.m. on both the first Friday and the following Saturday nights for the 2008 MQFF programme, two very privileged positions in the programme. Both Zach and Shaun are distinctly far removed from any gay or queer culture. The entire narrative has a clear absence of any political engagement. The scene with Shaun and Zach's first kiss displays Zach's sexually conservative nature, which is typical of this gay male archetype. The scene is set up like any indie romance film one would see on the film festival circuit. The soft folk-like backing track of Shane Mack's "Break" infers the relaxed attitude of both characters drinking a few beers on their beachside balcony (they are surfers after all!). Both characters fit every feature presented by Sender in *Business Not Politics*. Both Caucasian leads are gender appropriate, both are wearing loose skater-like clothing and are distinctly masculine with Zach referring to his mate as "dude" or "man"; Shaun resides in his parents' mansion, which both reside in at the conclusion of the film. The camera moves in on both sitting next to each other on the lounge. As Zach shows Shaun his artwork, the camera moves up to a bird's-eye view of the two. This signifies Zach's loosening up and letting his guard down as he is now lying flat next to Shaun; then, and only then, can Shaun move in for the kiss. We see their eyes meet and pause before they kiss. While this can be put down to Zach's closeted sexuality or dramatic tension, it's also a clear indicator of sexual conservativeness and shy masculinity, which is apparent in the many gay male romantic comedies listed above.

The representation of this gay male figure ultimately comes down to the relationship between the formal representation of cinema and dominant societal ideologies. Earlier, I introduced Comolli and Narboni's (1969) ideas on cinema and ideological criticism where film is part of an ideological superstructure, which is determined by capitalist economic systems. These films demonstrate the commodification of the gay male figure, where this capitalist economic system privileges a certain form of gay masculinity. When discussing this privileged gay male trend, we must remember that these films are not reproducing the reality of the gay male existence but are in fact reproducing the world created by these dominant ideologies. These films privilege dominant ideologies of race, gender, anachronistic notions of gay sexuality, and so on in "pure and unadulterated form" (815). As such, these films do not portray any real notion of contemporary gay reality but instead reflect the extent to which filmmakers themselves are imbued with said ideologies and how they merely do so for commercial pressure. Through work from Knget (2008), Chasin (2000), and Sender (2004) we know this gay male image is profitable. However, just because this *will* sell out a session at a queer film festival doesn't mean it *should*. This discussion raises Bazin's (1967) questioning of just what actually cinema is, where he argues that film is much like the photographic image, which we are "forced to accept as real the existence of the object reproduced, actually *re*-presented, set before us, that is to say, in time and space" (162). Bazin argues that the guiding fancy of realism (and film) is the "recreation of the world in its own image, an image unburdened by the freedom of interpretation of the artist or the irreversibility of time" (165–166). These "wax museum ideals," as Arnheim has argued (1957), fail to incorporate or satisfy artistic desires.

As such, Bazin's myth of the total cinema and the wax museum ideals Arnheim speaks of are a fallacy, as these films are never created within a vacuum. Films such as *Shelter* and *eCupid* are imbued with many dominant ideologies, particularly in relation to gender and race, in order to fulfil commercial possibilities. It is when these images are framed as realistic that when the homonormativity continues to be naturalised further. If we look back to the above-mentioned scene between Zach and Shaun in *Shelter*, we can see these dominant ideologies being naturalised through the realist construction of the scenes. The zooming in shot that opens the scene and the standard framing of the two guys fall within the cinematic genre of realism. This scene's style is invisible so as to not disrupt or create distance with the audience's identification. By not having an objective perspective, audience members are less likely to form an objective assessment of the identity politics at play. As such, the dominance of whiteness and gender appropriateness is harder to question (Fig. 4.2).

**Fig. 4.2**  The film still used in MQFF's 2011 programme for *La Mission*

The framing of the film in the programme must also be considered. The use of semi-naked attractive (usually white) men in many promotional photos is sometimes beyond the control of the festival:

> While we don't help ourselves with how we present the films in our program guide in terms of shirts off, we are kind of stuck with what filmmakers send us in terms of the ways they want the film to be marketed—and to be honest it sells tickets … last year's *La Mission* was a good example because we didn't have a sexy still of Benjamin Bratt, and we found it really hard to sell tickets to that film, which was frustrating as it's really good film. Most savvy filmmakers will tell us how they want their film marketed saying 'these are the three key stills I want you to use in this order.' Some just send whatever but most will say 'this is your program guide still' this is your 'website still' so they can be quite specific (Interview with Lisa Daniel 2011).

These are indicative of wider formations of homonormativity. Keeping in mind that MQFF is a social enterprise, the festival needs to sell tickets in order to remain operational and fulfil its social mission. In 2011's programme, *La Mission* (Peter Bratt 2009) was arguably the strongest gay male-themed feature-length film in the programme. The film was set in San Francisco's Mission District and depicted the tumultuous and strained relationship between tough guy Che Rivera (Bratt) and his son Jes (Jeremy

Ray Valdez) after discovering his son's sexuality. The mere fact that the film does not contain male figures (that Sender (2003) described as privileged in contemporary gay media) results in the film being considered less accessible for the mainstream gay audience. This is a key dilemma for the queer film festival programmer, says Daniel:

> Sometimes it's tempting to screen a film that has a really sexy pic but is in fact quite crappy. You know you can screen x film and sell a lot of tickets but you also know it's going to leave people feeling disappointed. I don't do that. It's too easy to make that decision and I think you lose punters the next year. If I went to a festival and saw three films and they were all rubbish I wouldn't go back! Especially if the program notes are telling me this film is really good. If we in Melbourne are going to screen films that aren't going to get a big audience then we write them up accordingly, 'this is a soapy film and if you like soapy stuff go and see it and if you don't like soapy stuff don't see it' (Interview with Daniel 2011).

### *Domesticity*

Homonormativity is the mimicry of heteronormative ideals. A significant manifestation of this is the attempted recreation of the nuclear family with little challenge to the wider ideology of familial politics. Assimilationist tactics of the LGBTI community are fuelled by a neoliberal political economy, in which hegemonic relations are the "boundaries through which money, political power, cultural resources, and social organization flow" (Duggan 2003, xii). Homonormalisation sees a departure from progressive politics, which would seek to examine the construction of the family and, rather, aims to be embedded within and mimic a conservative framework. By having an emphasis on normalised private domestic settings, homonormative narratives are not contesting pre-existing representations of gender and sexuality but instead accepting one's place within the patriarchy. This is a realignment of what constitutes as sexual normativity.

Melodrama *The Green* (Steven Williford 2010) centres on a couple striving for this domestic bliss in Connecticut. *The Green* was a sneak preview session for Frameline 35 as it was to be theatrically released. The film also screened in MQFF 2012 programme and received certain hype over bankable actor Cheyenne Jackson. Michael and Daniel have escaped the hustle and bustle in New York to lead a much simpler life in a small, leafy rural town. From the outset of the narrative, it is established that in order to achieve this quiet livelihood, both men must remain sexually conservative. Michael is a teacher at the local high school, and Daniel runs his own catering business. Both men have their relationships exist in a "don't ask, don't tell" state of affairs, where in order for them to be happy, they must keep things quiet. This is until a student accuses Michael of inappropriate conduct—cue typical of small-town hysteria. The parents of the boy pursue legal action, which makes matters worse for Daniel and Michael as the teacher's prior arrest for public indecency creates a fissure between the two. This false accusation results in the shattering of their rural dream. Construction work on their picturesque house halts, Daniel's clients cancel, and Michael has to hire a lawyer to fight the charges. Many reviewers missed the whole assimilating ideals of the lead couple:

> This is obviously a gay movie. However, it is far different from the sort of indie gay that tends to come at the viewer with either a glitter clutch full of camp, or armed with a big moral message with which it intends to enlighten you by beating you about the head and shoulders with said message, as though it were a cast iron skillet. Instead, we have a drama where the protagonist happens to be gay (Vaughan 2012, np).

What is perplexing about reactions to this film is that the leads' sexuality is deemed irrelevant.[11] Apparently, the overall narrative transcends the fact that we have a gay couple at the centre of such a scandal. By stating that these characters "just happen to be gay" significantly avoids the forced domestication of these characters. There is an internal homophobia at play here. In order for Michael and Daniel to achieve happiness, they must be sexually conservative. Any sexual passion between the two must occur within the private confines of the bedroom, which is further emphasised by Daniel's outrage at Michael's previous public indiscretions. By viewing this film as not being about sexuality or these characters as just "happening to be gay," we are implicit in this denial and repression of natural sexuality. This narrative is a clear demonstration of homonormativity as Daniel and Michael are attempting to mimic a conservative framework of what constitutes a family. Kentlyn (2008) believes that gay and lesbian couples in a domestic setting ("doing femininity") can be an illustration of a subversion of gender norms. However, if this domestic setting is more of a haven to hide one's sexual passions from the neighbourhood, then this can hardly be subversive or empowering.

A common trend for homonormative gay and lesbian films is the privileged status of the domestic setting with sexuality being confined to the home and an attempted embrace of the nuclear family. In Frameline 31, we had *Out at the Wedding* (Lee Friedlander 2007) and *East Side Story* (Carlos Portugal 2006), where both narratives centred on family and the importance of marriage. *Shelter* (Jonah Markowitz 2007) concluded with disillusioned young man Zach being welcomed into Shaun's home with his younger nephew Cody as a happy family, with the film concluding with a hackneyed montage of the three of them playing football on the beach. In Frameline 32, we had *Breakfast with Scot* (Laurie Lynd 2007), where Eric and Sam are a sexually conservative hyper-masculine couple (Eric is a retired hockey player and Sam is a sports lawyer) living in the suburbs with their newly adopted son Scot. Eric and Sam are much like Daniel and Michael from *The Green* in that the only affection expressed between the couple occurs within the home. Eric and Sam are played by heterosexual actors (Tom Cavanagh and Ben Shenkman) and have very little chemistry between them, which is illustrated by of their sexless kiss towards the end of the film. This is clearly a film for mainstream audiences, where any alternative sexuality must occur within the home and behind closed doors. Other films at Frameline that had a couple attempting to recreate the heteronormative ideal family were:

Frameline 33
   *Patrick Age 1.5* (Ella Lemhagen 2008)
   *Misconceptions* (Ron Satlof 2008)
Frameline 35
   *eCupid* (J.C. Calciano 2011)
   *Longhorns* (David Lews 2011)
   *Kawa* (Katie Wolfe 2011)
Frameline 36
   *Petunia* (Ash Christian 2011)
   *Margarita* (Dominique Cardona and Laurie Colbert 2012)
   *Unconditional* (Bryn Higgins 2011)

Are these gay domestic couples actively queering an environment traditionally thought of as a space for the nuclear family, or are we seeing deviance being domesticated? Domestic spaces in contemporary Western homes are mostly heterosexualised. Writing on the role gay men play in lifestyle television, Gorman-Murray (2006) writes:

[The] image of the 'domestic' gay man presents a *paradox*. While gay domesticity challenges and subverts the normative heterosexuality of the home, this association also provides a way to regulate and sanitize a dissident sexuality, linking gay masculinity with ideals of domestic family life acceptable to mainstream Australia. The image of the domestic gay man both *queers* ideas of home and *domesticates* a 'deviant' sexuality (Gorman-Murray 2006, 233).

This paradox is also evident in these films. While we do have domesticated couples queering a traditionally heterosexual environment, there is still an element of normalcy to them. They exude socially acceptable behaviour that won't upset the neighbours. This flip side that problematises the seemingly empowering queer domestic couple is a product of homonormativity as we are seeing an aspect of contemporary normalising trends.

## *Hierarchies of Sexual Identity*

The final category for homonormative cinema is the recreation of previous hegemonic relations within the LGBTI community. This is an internalisation of patriarchal norms. Contemporary lesbian and gay cinema sees a privileging of whiteness and being gender appropriate. On either side of the spectrum, cinema with LGBTI-related content can abandon progressive ideals in favour of a mainstream brand of identity politics, or cinema can be used to critique and challenge pre-existing views on sexuality and gender. Certain films mimic patriarchal norms favoured by a heteronormative society while others are more defiant. As previously mentioned, homonormativity sees a realignment of the stigmaphile and stigmaphobe positions. In his analysis of normalising trends in contemporary gay politics, Warner (1999) borrows the terms from Erving Goffman. Privilege is given to certain members of the LGBTI community based on wealth, status, gender identity, race, and so forth. This incorporation of a hegemonic order into the LGBTI community sees the movement of certain identities out of a stigmaphile space, where there is commonality in oppression, and into the stigmaphobe space of the mainstream.

A key trend in the hierarchy of sexual identities is the stereotypical representation of gay and lesbian characters. The ensemble casts are either entirely gender appropriate or their characters are clichés that we would normally expect from a film that caters for a mass (read: mainly heterosexual) audience.

Frameline 31
  *Out at the Wedding* (Lee Friedlander 2007)
  *Shelter* (Jonah Markowitz 2007)
  *2 Minutes Later* (Robert Gaston 2006)
  *A Four Letter Word* (Casper Andreas 2007)
  *Rock Haven* (David Lewis 2007)
Frameline 32
  *The Art of Being Straight* (Jesse Rosen 2008)
  *Saturn in Opposition* (Ferzan Ozpetek 2007)
  *Breakfast with Scott* (Laurie Lynd 2007)
Frameline 33
  *Give Me Your Hand* (Pascal-Alex Vincent 2009)
  *Hollywood Je T'aime* (Jason Bushman 2009)
  *Redwoods* (David Lewis 2009)
Frameline 34
  *Is It Just Me?* (J.C. Calciano 2010)
  *From Beginning to End* (*Do Comeco Ao Fim, Aluzio* Abranches 2009)
Frameline 35
  *August* (Eldar Rapaport 2010)
  *Bite Marks* (Mark Bessenger 2011)
  *eCupid* (J.C. Calciano 2011)
  *Flight of the Cardinal* (Roberty Gaston 2010)
  *The Green* (Steven Williford 2010)
  *Judas Kiss* (J.T. Tenapa 2011)
  *Longhorns* (David Lews 2011)
  *The One* (Caytha Jentis 2010)
  *Private Romeo* (Alan Brown 2010).

Many of these films also featured in the MQFF programme. These are images that reinforce dominant ideologies of both race and gender in their narratives and promote the film. During my internship with Frameline in 2009 for Frameline 33, it came as no surprise that the first films to sell out were the films that had sexually suggestive write-ups with a film still of a naked/semi-naked male.

Cis-normative programming strategies are another trend that creates hierarchies at queer film festivals. This is a key finding from Jonathan Williams's thesis on spectatorship and Melbourne trans counter-publics (2011). When criticising the MQFF for the problematic nature of their trans inclusion, Williams argues that the festival "frames transness as something other to, or in-between, 'girl' o 'boy'" (Williams 2011, 176). While cisgender narratives are primarily labelled as "gay" or "lesbian," trans-themed films between two transgender characters of the same gender would be labelled as just "trans" and separated from any sexuality. For Stryker (2008), this homonormative approach stems from "the misconstruing trans as either a 'gender or a sexual orientation" (148). This unintentional homonormativity desexualises transness and separates trans content from the rest of the programme. While Williams focuses his critiques on MQFF, I would argue that this is representative of the gender binary–driven focus of most queer film festivals.

These identity politics driven programming strategies are promoted as normal by a queer neoliberalism. This cis-normalisation and gay and/or lesbian cliché function as part of a wider discourse on socially acceptable sexuality that reinforces the hetero/homo binary (Cover 2000). These safe characters are much like Battles and Hilton-Morrow's account of *Will & Grace* (2002), whereby focusing on interpersonal relationships, the films prevent a "consideration of gay politics and leads to a failure to acknowledge the social consequences of gay and lesbians living in our heterosexual culture" (99). Many of the films listed in this section emulate normalising trends in contemporary politics in their standard subject matter. I believe that this is similar to Stryker's account of anti-homonormative transgender activism, where she argues that this conservatism occurs on the micro-political level, as gay interests are "aligned with dominant constructions of knowledge and power that disqualify the very modes of knowing threatening to disrupt the smooth functioning of normative space" (155). This is a product of neoliberalism as it makes queerness dormant and unable to shape social change. These films represent changing sexual politics influenced by identity-based consumption.

The positive effects these films deliver, however, flow from the film festival's status as a social enterprise. It is important for every non-profit organisation to think of its bottom line. If programmers ensure quality control, these "popcorn films" ensure financial stability for the queer film festival. Many staff members interviewed referred to programming as a balancing act, where you need the fluffy romantic comedies if you are going to be able to afford to programme more innovative films, such as documentaries or shorts that would have a more difficult time in finding an audience. The following are the attendance figures for gay male romantic comedies screened at the Castro at the 2011 festival (Table 4.1):[12]

**Table 4.1** Attendance figures for gay male romantic comedies screened at the Castro

| Film[13] | Attendance figure[14] |
| --- | --- |
| eCupid | 1080 |
| Going down in La La Land | 837 |
| August | 929 |
| The Green | 786 |
| Longhorns | 894 |
| Private Romeo | 1128 |

The gay rom-com dramas are a staple of any queer film festival and, as highlighted earlier, are indicative of the queer film festival's social entrepreneurial status. The terms "popcorn film" and a "bums on seats" film are often spoken at MQFF selection panel meetings. Much like Frameline, by programming these films, MQFF is considering its bottom line. These films, however, fulfil another role also linked with the social enterprise as discussed by selection panellist Liz Mutineer:

> Gay romantic films are really good for identification purposes. Although you wouldn't say romantic comedy are breaking any boundaries, I think it's really nice for people to see stories that people can identify with, such as love stories or comedies. When you go to the movies and watch a teen romantic comedy, queer audiences might find it harder to identify with. It normalises the idea of being gay. It really does. So, while there is the argument that they have just put in two gay characters where there used to be straight characters, I think it really depends on the filmmaker and the way it was written (Interview with Liz Mutineer 2011).

These films target a gap in the market, in that these films are a desirable product never receiving theatrical distribution and only limited access to movie rental stores and online streaming sites. While these films may not directly challenge dominant norms on sexuality and gender, their "light" status fulfils a dominant role in the queer film festival programme. As such, while films such as *Breakfast with Scott* or *eCupid* won't ever be considered innovative queer films, they do indeed help the festival to afford films that wouldn't be able to pack out the Castro. This is a quintessential trope of the social enterprise framework, where the social mission is assisted by economic means. In his analysis on blockbusters at film festivals, Julian Stringer highlights that "quality" non-US blockbusters have to "utilize the alternative distribution network that the globalized festival circuit represents... for purposes of enhanced prestige or commercial gain" (Stringer 2003, 206). I would argue that specifically gay-themed films depend on the queer film festival circuit when aiming to secure distribution, through avenues such as Netflix, Wolfe Video, or TLA Releasing. Neither these are art-house films, nor are the spectators engaging in cinephilia. These are films that rely on dominant homonormative media aesthetics to engage their audiences. Regardless, they still play a significant role in queer film festival programming strategies.

## SOCIAL EMPOWERMENT

### *Political Engagement and Alternate Film Forms*

There are often a noteworthy amount of feature-length films that depart from the previously mentioned politically sparse films. A number of these are activist-related documentaries. Frameline 34's programme consisted of 35 documentaries and 39 feature-length films. Popular documentaries from this programme included *8: The Mormon Proposition* (Reed Cowan 2010), *Postcards to Daddy* (Michael Stock 2010), centrepiece screening *Beautiful Darling: the Life and Times of Candy Darling, Andy Warhol Superstar* (James Rasin 2009), and showcase *The Topp Twins: Untouchable Girls* (Leanne Pooley 2009). Frameline 35's programme consisted of 37 documentary feature-length films, which is compared to 43 narrative feature films. Popular documentaries from this year included *Advocate for Fagdom* (Angélique Bosio 2011), *Becoming Chaz* (Fenton Baily and Randy Barbato 2011), *Wish Me Away*, and *Gen Silent* (Stu Maddox 2011). These figures present a significant portion of documentary films programmed, which demonstrates a strong presence of alternate film form in Frameline's programme.

Specifically politically engaged documentaries from Frameline 35 included *The Grove* (Andy Abrahams 2011), which traced the history of the AIDS Memorial Grove in Golden Gate Park, and *Still Around* (Jorg Fockele and Marc Smolowitz 2011) was an innovative feature-length collection of 15 short films about HIV/AIDS; *East Bloc Love* (Logan Mucha 2011) focuses on clandestine LGBT groups in Eastern Europe, from Belarus to Romania, Poland, Latvia, and Estonia, while *This Is What Love in Action Looks Like* (Morgan Fox 2010) is a personal account of a young boy's forced admittance to a teen-centred ex-gay rehabilitation clinic. These films remind us of the varying degrees of oppression LGBT individuals face internationally. A film such as *East Bloc Love*'s presence in the queer film festival is of the utmost importance as it reminds the San Franciscan audience of the LGBTI collective being a global community. This reminder of the oppression other queers face is important, says Alexis Whitham:

> When you have a niche film festival, that allows people to experience a world and a perspective that they wouldn't otherwise see, you get to see so much more of the queer community at large through the festival; China, Guatemala, any other country that is represented in the festival, what it looks like to be queer in Kansas versus San Francisco. I think it also serves as a really nice reminder for San Franciscans that other people are still going through things that maybe we aren't going through every day because we live in a bubble of acceptance for most of the time (Interview with Whitham 2011).

This active engagement with contemporary politics, as highlighted earlier by Whitham, is the first of two trends in this category. In Frameline 31, we had centrepiece film *The Bubble* (Eytan Fox 2006), which dealt with four friends amidst the Israeli/Palestine conflict; *Tan Lines* (Ed Aldridge 2006), which challenges homophobic Australian surfing culture; and *Finn's Girl* (Dominique Cardona and Laurie Colbert 2006), which deals with reproductive rights. In Frameline 32, we had *No End* (*Senza Fine*, Roberto Cuzzillo 2008), which directly deals with the discrimination caused by Italian laws on artificial insemination; *Tru Loved* (Stewart Wade 2007) was co-presented by the Gay–Straight Alliance Network. Frameline 33 had its closing night film *Hannah Free* (Wendy Jo Carlton 2009) raising issues regarding same-sex partner's rights in relation to the elderly. In Frameline 34, we had *The String* (*Le Fil*, Medhi Ben Attia 2010), which deals with French colonialism in French Tunisia. *Weekend* (Andrew Haigh 2011) from Frameline 35 offered us a detailed look at the budding connection between two very different gay men in London over one weekend. While Russell desperately tries to fit in with his straight friends, Glen challenges him by criticising hypocritical gays wanting to assimilate into established institutions of straight society. Frameline 36 opened with documentary *Vito* (Jeffrey Schwarz 2011) detailing the life of film historian and AIDS activist Vito Russo. One of their centrepiece films, documentary *Call Me Kuchu* (Katherine Fairfax Wright and Malika Zouhail-Worrall 2012), is a harrowing portrait of David Kato, who was a Ugandan activist fighting the illegality of homosexuality in Uganda. *Bye Bye Blondie* (Virginie Despentes 2011) asked what happened when two girl punk lovers reconnect as adults. Showcase *Facing Mirrors* (*Aynehaye Rooberoo* 2011) had a trans male

Iranian confronting his father's conservative views on gender. *Love Free or Die* (Macky Alston 2012) depicts Gene Robinson, an openly gay ordained Anglican Bishop. The shelling of the town Sderot, Tel Aviv, becomes the backdrop to *Joe & Belle* (Veronica Kedar 2011). Political corruption forms the subject matter of film *Senorita* (Vincent Sandoval 2011).

Similarly, MQFF programmes many feature-length narrative films that openly engage with contemporary politics. In 2008, it featured *The Bubble, Finn's Girl,* and *Clapham Junction* (Adrian Shergold 2007), which dealt with homophobic violence. In 2009, *Affinity* (Tom Fywell 2008) deals with gender inequality; *All My life* (Maher Sabry 2008) presents gay Egyptian life, a subject rarely seen in queer cinema; *Burn the Bridges* (*Quemar Las Naves,* Francisco Franco 2007) contains the taboo of subtextual incest. The year 2010 featured *Hannah Free* and *Children of God* (Kareem J. Mortimer 2009), which deal with racial and religious bigotry; *Eyes Wide Open* (*Einaym Pkuhot,* Haim Tabakman 2009) has a gay romance blossom in an Orthodox Jewish community; *He's My Girl* (*La Fulle historie d'amour,* Jean-Jacques Zilbermann 2009) and *Release* (Darren Flaxstone and Christian Martin 2010) both mix religion and sexuality; *Initiation* (*Blutsfreundschaft,* Peter Kern 2009) has queer characters confronting neo-fascism; and *Pedro* (Nick Oceano 2008) details the *Real World: San Francisco*'s Pedro Zamora's HIV/AIDS activism. In 2011, gay romance develops between two neo-Nazi punks in *Brotherhood* (*Broderskab,* Nicolo Donato 2009); *House of Boys* (Jean-Claude Schlim 2009) has a protagonist fighting HIV. *A Marine Story* (Ned Farr 2010) openly deals with "don't ask, don't tell." In 2012, *Off Beat* (Jan Gassmann and Max Fey 2011) saw homosexuality represented within the traditionally homophobic music scene of hip hop; *Beauty* (*Skoonheid,* Oliver Hermanus 2011) had the backdrop of South African Apartheid politics; *Circumstance* (Maryam Keshavarz 2011) followed a lesbian couple living in Iran. These films are all examples of key narrative features fighting any assumption of politically apathetic queer cinema with their protagonists directly engaging with political ideologies.

One such example is the nationalistic tensions and diaspora evident in the film *Sasha,* which screened at Frameline and MQFF. The Petrovic family is originally from Montenegro, but now live in Germany. The film commences with them returning home from a holiday in their motherland. The political undertones to this film, however, are not mentioned in the MQFF programme notes. For patrons seeing this at MQFF, the narrative is framed only as Sasha having a "sexy, openly gay piano teacher, Gebhard" who devastates Sasha by telling him he is leaving for Vienna. The film is presented as a dramatic comedy about unrequited love. The only mention of Sasha's family and cultural background is his "strict parents," his "rebellious brother's" blossoming relationship with Sasha's best friend Jiao, and his deadbeat uncle.

True to form, the film still plays out like a conventional dramatic comedy. If we look at the first scene between Gebhard and Sasha, we know immediately from their body language and the cinematography that they are both attracted to each other. By looking at the camera angles used in the scene, we can see the predominant shots used during their conversation at the piano. This is conventional framing using the shot/reverse shot technique to establish each figure's position. When one is speaking while sitting at the piano, we can see the other's shoulder. The classic 180° rule is never broken. By having the film's style as invisible during this scene, we can focus not on the construction of the film but the two men's dialogue and their eyeing each other up and down. After Gebhard delivers the upsetting news of his pending departure, Sasha runs out into the pouring rain with a swelling soundtrack. As he stands there leaning against the stone wall, the camera zooms in on his face. *Sasha's* style is fairly conventional.

The benefit from having such a standard tone to the film is that the patrons who are seeing the film for the relationship drama will not be alienated. As such, audience members can enjoy Sasha lusting after his "sexy, openly gay piano teacher" while also getting a taste of European politics. Sasha's parents are originally from Montenegro, a former member of the Federal Republic of Yugoslavia. Sasha's father Vlado and mother Stanka often reminisce of their birthplace but understand there are fewer opportunities for them and their kids in their hometown following the Bosnian War. Vlado is still proudly Montenegrin and forces this identity upon his family. At the beginning of the film while Bosnian policemen are interrogating the family, the cop accuses Sasha for being "pretty weak for a Serbian." To which Vlado bellows "he's Montenegrin!" In the car ride home, Sasha's deadbeat uncle Pero demands that the music playing better not be Turkish! The family's anti-Turkish sentiment continues with Vlado giving the Turkish appearance of the bathroom as his reason for a renovation. Vlado and Stanka express their diasporic longing for Montenegro through their constant reminding other characters of their homeland. Coupled with an invisible film style, audience members receive both the gay relationship drama (which is what would entice the audience to attend the screening) and a political narrative of a diasporic family. Politics is interwoven naturally through a classical realist style.

MQFF has also featured a number of queer Asian films in its programme, including *Spider Lilies* (*Ci Qing*, Zero Chou 2007), *Drifting Flowers* (*Piao Lang Qing Chun*, Zero Chou 2007), *Soundless Wind Chime* (Kit Hung 2009), and *Candy Rain* (*Hua Chile Na Nuhai*, Chen Hung-i 2008). Australia is considered not just as south of "the west" but also as south of Asia (Yue and Hawkins 2000). Asian cinema, be it queer or otherwise, performs an integral role in Australia's cultural milieu for this very reason. Likewise, Frameline has a strong Asian presence in its programme. In Frameline 37 in 2013, it had a Queer Asian Cinema programme, putting a "spotlight on burgeoning queer Asian cinema and the aesthetics, humor, contradictions, and politics of being queer in contemporary Asian film" (Frameline 2013). Furthermore, it regularly co-presents films with the San Francisco–based Centre for Asian American Media (CAAM). Specifically, Queer Asian films play a significant role in the queer film festival programme as they provide a non-Westernised notion of a queer identity. Indeed, the discipline of queer theory in itself is very much at risk of being "solipsistic and dominated by an unquestioned assumption that the most interesting and most important sites for queer analysis are to be found within the borders of the US nation-state" (Martin et al. 2008, 3). Therefore, by supporting Asian queer cinema, festivals can challenge this uneven distribution of cultural capital.

Interestingly, however, the term "queer Asian cinema" is very much a festival invention, according to Helen Hok-Sze Leung (2003). For Leung, queer Asian cinema is made of a diverse array of films, such as unintentionally queer films *Swordsman 2* (Ching Siu-tung and Stanley Tong 1992) and *Wu Yen* (Johnnie To and Wau Kai-fai 2001). Other Queer Asian films come from the independent and underground scenes, such as *Let's Love Hong Kong* (Hoa Yuk 2002) and *Maps of Sex and Love* (Evan Chan 2001) and works by filmmakers in the Asian diaspora.

If we look at Zero Chou's *Spider Lilies* (2007) closely, we can see how the film is forced to fall under a pan-Asian umbrella. The Taiwanese identities of both the film and the participants involved "converge to form a pan-Chinese LGBTQ community" with other films from Hong Kong, Taiwan, and China (Berry and Pang 2010, 100). This is even more so when the film is positioned in a film festival programme outside of East Asia. *Spider Lilies* along with Zero Chou's other film *Drifting Flowers* (2008), another queer film festival highlight, both embody alternate film forms that queer Asian cinema has become known for. *Spider Lilies* sees vivacious webcam girl Jade meet brooding tattooist Takeko, where they reignite a dormant love affair that causes ripples in each of their lives. The film's non-linear narrative jumps between time periods that led the film to be reviewed as "attractive but frustratingly abstract" and "muddled and cartoonish."[15] The film has a glaringly jarring style that juxtaposes the cuteness of Jade's website and online persona with Takeko's traumatic family history that is told through flashbacks. Likewise, *Drifting Flowers*, which was showcased in MQFF's 2009 programme, delivers a multilayered narrative that is emblematic of the art-house aesthetic that many queer Asian films are known for when compared to other Western films in MQFF's standard line-up.

This very label of a queer Taiwanese cinema is the result of a hybrid of local experiences and global cultural discourse. Queer can be translated into various words such as *tongzhi, guaitai,* and *ku'er* (Lim 2008), so when films, such as Chou's *Drifting Flowers* and *Spider Lilies*, are presented in an Australian or American film festival under the queer Taiwanese label, we are seeing the product of a "glocalized hybrid manifestation" (243). Chou's films represent the possibilities of a fluid film form and the disruption of Eurocentric programming.

While films such as *eCupid* adhere to a dominant homonormative ideology, films in this category engage in direct political action. Judgement as to how effectively these films actively deal with political action depends one's individual interpretation of each film. These films could attack dominant ideologies with a "breaking down of the traditional way of depicting reality" (Narboni and Comolli 1971, 32), or in the vein of *eCupid*, they may "not effectively criticize the dominant ideology within which they are embedded because they unquestioningly adopts its language and imagery" (817). The key word here is *unquestioningly*. These are films that use these very filmic tools to actively engage with politics in some form or another. *Weekend* markets itself as a film about two guys having a one-night stand and is in the vein of the many "two-people-talking-and-fucking-in-an-apartment" movies (Kagan 2012, np); however, what we also get is an intersection of the personal and the political. Says Glen to Russell: "Look, straight people like us as long as we conform. Imagine your friends; if you suddenly started getting all really political about being a fag [...] We mustn't upset the straights! Shh, watch out, let's not upset them, let's hide in our little ghettos!" This is a moment where a politically engaged character actively challenges a homonormative existence.

Another quintessential trend in queer cinema is that of films deliberately breaking free from mainstream Hollywood's ideal of continuity editing.

These are films that do break down dominant modes of representation. Trepidatiously, I refer to these films as art house. This use of the term "art house" follows Rosalind Galt and Karl Schoonover's interrogation of art cinema in a global context (2010). They define art cinema by its impurity, as it "perverts the standard categories used to divide up institutions, locations, histories, or spectators" (7). Through Galt and Schoonover's definition of the term, art cinema has an ambivalent relationship to both location and industrial categories of film. This is beyond the simplistic binary of Hollywood and serious European art-house faire. A more complex understanding between *art* and *global* is required. Andrew's call for a redefinition of art cinema "in a contextual, value-neutral way so that it is truly inclusive, capable of covering all permutations, past and present" (Andrews 2010, 64) is valued here, and I want to avoid being seduced by rigid classifications, as he so warns. Andrews identifies art house as anti-commercial, multi-generic, and not restricted to particular nations or high art. As such, when reviewing these festival programmes, I am open to any of these films being considered art house. For instance, evident in the programming were stylistically hybrid films that fused together a variety of different film forms:

Frameline 31
  *Glue* (Alexis Dos Santos 2006)
  *25 Cent Preview* (Cyrus Amini 2007)
  *The Doctor's Daughter* (Janine Fung 2005)
Frameline 32
  *The Lost Coast* (Gabriel Fleming 2008)
  *Otto; or Up There with Dead People* (Bruce LaBruce 2007)
  *The Sensei* (D. Lee Inosanto 2007)
Frameline 34
  *Howl* (Rob Epstein and Jeffrey Friendman 2010)
  *I Killed My Mother* (*J'ai tue ma mere*, Xavier Dolan 2009)
  *Owls* (Cheryl Dunye 2010)
  *The Adults in the Room* (Andy Blubaugh 2009)

Frameline often programmes films that are either experimental in form or have non-linear narratives.

Frameline 31
  *Starrbooty* (Mark Ruiz 2007)
  *Blueprint* (Kirk Shannon-Butts 2007)
  *Vampire Diary* (Mark James and Pil O'Shea 2007)

Frameline 32
>    *Solos* (Kam Lume and Loo Zihan 2007)
>    *La Leon* (Santiago Otheguy)
>    *Japan Japan* (Lior Shamriz 2007)

Frameline 33
>    *Lollipop Generation* (G.B. Jones 2008)
>    *Maggots and Men* (Cary Cronenwett 2009)
>    *Soundless Wind Chime* (Kit Hung 2009)

Frameline 34
>    *Paulista* (Roberto Moreira 2009)

Frameline 35
>    *Codependent Lesbian Space Alien Seeks Same* (Madeleine Olnek 2011)
>    *Without* (Mark Jackson 2011)
>    *Harvest* (*Stadt Land Fluss*, Benjamin Cantu 2011)

These are all films that reject the need to conform to a traditional film style in order to attract a wider audience. While art cinema does not have a set of "necessary-and-sufficient conventions at the formal level," it is important to refrain from defining art-house cinema purely in terms of a partial highbrow form of entertainment (Andrews 2013, 2). By rejecting dominant film forms, they are also rejecting a neoliberal desire for mass profit. These directly political films create a form of social legitimacy for Frameline as a social enterprise. By programming films that directly engage in challenging dominant ideologies of sex and gender, the social enterprise becomes an empowering "catalyst for social transformation" (Alvord et al. 2004, 262). This makes the film festival (and in particular these film sessions) morally legitimate:

> Social enterprise is being accorded a status of—if not quite a panacea—then at least a significantly important emergence in the societal management of key social needs (Dart 2004, 413).

As such, regardless of whether an experimental silent film, such as *Maggots and Men*, can bring in the same box office result as *eCupid*, it should still be programmed. The role of the social enterprise is to address the social needs of its targeted demographic. As Loist (2012) notes in her take on queer programming strategies, these festivals must consider not only matters of quality but also how these films engage with the requirements and desires of the LGBTI community. As such, it is appropriate and imperative for such a socially transformative film to have its place in the programme. These films are the making of the queer film festival's moral and social legitimacy.

Likewise, programming political films creates a form of social legitimacy for MQFF as a social enterprise. Being a social enterprise, MQFF's social role is to be a "catalyst for social transformation" (Alvord et al. 2004, 262). The queer film festival provides a space for Melbourne's LGBT community to directly engage with contemporary political issues and consume alternate film forms that would otherwise not be commercially viable. As such, MQFF is meeting a social need for its community. A noteworthy amount of films programmed by MQFF fulfil this social and artistic role. Two significant categories in MQFF's yearly programming assist in this field.

Firstly, MQFF's "Queeries" programme aims at providing LGBT narratives for younger identified audience members. Commencing in 1999 under the previous label of "Not Chicken" with the documentary *Surviving Friendly Fire* (Todd Neilson 1997), the sessions endeavoured to give a "voice to some of the many young people entering our queer family" (Watts 1999, 1). By being exempt from being rated by the Office for Film and Literature Classification, all sessions generally maintain that attendees must be 18 years and over. These sessions allow for younger audience members to attend a queer film festival with films that are suitable for that age group.

This is one indication of the short film holding value beyond being a mere stepping stone for the director into feature production. Traditionally, the short film was a training and testing ground for directors. The short film allows filmmakers on the fringes to overcome barriers in the industry. The queer short film has an important role in the queer film festival. Due to increased access to the technology required for a short film (as opposed to the hefty means required for a feature-length production), a contemporary digital democracy is forming, where "the ever-increasing availability of cheaper and easier film technologies has made picking up a camera and capturing stories on film that much more accessible" (Daniel and Jackson 2003, 7). An increasingly diverse array of queer filmmakers are making short films, which are distinctly different to the dominance of slick gay male features being made. On her take on the contemporary queer film festival, Margaret Daniel (2006) notes this dominance is:

[A] concession to audience desire for traditional feature length narratives, particularly romantic comedies built on classic Hollywood formulas. But these new films were often first-time outings missing the implicit social critique and skilled writing of their predecessors … A focus on European and European American gay male—centred narratives reflected the gender realities of access to the means of production, and who was and is primarily perceived as driving the box office (609).

As such, the digital democracy allowed by queer short films directly challenges the inherent heteronormative inequalities embedded in the means for feature film production. In MQFF's programme for many years now, many of the short sessions are identity-based sessions. The gay male sessions include *Short & Burly*, *Cocktales*, and *Sex, Drives and Videotape*. Lesbian short sessions are *Short & Girly*, *Boobtube*, and *Femme Fatalities*. Transgender-themed short films are in a session whose name changes from year to year. Previous titles have been both *Trans Phats* and *Transformations*. Mixed sessions have included *Oz Shorts*, *Celluloid Casserole*, *Oz Docs*, *Queeries*, and the recent addition of *Mix Tape*, which functions like a "best of the festival" session. This is common for most queer film festivals, including Frameline and HKLGFF. Granted some shorts programmes such as the standard "boy shorts" and "girls shorts" sessions aren't as imbued with the 'implicit social critique and skilled writing' as most queer short films being programmed nowadays; my own personal experience of programming for the MQFF, however, has proven these to be a minority.

## Denaturalising Domesticity

The films *Spork* (J.B. Ghuman Jr. 2010), *Three* (Tom Tykwer 2010), and *Drool* (Nancy Kissam 2009) offer narratives that challenge and deconstruct the familial domestic setting. Spork is a female-identified 13 year old who was born intersex. To overcome her social exclusion at middle school, she challenges the token group of mean girls (Betsy Byotch and her fellow Byotches) at the school talent quest. Tootsie Roll, Spork's neighbour in the trailer park, agrees to coach Spork and teach her a dance routine. The film reads like a queered *Napoleon Dynamite*. Spork and her guardian, older brother Spit, live in a small trailer situated in what seems like an empty landscape. Next door is Tootsie Roll and her mother (who briefly appears for one scene only). Spork's mum's grave lies in their backyard, with Spork often braving her allergic reaction to the weeds that grow nearby to visit it.

**Fig. 4.3** Spork's bedroom is a manifestation of her insecurity

The narrative is a coming of age tale, with Spork and her brother (and his friend and their girlfriends) all managing to make a somewhat harmonious living space in the one trailer. The one bedroom in the trailer (Fig. 4.3) functions as Spork's escape from the outside world with no explanation given to where Spit (or Tootsie Roll's mother) sleep. The living quarters function as a surreal manifestation of Spork's hideout from the real world. The room, full of toys, child-like posters, her deceased dog (now stuffed), and the basketball with Betsy Byotch's blood smeared on it, functions as an alternate universe. Being a coming of age tale, the challenge for Spork is to embrace her gender difference and move on from this child-like hideout. As such, the home for Spork is the manifestation of her social dysfunction. By gaining confidence and friends, she is less reliant on this private world.

Tom Tykwer's *Three* sees the growth of a bisexual love triangle into a poly-amorous relationship. Hanna and Simon appear to be living the perfect life. Living together in Berlin, they are both successful in their chosen fields (he an architect, she a television presenter) and are fast approaching their 20th anniversary. For both, however, this contentment leads to restlessness, and they ultimately commence an affair (unknowingly) with the same man Adam, a work colleague of Hanna and a man who Simon regularly swims with. Hanna and Simon go through a process of opening up their pre-existing understanding of romance and monogamy and a rediscovery of their sexual selves. While Simon is undergoing surgery for testicular cancer and dealing with the death of his mother, Hannah is spending time with Adam, drinking, attending a soccer match, and slowly overcoming her initial hesitation in starting an affair. The conclusion of the narrative, with the fruition of the titular triptych, displays a queer possibility for love and romance free from boundaries. The three love connections that take place, Adam and Simon, Simon and Hanna, Hanna and Adam, are all treated with equal amounts of passion and sensuality. Each physical connection is complemented by an emotional and intellectual connection. Adam challenges Hanna over genetic research, Hanna helps Simon through chemotherapy and the passing of his mother, and Adam eases Simon into a new sexual selfhood. This triptych relationship is a deconstruction of the heteronormative ideal and at the conclusion this is a celebration. Many films programmed by Frameline are indicative of this defiant queer trend of rejecting the normalising ideal of a stable home in the suburbs and instead opt for radical constructions of alternate families.

Frameline 31
  *The Witness* (*Les Temoins*, Andre Techine 2007)
  *The Bubble* (Eytan Fox 2006)
  *Itty Bitty Titty Committy* (Jamie Babbti 2007)
  *Another Woman* (*Une autre femme*, Jerome Fouton 2002)
  *Nina's Heavenly Delight* (Pratibha Parmar 2006)
  *You Belong to Me* (Sam Zalutsky 2006)
  *Lez Be Friends* (Glenn Gaylord 2007)
  *Finn's Girl* (Dominique Cardona and Laurie Colbert 2006)
  *El Calentito* (Chus Gutierrez 2005).
Frameline 32
  *Saturn in Opposition* (Ferzan Ozpetek 2007)
  *Dolls* (*Pusinsky*, Karin Babinska 2007)
  *Tru Loved* (Stewart Wade 2007)
  *Cthulhu* (Daniel Gildark 2007)
Frameline 33
  *Night Fliers* (Sara St. Martin Lynne 2009)
  *I Can't Think Straight* (Shamim Sarif 2007)
  *"Family"* (Faith Trimel 2008)
  *The Baby Formula* (Alison Reid 2008)
  *Born in in '68* (*Nes en 68*, Olivier Duscastel and Jacques Martineau 2009)
  *Lion's Den* (*Leonera*, Pablo Trapero 2009)
Frameline 34
  *Hideaway* (*Le Refuge*, Francois Ozon 2009)

*I Killed My Mother* (*J'ai tue ma mere* 2009)
Frameline 36
    *Cloudburst* (Thom Fitzgerald 2011)
    *Kiss Me* (*Kiss Mig*, Alexandra-Therese Keining 2011)
    *My Best Day* (Erin Greenwell 2012)
    *Frauensee* (Zoltan Paul 2012)

All these films challenge the idea of the ideal neoliberal citizen and this conservative perspective of sexuality only being kept for the bedroom. Non-heterosexual identities traditionally existed independently from familial settings (Cook 2010). Gay men and lesbians existed in alienation from the nuclear family. They are families of choice that are an "overt politicization of kinship" (Weston 1991, 106) that enable queers to actively form kin-like networks of relationships, friendships, and commitments "beyond blood" (Weeks 2001, 9). There is a plurality to this concept of the queer family. Alternative families are constructed that do not try to emulate any heteronormative ideals of two gender-appropriate individuals and a baby. They are made on their own terms.

Queer films challenge the homonormative privileging of domesticity and the nuclear family with narratives that deconstruct the familial domestic setting. We have recently seen a rising trend in gay- and lesbian-themed films of families that are recreating the heteronormative ideal, albeit with same-sex parents. This is a recreation of a familial setting, which originally excluded non-heterosexual identities. Queer existence was mutually exclusive with domesticity. While same-sex coupling can be seeing as political kinship, it is also a moving of gay and lesbian domesticity from a stigmaphile position to a stigmaphobe position that is privileged over other forms of kinships of choice in queer media, notably in queer cinema.

Another highlight on the queer film festival circuit that centred on families of choice was *Drool* (Nancy Kissam 2009). The film sees a kin-like network of relationships, friendships, and commitments formed that are beyond blood (Weeks 2001). The film sees Anora Fleece trapped in a loveless marriage, where her days are filled with household chores and raising two selfish, bratty kids. Her world changes when, after being caught kissing the neighbourhood cosmetics saleswoman Imogene, she shoots and murders her violent husband. *Drool* is a road movie where Anora and Imogene take the kids to see her boss Kathy K. of "Kathy K. Cosmetics." The family setting of Anora, Imogene, the kids, Kathy K., and the two pool boys exists in harmony, directly contrasting the tense, violent depiction of

**Fig. 4.4** The dinner scenes at the beginning and conclusion of the film demonstrate the difference in colour palette

Anora's life with her late husband. This freedom is evident in how the two spaces are presented formally. Kathy K.'s house is a paradise, full of rich green flora and banquets of food, while the Fleece family home is dull and claustrophobic, with tight camera shots and a colour palette of beige. Even when outside, Anora is tightly framed by her washing. This begins to break up only when Imogene enters the family home in shockingly bright purple. This narrative and film form places this kin-like network in a desirable light. Even though the assortment of misfits in Kathy K.'s house is beyond blood and doesn't resemble a patriarchal ideal, it is positioned as loving and safe, a place where Anora is safe to be herself (Fig. 4.4).

Extending from the formalist interrogation of homonormative cinema, the film's aesthetic distinctly draws attention to itself. The domestic setting of both Imogene and Kathy K. present bright, bold colours of green and purple to differentiate Imogene's world from Anora's recently murdered husband (Fig. 4.5). This change provides significant weight to the film's meaning. As such, this subtly alters the formal properties evident at the commencement of the film. This highlights the artificiality of cinema while also the constructionist nature of the nuclear family. As Bazin (1967) argues, the guiding fancy of realism (and film) is the "recreation of the world in its own image, an image unburdened by the freedom of interpretation of the artist or the irreversibility of time" (165–166). This is a denaturalisation of dominant familial representations. The introduction of Imogene's purple palette is overwhelming and is very much in the tradition of style drawing attention to itself. This is a blatant Brechtian "distanciation" technique forcing the audience member into a subjective spectatorship position, a position that allows them to think critically on the social construction of family and the domestic setting.

**Fig. 4.5** Imogene and Kathy K.'s domestic space is open and colourful compared to Anora's claustrophobic and dull home

### Queer Diversity

Programming a diverse array of films is important for any film festival. In Frameline 35's programme, two key films stood out as defiant, *Gun Hill Road* (Rashaad Ernesto Green 2011) and *Mangus* (Ash Christian 2011). *Gun Hill Road* was an innovative choice for opening night. Quite often, queer film festivals will open with a conventional gay feature, as that is the safest option for obtaining a sell-out session. I am reminded of Sarah Deragon's comment of opening night being a sign of Frameline's innovation:

> I feel opening night was incredibly innovative. Introducing a trans story to the rest of the community who don't necessarily not care but don't know or have not seen it before. I have never seen homemade silicone injections on screen before! (Interview with Deragon 2011).

Various audience members interviewed were also delighted to see a transgender film selected for the opening night position:

I saw *Gun Hill Road*, the opening night film. I thought that was fantastic. I thought it was really well done. It was a bit heavy for an opening night film though (Interview with "Maria" 2011).

I saw the opening night film *Gun Hill Road*. It was really good. I was really glad to see a trans film opening the festival. I also went to the party for that night. I thought the party was really fun. That one was more of a trans party than what the actual trans party was for this year.[16] More people showed up to that one for this year because it was opening night (Interview with "Sam" 2011).

This is a clear display of Frameline functioning as a successful social enterprise in that social value and providing the Bay Area community with quality queer cinema are deemed just as valuable as profit and ticket sales. As Sam states in his interview, the opening night after party felt like it was in fact the Transtastic shorts after-party. Perhaps this is a comment on the fluidity and queerness of the space as opposed to it being dominated by a rigid gay and lesbian presence.

The film *Mangus* embodies a queer aesthetic that makes it difficult to neatly fit into the rigid categories of "LGBTI." Mangus Sedgwick's one goal in life is to perform as Jesus in his high school production of *Jesus Christ Superstar*, a goal that is put on hold when he ends up in a wheelchair after an unexpected accident. Mangus is straight and has a lesbian sister named Jessica Simpson (played by the brilliant Heather Matarazzo); however, the character Jessica Simpson is not just the reason why the film is programmed in a queer film festival. The film has a very queer aesthetic and a camp, dark humour. The film revels in its excess and opacity. For Williford (2009), the queer aesthetic is ambiguous, in that it "resists identification, choosing to play at the borders of the visible, attempting to assert the possibility of the unidentified or misidentified subject and to eroticize the threat that an action or condition may displace a subject from an identity/category" (12).

The film stars cult comedy icons Jennifer Coolridge and Matarazzo and cameos from queer icons Leslie Jordan as the drama teacher and John Waters as a vision of Jesus visiting him in a time of need. The film is queer (and not gay or lesbian) in that there is a fluidity of identity and a celebration of a rejection of societal norms. The film is a coming-of-age narrative in that an outsider initially shunned by society gains self-acceptance and confidence that allows him to achieve his goal. This is the queer experience that allows this story's moral compass to be adaptable to a variety of queer identities.

The viewing experience transcends LGBTI identity boundaries. Furthermore, with Frameline giving this film a Showcase time slot on a Saturday evening for the 2011 festival, the post-identity aesthetic of the film is thus given a privileged position in Frameline.

In the contemporary queer film festival, we can see a tension between films that reinforce pre-existing hegemonic identity constructions and those narratives that present hierarchical manifestations. We can, however, make this justification problematic by asking whether or not these films actually result in sustainable change to this normalising trend in contemporary gay and lesbian politics. Whether or not this representation actually challenges the status quo is open to interpretation. The film *Were the World Mine* (Tom Gustafson 2008) presents the stark difference between fluid identities of queer and the rigidity of gay and lesbian identities. An easy misreading of *Were the World Mine* is seeing Timmy (Tanner Cohen) being, as they say, the only gay in the village. Although at his privileged all boys' school he is bullied, he is certainly not alone in his queerness. The narrative sees the school's play of *A Midsummer's Night Dream* come to life in the small American town. Timmy plays the lead role of Puck and casts his own spell on everyone around him, including his crush Jonathan, resulting in everyone becoming magically gay or lesbian (conveniently converted for hilarity's sake). The narrative presented prior to Timmy's spell however presents plenty of queer elements. Timmy's queerness does not exist in isolation prior to him casting his spell. A queer subtextual reading could certainly be read into the scene between Nora Fay and Timmy's mother Donna during her make-up tutorial. Nora gently holds Donna's hand as she instructs her how a strong woman should present herself. During the rehearsals, Timmy's classmates (the ones who bully Timmy) audition for the school play desperately trying to be more masculine yet end up cast in various roles ("Who's Thrisby? Is that a chick's role?"). Outside of school, Timmy associates with friend Frankie, who defines herself as "flexi-sexual" ("I'm straight but shit happens"), and Max, a straight male who spends his time in a dress in the first scene when at Timmy's house. The soundtrack features effeminate gay male singers Patrick Wolf, Mika, and the Guts (with Tanner Cohen as lead vocals). When Timmy is cast as Puck, Donna cuts up her wedding dress for Puck's wings. This is not only a rite of passage for Donna as she accepts her son "playing a fairy" but also a traditionally heterosexual symbol being reworked for her son's queer performance (Fig. 4.6).

**Fig. 4.6** Timmy's world in *Were the World Mine* is incredibly queer even before the spell takes place

Ultimately, however, once the spell takes place, Timmy's world becomes rigidly gay and lesbian. Instead of Frankie casually stating she's flexi-sexual, she proclaims "I'm not a lesbian" to Jonathan's spellbound ex-girlfriend. Maxi performs his masculinity even more so when he is gay and under the spell than at the beginning of the film. In a discussion between Donna and Timmy:

> Donna: Why are you gay? Did I do something wrong?
> Timmy: You didn't make me queer.

This exchange sums up Timmy's world when there is free will and no spell. It's queer and fluid as opposed to the rigidity of the spell. Mrs Tebbit orders Timmy and Jonathan to "awaken and empower what's within." In Timmy's dream sequences with the camp musical numbers, both Timmy and Jonathan occupy both masculine and feminine positions. These male bodies directly challenge the hegemonic masculinity in films such as *Shelter* or *eCupid*. The film also proved extremely popular as it sold out the opening night slot of MQFF 2009. A significant number of films in Frameline's programming challenge the dominant hegemony of a homonormative culture.

Frameline 31

*Itty Bitty Titty Committee*

*Glue* (Alexis Dos Santos 2006)

*The Two Sides of the Bed* (*Los dos lados de la cama*, Emilio Martinez Lazaro 2005)

*Blueprint* (Kirk Shannon-Butts 2007)

*The DL Chronicles* (Deondray Gossett and Quincy Le Near 2007)

*El Calentito* (Chus Gutierrez 2005)

*Shelter Me* (*Riparo*, Marco Simon Puccioni 2006)

*Twilight Dancers* (Mel Chionglo 2006)

*Rick and Steve: The Happiest Gay Couple in the World* (Q. Allan Brocka 2007)

*Vivere* (Angelina Maccarone 2007)

Frameline 32

*Before I forget* (*Avant que j'oublie*, Jacques Nolot 2007)

*Solos* (Kam Lume and Loo Zihan 2007)

*Another Gay Sequel: Gays Gone Wild* (Todd Stephens 2008)

*The Gay Bed and Breakfast of Terror* (Jaymes Thompson 2007)

*Manuela y Manuel* (Raul Marchand 2007)

*Dolls* (*Pusinsky*, Karin Babinska 2007)

*Ready? OK!* (James Vasquez 2008)

*Butch Jamie* (Michelle Ehlen 2007)

*XXY* (Lucia Puenzo 2007)

Frameline 33

*"Family"* (Faith Trimel 2008)

*Mississippi Damned* (Tina Mabry 2009)

*Drool* (Nancy Kissam 2009)

*I Can't Think Straight* (Shamim Sarif 2007)

*Soundless Wind Chime* (Kit Hung 2009)

*Maggots and Men*

Frameline 34

*The Sea Purple* (Donatella Maiorca 2009)

*Plan B* (Marco Berger 2009)

*The Consul of Sodom* (*El Consul de Sodoma*, Sigfrid Monleon 2009)

*Owls* (Cheryl Dunye 2010)

*Open* (Jake Yuzna 2009)

*Elvis and Madonna* (Marcelo Laffitte 2010)

Frameline 35

*Absente* (*Ausente*, Marco Berger 2011)

*Codependent Lesbian Space Alien Seeks Same* (Madeleine Olnek 2011)
*Gun Hill Road* (Rashaad Ernesto Green 2011)
*Harvest* (*Stadt Land Fluss*, Benjamin Cantu 2011)
*Madame X* (Lucky Kuswandi 2011)
*Mangus* Ash (Christian 2011)
*Spork* (J.B. Ghuman Jr. 2010)
Frameline 36
   *Cloudburst*
   *Facing Mirrors*
   *My Brother the Devil* (Sally El Hosaini 2012)
   *Fourplay* (Kyle Henry 2012)
   *Morgan* (Michael Akers 2011)
   *Offbeat* (Jan Gassmann 2011)

These films challenge pre-existing dominant norms evident in both mainstream gay and lesbian culture *and* heterosexual culture. They are providing voices for identities traditionally marginalised in the gay mainstream. In Michael Warner's *The Trouble with Normal* (1999), when he lists all of the identities marginalised by the gay marriage movement, we see a hierarchy of sexual shame within the contemporary queer community. This is a result of the transition from the confrontational to the normalising politics that Duggan (2003) identifies in her discussion of homonormativity. Ultimately, in the contemporary pursuit of gay marriage rights, those that do not fit the ideal image of the monogamous gay couple are deemed less worthy of equality. These characters and narratives are actively challenging pre-existing hegemonic constructions of identity and are confrontational to normalising trends in gay culture.

This UN-style queer diversity can be inherently problematic, however. While it is wonderful to have such a diverse array of film styles and identities presented in the programme, does it actually challenge the status quo? If we compare the films screened in the much larger Castro Theatre to the Mission Theatre, a distinct trend is apparent. For the Frameline 35 film programme, I tallied the feature narrative films at each of the three main Frameline theatres according to the "central" identity of the film according to the programme (Figs. 4.7, 4.8, and 4.9):

Gay male features have an overwhelming representation at the Castro with the Roxie and the Victoria theatres being more equally distributed.

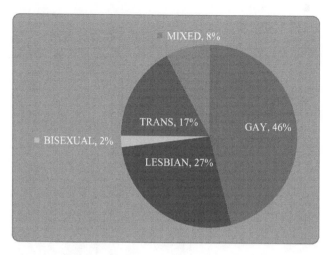

**Fig. 4.7** The Castro Theatre's programming

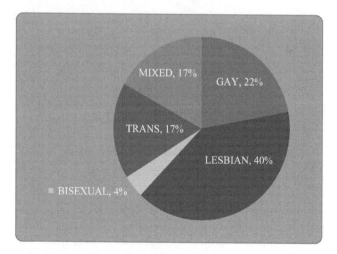

**Fig. 4.8** The Roxie Theatre Programing

This distribution was acknowledged in many interviews. Although the Castro's homonormativity and conservative nature will be discussed in the following chapter, I would like to raise here the audience's perception of this difference between neighbourhoods:

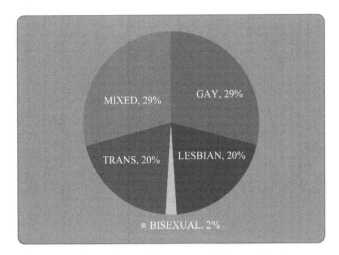

**Fig. 4.9** The Victoria Theatre Programming

It's alienating ... You've got the pink dollar up the hill and us down here, which I actually like having that separation coz I like knowing where my hood is and I don't wanna go and hang out in that area (Interview with "Polly" 2011).

It's white, it's dudes with double incomes, it's not my gay. Those people are not my gay and the girls who hang out with the gay boys there are not my gay either. I don't like going there. I don't think I would ever go to any of the bars really at all ... They're 'straight gay,' they happen to suck cock or eat pussy but they're not queer, they're not dirty. I like people who are gritty with a little more flavour, who are a little more into politics (Interview with "Alex" 2011).

There has been a recent cultural shift with Frameline in its recent adoption of the LGBTQ label. The theoretical difference between this label and LGBT is significant. The label LGBT creates legitimated identities, which recalls the ethnic model approach to sexuality whose main agenda was assimilation and winning civil rights (Seidman 1993). The queer identity is a movement away from identity politics being intrinsically natural and a post-structuralist critique on the limitations that these rigid categories create (Jagose 1996). The LGBT label reinforces the homo/hetero and male/female binary. The addition of the Q however is an acknowledgement of the limitations of simply having the LGBT label. Volunteer coordinator Feliciano highlights the growing cultural shift of Frameline from the lesbian and gay dichotomy to a queerer atmosphere:

> On a larger scale, within the festival and within the community, is the shift from LGBT to queer ... In a lot of ways I would love this festival and other festivals to be queerer focused or moving towards a queerer focus. Frameline is the LGBT film festival. While that systematic and institutional change hasn't been made, I do think it is happening within the films that are being submitted (Interview with Feliciano 2011).

For a large cultural institution that plays a significant role in the San Francisco and Bay Area LGBT community, this approach to identity can become very problematic as Lares continued to discuss in her interview:

> I identify as queer. For me that means transcending boundaries and binaries ... I think LGBT really enforces those binaries or there is a subtle implication that those binaries exist and should be abided by. You have lesbian for women, gay for men and bi for people who like both and trans for people are one thing then become the other. It doesn't leave a lot of room for grey. And I think for me queer is all about grey. It's all about like "I'm going to be butch one day, femme the next day, strap it on tomorrow and the next day I'm gonna take it." You know what I mean? It's about exploring all the different ways gender can influence our identities and experiences. Queer is a tricky term as it doesn't mean the same for everybody. For me it's a really radical term and it's a really radical identity. I don't think that that is how everybody experiences it as I think queer is synonymous for LGBT for some people (Interview with Feliciano 2011).

This ability for Frameline to embrace a queer ideology in a formal sense can be seen as a movement away from sexual shame. Warner states that leading gay organisations are "becoming more and more enthralled by respectability. Instead of broadening its campaign against sexual stigma beyond sexual orientation, (...) it has increasingly narrowed its scope to those issues of sexual orientation that have least to do with sex" (1999, 25). According to Warner's argument on sexual shame, the dignified homosexual not only feels shame for his sexual difference but shame for "every queer who flaunts his sex and his faggotry, making the dignified homosexual's stigma all the more justifiable in the eyes of the straights" (32). By adding the Q, however,

Frameline is beginning to accept queer's radical possibilities a spot at the table in an institutional sense.

MQFF, however, differs greatly from Frameline. As outlined in Chap. 2, the festival changed its name from The Melbourne Gay and Lesbian Film and Video Festival to The Melbourne Queer Film and Video Festival thus making it the first of its kind to make the change. This innovative approach to embracing queer at such an early stage is seen as an inclusive act to make the festival accessible to more members of the queer community. This begs the question, however. Does using the term "queer" as an umbrella term result in the term "queer" losing its radical potential? Much like my case study of Frameline, just how socially empowering is coalition politics?

The term "queer" has undergone radical transformation over the past 20 plus years since it burst dramatically onto the academic scene. As established in the beginning of this chapter, the early writings of Michel Foucault (1977), Gayle Rubin (1975), Leo Bersani (1995), Eva Kosovsky Sedgwick (1985, 1990), and Judith Butler (1990) all wrote about sexuality in terms of power and resistance. Pleasures in alternative sexuality and the formation of a radical culture all posed confrontations to normative frameworks of gender and sexual orientation, particularly in the rigidity of "gay and lesbian." Socially, queer was born out of a confrontational politics, akin to ACT UP and Queer Nation, which proposed solidarity of persons beyond identity.

There is indeed a fissure between the social and academic uses of queer. Warner states that "technical clarity and journalistic accessibility are not the same" (2012, np) and states how unfair it is for Butler and Sedgwick to be singled out for their difficult academic prose. However, inaccessibility has resulted in these works not being circulated beyond academic and activist circles. This has resulted in an even more ambivalent status for queer, thus making it harder to define. Neoliberalism has also played a hand at commodifying the word with television shows such as *Queer Eye for the Straight Guy* and *Queer as Folk* thus emptying "its radical political history of such movements as Queer Nation" (Tilsen and Nylun 2010, 69). Some argue that by using queer as an umbrella term for LGBT, we are undermining and narrowing the original intent for queer:

> Being queer is not a matter of being gay, then, but rather of being committed to challenging that which is perceived as normal. There is no fool-proof membership criterion for queerness other than the willingness to seek out sites of resistance to normalcy in any possible location (Rudy 2000, 197).

While queer is an excellent exploratory device that critiques normative identity practices by distancing it entirely from identity politics, this undermines the lived experiences of those that do not live their everyday lives as heterosexual. As such, queer can be used as an umbrella term to unite previously fractioned members of the LGBTI community and still retain its political force. The theme for MQFF 2011 festival after all *was* activism. Granted queer is "less an identity than a *critique* of identity" (Jagose 1996, 131), queer subjects "trouble and subvert such categories to create and defend spaces for non-normative desires and practices" (King 2008, 422). Therefore, the *queer* film festival unites various non-normative subjects to experience films and narratives of subjects that resist normative representations existing in mainstream media. By embracing a diversity of queer stories, MQFF is refusing to go down the normative path highlighted by Warner (1999), where he asks: "What could be a better way of legitimating oneself than to insist on being seen as normal? ... The problem always is that embracing this standard merely throws shame on those who stand farther down the level of respectability" (60). A queer label for a film festival does allow for a plethora of fluid identities that are contingent and multiple, identities that would be limited under the rubric of LGBT or even LGBTQ. This is the ultimate definition of the queer film festival.

This use of queer as an umbrella term for this plethora of fluid identities does not necessarily make the organisation immune from still privileging the white gay male figure. This line of inquiry that problematises queer diversity is an intersectional analysis. While there is evidence of diverse identities programmed in the festival, key programming slots (Friday and Saturday evenings) are still given to accessible commercial films with protagonists that are products of the homonormative movement in LGBTI politics. As such, does the very presence of alternative narratives in the programme that embrace post-identity politics actually challenge such hegemony? For Halberstam (2005), shame is an important political tactic to "make privilege (whiteness, masculinity, wealth) visible" (220). Does queer lose its radical potency if these "current social arrangements of power preserve and protect certain forms of legitimacy for white, phallic subjects?" (226). By positioning certain films at key programming times (gay male films on a Friday or Saturday night and trans films on a Sunday afternoon), is the queer film festival recreating a hierarchy of sexual shame as discussed by writers such as Warner (1999), where public discourse portrays certain sexual behaviour as intolerable? This notion of sexual shame produces a hierarchy of respectability.

This theoretical and social ambiguity extends further beyond the mere labelling of the festival. Queer has now been co-opted to produce value in the creative industry. This is a significant shift from queer being a theoretical tool to critically examine the "normalizing mechanisms of state power to name its sexual subjects" (Eng et al. 2005, 1). The City of Melbourne's support of MQFF is a product of contemporary queer liberalism, where "our current historical moment is marked by a particular coming together of economic and political spheres that form the basis for liberal inclusion" (10). In an age where we see a mainstreaming of gay and lesbian politics and identities, this relationship between a self-identified queer organisation and the local government raises many lines of inquiry into whether queer studies remain yet unfulfilled. This becomes even more so where queer is used as an LGBT umbrella term and runs the risk of adhering to possessive individualism that privileges white, gay, and biologically male identities (Halberstam 2005). This professional, official status afforded to MQFF becomes a significant factor in whether the organisation can fulfil its political and social mission.

## A Brief Comment on Documentary Cinema and Short Films

Thus far, the socially empowering films that have been mentioned have mostly been feature-length narratives. It is necessary to outline that in their very form, documentaries and short films are socially empowering due to not being a profitable format. With the exception of the "fun in boys shorts" programme and a handful of centrepiece documentaries,[17] these are cinematic formats that don't lend themselves to large box office returns, as "theatrical distribution still remains the holy grail for many documentary filmmakers" (Keenlyside 2001, np) and indeed documentaries have always had a complicated relationship with the marketplace. While documentaries are now venturing beyond "the confines of the elite urban audiences" (Arthur 2005, 18), funding and lack of visibility have always been challenges for short and documentary film. Paul Arthur accounts for the increasing appeal and commercial viability for the documentary and discusses the ethical dilemma with commercial documentarians. Are they simply "telling" the truth or "parading" it? Regardless, the documentary remains a powerful tool for political and social advocacy (Arthur 2005; Silbey 2006). Much like the queer film festival itself, the determination of success is much more complex than financial returns. It is for this reason that short films and documentaries are labelled as socially empowering films in the programme. In a general sense, these are non-homonormative genres.

## HKLGFF AND THE GLOBAL GAY DIVIDE

In my analysis of HKLGFF as a social enterprise, it became apparent that the festival did not meet some criteria to the same extent as Frameline or MQFF. In Chap. 3, the three festivals were analysed according to six themes of the social enterprise. Notably, there was little evidence to claim that HKLGFF addresses existing gaps within the film distribution market. Arguably, this would also impact upon the social empowerment created by the festival. Two significant factors were identified for HKLGFF as contemporary challenges for the festival. First, the programming is male dominated. While most LGBT-themed film festivals do programme more gay male content than other identity categories, HKLGFF tends to programme *notably* more gay male content. Second, the festival programmes significantly more Western content than local films. This Westernisation of the festival is compounded by the minimal use of Chinese subtitles, although this was identified as being economically difficult and unavoidable for the festival in Chap. 3. These two issues are evident of the influence a global gay mentality has on the programming. This greatly influences the homonormativity of the festival's content.

When considering the HKLGFF's programme, it is my contention that an international gay male identity dominates the programme. Western media's role in globalisation has played a significant role in the permeation of this culture (Boellstorff 2001). Furthermore, this "global gay identity is looking more and more like the Western gay identity" (Sutton 2007, 53). Globalisation pushes this stereotypical Western discourse of the gay male internationally (Das and Harry 1980). In his study of constructivist accounts of homosexuality, Altman (2001) contends that this is an analysis in "how people incorporate it into their sense of self" (86).

While much has been written on this topic, this analysis will refrain from relying on Euro-American scholars. It is important to acknowledge the danger of Western bias with this line of inquiry as "the theoretical lenses (Western) scholars used to view erotic cultures can predispose them to seeing either similarity or difference" (Jackson 1998, 955), in that erotic cultures are analysed in terms of Western modes of thought. It is this line of thought that Helen Hok-Sze Leung follows when calling for us to irreverently *inhabit* rather than *avoid* the gap between "queer" and "theory" when considering trying to find what is local about the global queer, specifically in Hong Kong (Leung 2007). When analysing a local culture, it is important to not be confined by the predominantly American boundaries of "theory" as this reinforces the dominance of Western discourse at an international level.

Evidence of a homonormative culture has developed in Hong Kong. In his analysis of Hong Kong elderly gay men's use of spaces, Travis Kong (2012) argues that the rise of homonormativity in Hong Kong's gay scene is tied to "urban renewal and redevelopment," resulting in an "apparently successful 'territorialization' of tongzhi spaces and the pink economy (nurturing) the new tongzhi image of the 'good consumer citizen'" (908). Following the decriminalisation of homosexuality in 1991, spaces designed for tongzhi consumption—bars, clubs, saunas, and so on—have flourished. Kong argues that this new tongzhi image is directly tied to consumption and is derived of the "global queer identity" as outlined by Altman (1997). Kong sees a division in the contemporary Hong Kong gay community, between those that fit this ideal and those that don't. These divisions, such as class, body image, and age, manifest due to the influence of contemporary homonormative politics. This division in the Hong Kong LGBT community is obviously not unique to Hong Kong but rather directly tied to conservative trends in LGBTI communities worldwide. As such, when analysing HKLGFF's programme, it is in terms of the influence of a homonormative, global gay identity.

HKLGFF has been accused of a consistent dominance of male content in the festival. Numerous critics of the festival have addressed this (Yau 2006; Tang 2011). The issue of potential content quotas arose in my interview with HKLGFF director Joe Lam:

> We try to program lesbian films. The market is so small though and there aren't very many good lesbian films every year. Last year there were more. We put in fourteen lesbian and transgender films but the box office was bad. So this year we had to program less lesbian films. It depends on how good the film is. Of course the gay films are going to be popular than lesbian films. We try to program 30–35 films every year and we tried to program around seven lesbian films and maybe two transgender films (Interview with Joe Lam 2014).

For HKLGFF 2014, there were 27 gay-themed films programmed. This includes three separate gay short film sessions, one of which problematically included the short documentary *Lives under the Red Light* (Vanna Hem 2013), which looked at the lives of three ladyboys working in the sex industry in Phnom Penh. Compared to the 27 gay-themed films, most of which had multiple sessions, HKLGFF programmed only 6 lesbian-themed films.[18] Also programmed where two trans-themed films, *Something Must Break* (Ester Martin Bergsmark 2014) and *52 Tuesdays* (Sophie Hyde 2013), the latter of which also contains the character Billie exploring her sexuality. Two bisexual-themed films, *Appropriate Behavior* (Desiree Akhavan 2014) and *Regarding Susan Sontag* (Nancy D Kates 2014), were also programmed.

This trend is inconsistent, however, if we compare the 2014 festival to previous years. In its 2012 festival, HKLGFF featured 16 gay-themed films, including 2 short sessions, 12 lesbian-themed films, 2 transgender films, being *Sexing the Transman* (Buck Angel 2011) and *Laurence Anyways* (Xavier Dolan 2012), and 1 bisexual-themed film—*Joshua Tree 1951: A Portrait of James Dean* (Matthew Mishory 2012).[19] Its 2011 festival, however, recalls this male dominance. The festival featured 23 gay-themed sessions (2 of which were short sessions), 6 lesbian-themed sessions, 2 - transgender-themed sessions, being *Gun Hill Road* and *In a Bottle* (Raja Azmi Raja Sulaiman 2011), and the drag-themed film *Be a Woman* (Fan Popo 2011).

Likewise, there is inconsistency with the programming of sinitic content. When considering the 2014 programme, the only Chinese films appeared in the shorts sessions. Programmed by Ginger Yang and Denise Tang, the Girls Shorts: Underground Love session consisted of five films, three of which were in Mandarin with English and Chinese subtitles—the films being *Once a Time with You* (Helen Zhu 2014), *Under Ground* (Sha Huang 2014), and *Penguins at North Pole* (Kassey C. M. Huang 2014). The third boys shorts programme, entitled Red, also featured the film *For Love, We Can* (Lam Chi Lung 2014). In 2013, the festival featured Taiwanese documentaries from Susan Chen—*Lesbian Factory* (2010) and *Rainbow Popcorn* (2013). In 2012, the festival featured *Mama Rainbow, I'm Here* (Tracy Choi 2012)—a documentary looking at two women coming out in Macau, which screened alongside the Hong Kong short *Lopsided* (Ka Ho Chow and Tsz Ngo Poppy Yeung 2012)—and the Girls Short session Cutting through Time and Space featured Taiwanese short *The FEMily*. The 2011 festival featured Beijing-based romantic drama *Bad*

*Romance* (Francois Chang 2011), *Be a Woman*, and Taiwanese HIV/AIDS documentary *The Hope of Love* (Jeng-Shiun Chen 2011), which screened with short from Hong Kong filmmaker Kit Hung *Always My Child* (2011).

Very few films have Chinese subtitles for local audiences. In the entire 2014 programme, only three feature-length films had Chinese subtitles, which were opening night boys film *Love Is Strange* (Ira Sachs 2014),[20] closing night film *The Way He Looks* (*Hoje Eu Quero Voltar Sozinho*, Daniel Ribeiro 2014) and *52 Tuesdays;* all three films were picked up by distributors in the region (Fortissimo, Cinehub and Edko Films). In the 2012 festival, *Mama Rainbow* and *I'm Here* were in Mandarin and Cantonese with English subtitles respectively. The short film *Lopsided*, which screened before *I'm Here*, was in Cantonese with Chinese and English subtitles. In 2011, both *Bad Romance* and *Be a Woman* were in Mandarin with English and Chinese subtitles. The documentary *The Hope of Love* was in Mandarin with Chinese subtitles.

The 2014 festival also featured four other Asian films, consisting of *Anita's Last Cha-Cha* (*Ang Huling Cha-Cha Ni Anita*, Sigrid Andrea P. Bernado 2014), *Frangipani* (Chandrasekaram Visakesa 2014), *Unfriend* (Joselito Altarejos 2014), and *Appropriate Behavior* from Brooklyn-based writer-director Desiree Akhavan, a bisexual, underachieving 20-something who is not out to her Iranian parents. In 2013, Nepalese film *Soongava: Dance of the Orchids* (Subarna Thapa 2012) screened with short documentary *Two Girls against the Rain* (Sao Sopheak 2012).

Two other North American films with Chinese casts were quite popular during the festival, both with quite similar themes. The Canadian *John Apple Jack* (Monika Mitchell 2013) and American *Eat with Me* (David Au 2014) both had very Western approaches to Chinese culture:

> It's quite common for Chinese-American films to have an issue with the mom or dad finding out their son is gay and how they would act; there is a relationship with a Westerner, which has been quite common over the past few years. Maybe that's what they are dealing with all the time. Maybe they all have Chinese restaurants in the US! (Interview with Joe Lam 2014).

*John Apple Jack* sees protagonist John, a white, arrogant heir to a successful restaurant chain, discover that his sister's fiancé is Jack, his childhood crush. As his love for his childhood friend reignites, his life spirals out of control. Jack is a chef specialising in Chinese cuisine, while another supporting Asian character is Marco Chow, the secretary John is currently sleeping with.

Marco is stereotypically effeminate, defined purely in terms of his excessive sexuality and vindictiveness when dumped by John. Similar themes occur in *Eat with Me*. Feeling underappreciated at home, Emma moves in with her son Elliot, who runs an unsuccessful Chinese restaurant facing bankruptcy in downtown LA. While Emma gains confidence and yearns to be closer with her son, Elliot is fearful of coming out to her and the growing commitment with his new lover. Luckily, they both have their passion for food to bring them together.

HKLGFF 2012 had a substantial amount of Asian content: South Korean romantic comedy *Two Weddings and a Funeral* opened the festival with romantic drama *Yes or No 2: Come Back to Me* (Saratswadee Wongsomphet 2012); Thai drama *It Gets Better* (Tanwarin Sukkhapisit 2012) closed the festival; other Asian films for 2012 included the South Korean film *Mirage* (Jung-ho Yang 2011), Indonesian film *Arisan! 2* (Nia Dinata 2011), Japanese lesbian drama *Yoshiko & Yuriko* (Sachi Hamano 2011), Iranian drama *Facing Mirrors* (Negar Azarbayjani 2011), *Tsuyako* (Mitsuyo Miyazaki 2011), which screened in the Cutting through Time and Space shorts session, and finally South Korean director Kim Jho Kwang-soo's shorts trilogy *Boy Meets Boys* (2008), *Just Friends?* (2009), and *Love 100° C* (2010).

HKLGFF 2011 opened the festival with *Lost in Paradise* (Vu Ngoc Dang 2011) and *Yes or No* (Saraswadee Wongsompetch 2010). Iranian *Circumstance* closed the festival alongside the American drama/comedy *Beginners* (Mike Millis 2011). Other Asian films were the South Korean films *The Depths* (Ryusuke Hamaguchi 2011) and *Ashamed* (Kim Soo-hyun 2011), Malaysian *In a Bottle*, and the French documentary on Japanese icon Akihiro Miwa *Miwa: A Japanese Icon* (Pascal-Alex Vincent 2011). The 2011 festival also featured a Boys Short session on "Asian Faces," featuring four Asian-American shorts, one Asian-Canadian, and shorts from Thailand, Japan, and India.

From Looking at HKLGFF's programming against the principal elements it has been criticised—namely male dominance, lack of local content, and minimal subtitles—the theme of inconsistency stands out. This is obviously the festival programmer responding to the current state of queer cinema at any given time. If sufficient lesbian titles are available that meet the programmer standards, then that year will not be male-centric. It is evident that economic value has a significant influence on the festival's content. As such, we can identify homonormativity here through this neoliberal outlook as the very purpose of HKLGFF's programming is to seek profit. This was apparent in my interview with festival director Joe Lam. This emphasis on the economics of the festival ignores the overarching social structures at play that produce this economic inequality in the queer film festival circuit. As Kong has identified with the rise of new Tongzhi spaces being carved out by homonormativity, so too is the programme influenced by a focus on economic value over an "arts for art's sake" approach. As highlighted earlier in this book, this was a Bourdieusian framework employed by De Valck to analyse the International Film Festival Rotterdam (2014). Perhaps a more appropriate term for our analysis would be "arts for social empowerment sake." This is a particularly US-style neoliberalism that is expressed in the programming in that it cannot be separated from globalisation. International power relations that are privileged within the hegemonic framework of homonormativity influence the conditions experienced by HKLGFF. This commercial media system, which emphasises profit and privatisation, is an integral part to this neoliberal imperialism (McChesney 2001). This ultimately sees a sexual politics influenced by neoliberalism, whereby "sexual politics, communities and identities are shaped by economic process" (Richardson 2005, 517). Ultimately, content featuring lesbians, transgender characters, and people of colour are dictated by economic conditions. There is clearly not a shortage of this content, which is evident in the films programmed by MQFF and Frameline. However, the inconsistency in HKLGFF's programming is evident that the content is dictated by this need for profit.

## Conclusion

It is clear the festival successfully straddles the difficult line between being an elite cultural event and a closely engaged community experience. By comparing Frameline with MQFF, we can see elements that are common to the queer film festival while also specific differences with the two cities. Both festivals tend to position films that adhere to homonormative ideologies in key programming slots. These films see a naturalisation of white, gender-appropriate, sexually conservative identities. These films use a realist aesthetic that is imbued with dominant cultural ideologies. Films such as *eCupid* and *Shelter* are representative of this trend in gay cinema that recycles these conservative tropes that adhere to contemporary normalising gay politics. Even though *Leave It on the Floor* always produces a fun, raucous screening, the film fails to address the similar political concerns of its antecedent *Paris Is Burning*.

Another significant conclusion from this comparison refers to the very definition of the queer film festival itself. There is very little difference between Frameline's *LGBTQ* film festival and the Melbourne *Queer* Film Festival. Both festivals align their programming primarily on traditional gender lines, particularly in terms of shorts programming, passes,[21] and the tagging of films online. While this may seem to contradict the essence of queerness, the reinforcement of the gender binary in queer film festival programming is imperative for two reasons. First, these social enterprises must respond to the purchasing behaviour of the consumers. Second, this reduces the chance of lesbian and transgender content being overwhelmed by gay sessions, which is evident in the HKLGFF programming.

Both festivals, however, highlight socially progressive films in their programmes with centrepiece, opening, and closing screenings. Frameline opened its 35th festival with *Gun Hill Road*. That same year the festival programmed *Three* and *Wish Me Away* as its centrepiece films and also had *Becoming Chaz, Mangus, Spork, Tomboy,* and *Weekend* as showcase films alongside *Leave It on the Floor*. These films are socially progressive in their content. MQFF also prioritises a socially progressive agenda with its *Queeries* sessions aimed at LGBT youth and the Selector's Choice session, where exceptional films that are a "hard sell" are given a priority position in the programme layout. In terms of a homonormative focus on the domestic setting, both festivals programmed a selection of films that saw a neoliberal mimicking of the heteronormative familial ideal. Both festivals programmed a similar amount of films in this regard, while also programming narratives of families of choice, such as the popular film *Drool*.

Neoliberalism produces safe gay characters that are sexually stagnant and stable. Ultimately, both festivals acknowledge that these films are financially safe. My internship for Frameline highlighted this very trend, where if a film has a sexually suggestible programme write-up alongside a conventionally attractive male, it will no doubt sell out. These films are traditionally given peak time slots in the programme (Friday and Saturday evenings). As a social enterprise, this is an imperative move in order to ensure fiscal responsibility. Engaging in these business practices, programming the more commercial films at peak periods ensures financial viability that will allow the organisation to programme films that *are* a hard sell, for instance *Maggots and Men*, which premiered at the Castro Theatre. Consequently, this financial strength allows for an increasing amount of queerer films that challenge these dominant ideologies on sex, gender, race, and so on.

This UN-style queer diversity, however, can be problematic as it can be argued that this programming doesn't actually challenge the status quo. As an umbrella term, queer has the possibility to unite non-normative subjects to experience films and narratives of subjects that resist normative representations existing in mainstream media. I say "possibility" as this coalitional form of politics still runs the risk of erasing queer's radical potential. The alternative to this queer diversity, however, is HKLGFF's programming that is heavily influenced by a neoliberal drive for profit. By looking at the programme in the light of defining the queer film festival as a social enterprise, size and financial gain need not be the sole determinant of success or priority, thus a small screening on a Sunday afternoon need not be deemed as less important to the festival's success. Success must not be defined by profit.

## NOTES

1. An example given is Anthony Giddens's *The Constitution of Society* (1984).
2. On Mimicry, Bhabba writes that it is "the sign of a double articulation; a complex strategy of reform, regulation, and discipline, which 'appropriates' the Other as it visualizes power. Mimicry is also the sign of the inappropriate, however, a difference or recalcitrance which coheres the dominant strategic function of colonial power, intensifies surveillance, and poses an imminent threat to both 'normalized' knowledges and disciplinary powers" (1984, 126).
3. http://bullybloggers.wordpress.com/2010/07/15/the-kids-arent-alright/
4. *High Art* (Lisa Cholodenko 1998).
5. http://colorlines.com/archives/2010/07/the_kids_are_all_right_but_not_the_race_politics.html, the comments following the post are an interesting display of the difference between a gay community and a queer movement.
6. Luis the gardener is fired; Tanya, Paul's girlfriend, is dumped; and Jai, Joni's love interest, is left bewildered at Joni's drunken advances at a pool party.
7. Other gay male comedies in Frameline 35th Festival were *Bite Marks* (Mark Bessenger 2011), *Going Down in La-La Land* (Casper Andreas 2011), *Judas Kiss* (J.T. Tepnapa 2011), *Longhorns* (David Lewis 2011), and *The One* (Caytha Jentis 2010)
8. Clothing label Abercrombie and Fitch are notorious for featuring predominantly white men in their catalogues.
9. Colby Scott's article on gay.com discusses such issues arguing "Having been born within the mainstream society, we come to the LGBT

community with all the baggage society has instilled in us": http://
www.gay.net/news/2012/02/16/skin-deep-gay-racism-comes-out

10. In reference to pop singer Lady Gaga.

11. This reaction can be seen in various reviews of the film, such as Mark
Vaughan (2012), Marc Eastman (2011), and James Plath (2012).

13. I have excluded *Weekend* from this list due to the film having subject
matter that directly engages with contemporary normalisation politics. The film received an attendance figure of 732 as the distributor
requested an afternoon screening with a limited viewing audience as
opposed to an evening Castro screening, which would have resulted
in the attendance figure being significantly larger.

14. The Castro seats 1400, so these films (with the perhaps exception of
*The Green*) are considered larger screenings.

12. I am greatly indebted to Frances Wallace, current executive director
of Frameline, for providing me with these figures.

15. Taken from a variety of reviews from *Love HK Film* and *After Ellen*,
an American lesbian pop culture news site.

16. Frameline hosts a party following the *Transtastic* short films
annually.

17. Such examples would be Frameline 35 sell-out documentaries *Chaz*
(Fenton Bailey & Randy Barbato, 2011) and *Wish Me Away*
(Bobbie Birleffi & Beverly Kopf, 2011).

18. I have included the film *20 Lies, 4 Parents & a Little Egg* (Hanro
Smitsman 2013) in both the gay and lesbian figures as the film
featured both gay and lesbian parent figures.

19. I have included the films *Two Weddings and a Funeral* (Kim Jho
Kwang-soo 2012), *Mama Rainbow* (Fan Popo 2012), and *Les Invis-
ibles* (Sebastien Lifshitz 2012) as being both gay and lesbian themed.

20. *Love Is Strange* also had a subsequent screening.

21. MQFF has previously had "lazy lesbians," "lazy trans," and "lazy
buggers" passes, where ticker holders would get access to five
sessions.

## Works Cited

Aaron, Michele. 2004. *New Queer Cinema: A Critical Reader*. New Brunswick, NJ:
Rutgers University Press.

Alexander, Susan M. 2003. Stylish Hard Bodies: Branded Masculinity in Men's
Health Magazine. *Sociological Perspectives* 46(4): 535–554.

Altman, Dennis. 1997. Global Gaze/Global Gays. *GLQ: A Journal of Lesbian and
Gay Studies* 3(4): 417–436.

————. 2001. *Global Sex.* Chicago: University of Chicago Press.

Alvord, Sarah H., L. David Brown, and Christine W. Letts. 2004. Social Entrepreneurship and Societal Transformation. *The Journal of Applied Behavioural Sciences* 40(3): 260–282.

Andrews, David. 2010. Toward an Inclusive, Exclusive Approach to Art Cinema. In *Global Art Cinema: New Theories and Histories,* ed. Rosalind Galt, and Karl Schoonover, 62–75. Oxford: Oxford University Press.

————. 2013. *Theorizing Art Cinemas: Foreign, Cult Avant-Garde, and Beyond.* Austin, TX: University of Texas.

Arnheim, Rudolf. 1957. Film as art. Berkeley; Los Angeles; London: University of California Press.

Arthur, Paul. 2005. Extreme Makeover: The Changing Face of Documentary. *Cineaste* 30(3): 18–24.

Artz, Lee, and Bren Ortega Murphy. 2000. *Cultural Hegemony.* New York: Sage.

Battles, Kathleen, and Wendy Hilton-Morrow. 2002. Nobody Wants to Watch a Beacon: *Will & Grace* and the Limits of Mainstream Network Television. *Queers in American Popular Culture* 1: 187–208.

Bawer, Bruce. 1993. *A Place at the Table: The Gay Individual in American Society.* New York: Poseidon Press.

Bazin, Andre. 1967. *What Is Cinema?* Vol. 1. Trans. Hugh Gray. Berkeley, CA: University of California Press.

Becker, Ron. 2006. Gay-Themed Television and the Slumpy Class the Affordable, Multicultural Politics of the Gay Nineties. *Television & New Media* 7(2): 184–215.

Berry, Chris, and Laikwan Pang. 2010. Remapping contemporary Chinese cinema studies. *China Review* 10(2): 89–108.

Bersani, Leo. 1995. *Homos.* Cambridge, MA: Harvard University Press.

Bhabba, Homi. 1984. Of Mimicry and Man: The Ambivalence of Colonial Discourse. *October* 28(Discipleship: A Special Issues on Psychoanalysis): 125–133.

Blasius, Mark. 2001. *Sexual Identities, Queer Politics.* Princeton, NJ: Princeton University Pres.

Boellstorff, Tom. 2001. Dubbing Culture: Indonesian Gay and Lesbi Subjectivities and Ethnography in an Already Globalized World. *American Ethnologist* 30: 225–242.

Brown, Wendy. 2006. *Regulating Aversion: Tolerance in the Age of Identity and Empire.* Princeton, NJ: Princeton University Press.

Butler, Judith. 1990. *Gender Trouble: Feminism and the Subversion of Identity.* New York: Routledge.

Butler, Judith. 1993. *Bodies that matter: On the discourse limits of sex.* New York and London: Routledge.

————. 2004. *Undoing Gender.* New York: Routledge.

Chambers, Samuel A. 2003. Telepistemology of the Closet; or, The Queer Politics of *Six Feet Under. The Journal of American Culture* 26(1): 24–41.

———. 2006. Heteronormativity and the *L Word*: From a Politics of Representation to a Politics of Norms. In *Reading the L Word. Outing in Contemporary Television*. New York: IB Tauris.

Chasin, Alexandra. 2000. *Selling Out: The Gay and Lesbian Movement Goes to Market*. New York: Palgrave.

Ciasullo, Ann M. 2001. Making Her (in) Visible: Cultural Representations of Lesbianism and the Lesbian Body in the 1990s. *Feminist Studies* 27(3): 577–608.

Comolli, Jean-Louis, and Jean Narboni. 1971. 'Cinema/ Ideology/ Criticism', translated by Susan Bennett. *Screen* 12(1): 27–36.

Connolly, William. 2002. *Identity/Difference: Democratic Negotiations of Political Paradox*. Minneapolis, MN: University of Minnesota Press.

Cook, Matt. 2010. Families of Choice? George Ives, Queer Lives and the Family in Early Twentieth-Century Britain. *Gender & History* 22(1): 1–20.

Cover, Rob. 2000. First Contact: Queer Theory, Sexual Identity, and "Mainstream" Film. *International Journal of Sexuality and Gender Studies* 5(1): 71–89.

Daniel, Margaret R. 2006. Camps and Shifts. *GLQ: A Journal of Lesbian and Gay Studies* 12(4): 607–611.

Daniel, Lisa, and Claire Jackson. 2003. *The Bent Lens: A World Guide to Gay & Lesbian Film*. Melbourne: Allen & Unwin.

Dart, Raymond. 2004. The Legitimacy of Social Enterprise. *Nonprofit Management and Leadership* 14(4): 411–424.

Das, Man S., and Joseph Harry. 1980. *Homosexuality in International Perspective*. New Delhi: Vikas Publishing House.

De Valck, Marijke. 2014. Supporting Art Cinema at a Time of Commercialization: Principles and Practices, the Case of the International Film Festival Rotterdam. *Poetics* 42: 40–59.

Dean, Jodi. 2009. *Democracy and Other Neoliberal Fantasies: Communicative Capitalism and Left Politics*. Durham, NC: Duke University Press Books.

Duggan, Lisa. 2002. The new homonormativity: The sexual politics of neoliberalism. In *Materializing democracy: Toward a revitalized cultural politics*, ed. Russ Castronovo and Dana D. Nelson, 175–194. Durham, NC: Duke University Press.

Duggan, Lisa. 2003. *The Twilight of Equality: Neoliberalism, Cultural Politics, and the Attack on the Democracy*. Boston, MA: Beacon Press.

———. 2011. Forward. In *Hegemony and Heteronormativity: Revisiting the political in queer politics*, eds. Maria do Mar Castro Varela et al., xxv–xxvii. Surrey: Ashgate.

Dyer, Richard. 1997. *White*. New York: Routledge.

Eastman, Marc. 2011. The Green DVD Review. *R U Screening?* Accessed on 15 August 2012 at: http://www.areyouscreening.com/2011/12/06/the-green-dvd-review

Eng, David, L., Judith Halberstam, and Esteban Muñoz. 2005. What's Queer About Queer Studies Now? *Social text* 23(3/4): 1–17.

Emig, Rainer. 2000. Queering the Straights: Straightening Queers: Commodified Sexualities and Hegemonic Masculinity. In *Subverting Masculinity: Hegemonic* and *Alternative Versions of Masculinity in Contemporary Culture*, 207–226. Amsterdam: Rodopi Press.

Farley, Anthony Paul. 1997. Black Body as Fetish Object. *Oregon Law Review* 76: 457.

Foucault, Michel. 1977. *The History of Sexuality: An Introduction*, vol 1. New York: Vintage.

Foucault, Michel. 1980. *Power/knowledge: Selected interviews and other writings, 1972-1977*. Pantheon.

Galt, Rosalind, and Karl Schoonover. 2010. Intoduction: The Impurity of Art Cinema. In *Global Art Cinema: New Theories and Histories*, ed. Rosalind Galt, and Karl Schoonover, 3–30. Oxford: Oxford University Press.

Gamson, Joshua. 1996. The Organizational Shaping of Collective Identity: The Case of Lesbian and Gay Film Festivals in New York. *Sociological Forum* 11(2): 231–261.

Ghaziani, Amin. 2008. *The Dividends of Dissent: How Conflict and Culture Work in Lesbian and Gay Marches on Washington*. Chicago: University of Chicago Press.

Giddens, Anthony. 1984. *The Constitution of Society: Outline of the Theory of Structuration*. Los Angeles, CA: University of California Press.

Goffman, Erving. 1963. *Stigma: Notes on the Management of Spoiled Identity*. Englewood Cliffs, NJ: Prentice Hall.

Gorfinkel, Elena. 2006. Wet Dreams: Erotic Film Festivals of the Early 1970s and the Utopian Sexual Public Sphere. *Framework* 47(2): 59–86.

Gorman-Murray, Andrew. 2006. Queering Home or Domesticating Deviance? Interrogating Gay Domesticity Through Lifestyle Television. *International Journal of Cultural Studies* 9(2): 227–247.

Gross, Larry. 2005. The Past and the Future of Gay, Lesbian, Bisexual, and Transgender Studies. *Journal of Communication* 55: 508–528.

Halberstam, Judith. 2005. Shame and White Gay Masculinity. *Social Text*, 23(3–4, 84–85): 219–233.

Halberstam, Jack. 2010. The Kids Aren't Alright!. *The Bully Bloggers*. Accessed on 16 March 2011 at: http://bullybloggers.wordpress.com/2010/07/15/the-kids-arent-alright/

Halperin, David M. 1995. *Saint Foucault: Towards a Gay Hagiography*. New York: Oxford University Press.

Hernandez, Daisy. 2010. The Kids Are Alright but Not the Queer Movement. *The Color Lines*. Accessed on 4 April 2012 at: http://colorlines.com/archives/2010/07/the_kids_are_all_right_but_not_the_race_politics.html

Jackson, Peter A. 1998. Reading Rio from Bangkok: An Asianist Perspective on Brazil's Male Homosexual Cultures. *American Ethnologist* 27: 950–960.

Jagose, Annemarie. 1996. *Queer Theory*. Carlton: Melbourne University Press.

Jakobson, Janet. 1998. Queer Is? Queer Does?: Normativity and Resistance. *GLQ: A Journal of Lesbian and Gay Studies* 4(4): 511–536.

Jenkins, Tricia. 2005. "Potential Lesbians at Two O'clock": The Heterosexualization of Lesbianism in the Recent Teen Film. *The Journal of Popular Culture* 38(3): 491–504.

Kagan, Dion. 2012. High-Stakes Verite: Andrew Haigh's *Weekend*. *Kill Your Darlings*. Accessed on 4 February at: http://www.killyourdarlingsjournal.com/2012/02/high-stakes-verite-andrew-haighs-weekend/

Keenlyside, Sarah. 2001. Post-Sundance 2001: Docs Still Facing Financing and Distribution Challenge. *IndieWire*. Accessed on 7 September at: http://www.indiewire.com/article/festivals_post_sundance_2001_docs_still_face_financing_and_distribution_cha

Kentlyn, Sue. 2008. The Radically Subversive Space of the Queer Home:'Safety House' and 'Neighbourhood Watch'2. *Australian Geographer* 39(3): 327–337.

Kim, Jeongmin. 2007. Queer Cultural Movements and Local Counterpublics of Sexuality: A Case of Seoul Queer Films and Videos Festival. Trans. Sunghee Hong. *Inter-Asia Cultural Studies* 8(4): 617–633.

King, Samantha. 2008. What's Queer About (Queer) Sport Sociology Now? A Review Essay. *Sociology of Sport Journal* 25(4): 419–442.

Klinger, Barbara. 1986. 'Cinema/Ideology/Criticism' Revisited: The Progressive Genre. In *Film Genre Reader*, ed. Barry K. Grant, 74–90. Austin, TX: University of Texas.

Knegt, Peter. 2008. *Forging a Gay Mainstream: Negotiating Gay Cinema in the American hegemony*. Master's Thesis. Montreal, QC: Concordia University.

Kong, Travis. 2012. A Fading *Tongzhi* Heterotopia: Hong Kong Older Gay Men's Use of Spaces. *Sexualities* 15(8): 896–916.

Lam, Joe. 2014. Interview by Stuart Richards, personal interview, Hong Kong. 22nd September.

Leung, Helen Hok-Sze. 2003. Queer Asian Cinemas. In *The Bent Lens: A World Guide to Gay & Lesbian Film*, ed. Lisa Daniel, and Claire Jackson, 14–17. Melbourne: Allen & Unwin.

———. 2007. Archiving Queer Feelings in Hong Kong. *Inter-Asia Cultural Studies* 8(4): 559–571.

Lim, Song Hwee. 2008. How to be Queer in Taiwan: Translation, Appropriation and the Construction of a Queer Identity in Taiwan. In *AsiaPacifiQueer: Rethinking Genders and Sexualities*, ed. F. Martin, P.A. Jackson, M. McLelland, and A. Yue, 235–250. Urbana, IL: University of Illinois Press.

Loist, Skadi. 2012. A Complicated Queerness: LGBT Film Festivals and Queer Programming Strategies. In *Coming Soon to a Festival Near You: Programming Film Festivals*, ed. Jeffrey Ruoff. St Andrews: St Andrews Film Studies.

Ludwig, Gundula. 2011. From the 'Heterosexual Matrix' to a 'Heteronormative Hegemony': Initiating a Dialogue between Judith Butler and Antonio Gramsci about Queer Theory and Politics. In *Hegemony and Heteronormativity: Revisiting the Political in Queer Politics*, ed. Maria do Mar Castro Varela, Nikita Dhawan, and Antke Engel, 43–62. Surrey: Ashgate.

Martin, Fran, Peter Jackson, Mark McLelland, and Audrey Yue (ed). 2008. *AsiaPacifiQueer: Rethinking Genders and Sexualities.* Urbana, IL: University of Illinois Press.

McBride, Dwight A. 2007. Why I Hate That I Loved Brokeback Mountain. *GLQ: A Journal of Lesbian and Gay Studies* 13(1): 95–97.

McChesney, Robert. 2001. Global Media, Neoliberalism & Imperialism. *International Socialist Review,* August/September. Accessed at: http://www. thirdworldtraveler.com/McChesney/GlobalMedia_Neoliberalism.html

Muñoz, José Esteban. 2005. Queer Minstrels for the Straight Eye: Race as Surplus in Gay TV. *GLQ: A Journal of Lesbian and Gay Studies* 11(1): 101–102.

Murphy, Kevin P., Jason Ruiz, and David Serlin. 2008. Queer Futures: The Homonormativity Issue. *Special Issue: Radical History Review,* 100.

Ohmann, Richard. 1996. *Selling Cultures: Magazines, Markets and Class at the Turn of the Century.* New York: Verso.

Perspex. 2006. The First Asian Lesbian Film and Video Festival in Taipei Celebrates a New Form of Social Activism. *Inter-Asia Cultural Studies* 7(3): 527–532.

Phelan, Shane. 1989. *Identity Politics: Lesbian Feminism and the Limits of Community.* Philadelphia, PA: Temple University Press.

———. 1994. *Getting Specific: Postmodern Lesbian Politics.* Minneapolis, MN: University of Minnesota Press.

Plath, James. 2012. The Green—DVD Review. *Movie Metropolis.* Accessed on 14 August 2012 at: http://moviemet.com/review/green-dvd-review

Puar, Jasbir. 2005. Queer Times, Queer Assemblages. *Social Text* 23: 121–139.

Rahman, Momin. 2004. Is Straight the New Queer? David Beckham and the Dialectics of Celebrity. *M/C (media/culture)* 7(5). Accessed online at: http://journal.media-culture.org.au/0411/15-rahman.php

Rhyne, Raghan. 2006. The Industry and the Ecstasy: Gay and Lesbian Film Festivals and the Economy of Community. eds. Straayer, Chris and Thomas Waugh, "Queer Film and Video Festival Forum, Take Two. Critics Speak Out" *GLQ: A Journal of Lesbian and Gay Studies* 12(4): 617–619.

Rich, Adrienne. 1980. Compulsory Heterosexuality and Lesbian Existence. *Signs* 5 (4): 631–660.

Rich, B. Ruby. 1999. Collision, Catastrophe, Celebration: The Relationship between Gay and Lesbian Film Festivals and Their Public. *GLQ: A Journal of Lesbian and Gay Studies* 5(1): 79–84.

———. 2000. Queer and Present Danger. *Sight and Sound,* 80, March. http://www.bfi.org.uk/sightandsound/feature/80

Richards, Stuart. 2016. Overcoming the Stigma: The Queer Denial of Indiewood. *Journal of Film and Video* 68(1): 19–30.

Richardson, Diane. 2005. Desiring Sameness? The Rise of a Neoliberal Politics of Normalisation. *Antipode* 37(3): 515–535.

Rubin, Gayle. 1975. The Traffic in Women: Notes on the 'Political Economy' of Sex. In *Toward an Anthology of Women,* ed. Rayna Reiter. New York: Monthly Review Press.

Rudy, Kath. 2000. Queer theory and feminism. *Women Studies* 29: 195–216.
Sedgwick, Eve Kosofsky. 1985. *Between Men: Male Homosocial Desire and English Literature*. New York: Columbia University Press.
———. 1990. *Epistemology of the Closet*. Berkeley, CA: University of California Press.
Seidman, Steven. 1993. Identity politics in a postmodern gay culture: Some conceptual and historical notes. In *Fear of a Queer Planet*, ed. Michael Warner, 105–142. Minneapolis: University of Minnesota Press.
Sender, Katherine. 2003. Sex Sells: Sex, Class, and Taste in Commercial Gay and Lesbian Media. *GLQ: A Journal of Lesbian and Gay Studies* 9(3): 331–365.
———. 2004. *Business, Not Politics*. New York: Columbia University Press.
Silbey, Jessica M. 2006. Videotaped Confessions and the Genre of Documentary. *Fordham Intellectual Property Media & Entertainment Law Journal* 16(3): 789–808.
Stone, Amy L. 2009. Diversity, Dissent, and Decision Making: The Challenge to LGBT Politics. *GLQ: A Journal of Lesbian and Gay Studies* 16(3): 465–472.
Stringer, Julian. 2003. Neither one nor the other: Blockbusters at film festivals. In *Movie blockbusters*, ed. Julian Stringer, 202–214. London and New York: Routledge.
Stryker, Susan. 1996. San Francisco International Lesbian and Gay Film Festival. In *The Ultimate Guide to Lesbian and Gay Film and Video*, ed. Jenni Olson, 364–370. San Francisco, CA: Serpent's Tail.
———. 2008. Transgender History, Homonormativity, and Disciplinarity. *Radical History Review* 100: 145–157.
Sutton, Tyler H. 2007. The Emergence of a Male Global Gay Identity: A Contentious and Contemporary Movement. *Totem: The University of Western Ontario Journal of Anthropology* 15(1): 51–58.
Tang, Denise Tse Shang. 2011. *Conditional Desires: Honk Kong Lesbian Desires and Everyday Life*. Hong Kong: Hong Kong University Press.
Tilsen, Julie, and Dave Nylund. 2010. Homonormativity and Queer Youth Resistance. In *Counseling Ideologies: Queer Challenges to Heteronormativity*. London: Ashgate.
Varela, Maria do Mar Castro, Nikita Dhawan, and Antke Engel. 2011. Hegemony and Heteronormativity: Revisiting "The Political" in Queer Politics. In *Hegeomony and Heternormativity: Revisiting "The Political" in Queer Politics*, ed. Maria do Mar Castro Varela, Nikita Dhawan, and Antke Engel, 1–24. Surrey Hills: Ashgate.
Vaughan, Mark. 2012. Modern Day Witch Trials in Small Towns: Substitute 'Gay' for 'Witch'. *epinions.com*. Accessed on 14 August 2012 at: http://www.epinions.com/review/The_Green_epi/content_587374169732?sb=1
Ward, Elizabeth Jane. 2008. *Respectably Queer: Diversity Culture in LGBT Activist Organizations*. Nashville, TN: Vanderbilt University Press.
Warner, Michael. 1993. *The Fear of a Queer Planet*. Minneapolis, MN: University of Minnesota Press.

216 S.J. RICHARDS

———. 1999. *The Trouble with Normal: Sex, Politics and the Ethics of Queer Life*. New York: Free Press.

———. 2012. *Queer and Then? The Chronicle of Higher Education. Accessed online on 24 January at* .http://chronicle.com/article/QueerThen-/130161/

Watts, Richard. 1999. Introduction. *Melbourne Queer Film Festival* (program).

Weeks, Jeffrey. 2001. *Same Sex Intimacies: Families of Choice and other Life Experiments*. New York: Routledge.

Weston, Kath. 1991. *Families We Choose*. New York: Columbia University Press.

Williams, Raymond. 1977. *Marxist and Literature, Marxist Introductions*. London: Oxford University Press.

Williams, Jonathan. 2011. *Trans Cinema, Trans Viewers*. PhD Thesis. Melbourne: The University of Melbourne.

Williford, Daniel. 2009. Queer Aesthetics. *Borderlands* 8(2): 1–15.

Yau, Ching. 2006. Bridges and battles. *GLQ: A Journal of Lesbian and Gay Studies* 12(4): 605–607.

Yep, Gust, and Elia John. 2007. Queering/Quaring Blackness in *Noah's Ark*. In *Queer Popular Culture: Literature, Media, Film & Television*, ed. T. Peele, 27–40. New York: Palgrave Macmillan.

Yep, Gust A., and John P. Elia. 2012. Racialized masculinities and the new homonormativity in LOGO's Noah's Arc. *Journal of homosexuality* 59(7): 890–911.

Yue, Audrey, and Gay Hawkins. 2000. Going South. *New Formations* 40: 49–63.

Žižek, Slavoj. 1999. The Ticklish subject: The Absent Centre of Political Ontology. London; New York: Verso.

## INTERVIEWS

Daniel, Lisa. Interviewed by Stuart Richards, personal interview, Melbourne, 5 August 2011.

Deragon, Sarah. Interviewed by Stuart Richards, personal interview, San Francisco, 2 July 2011.

Feliciano, Lares, Sam Berliner and Nissa Poulson. Interviewed by Stuart Richards, personal interview, San Francisco, 7 July 2011.

Maria. Interviewed by Stuart Richards, confidential, San Francisco, 11 July 2011.

Mutineer, Liz. Interviewed by Stuart Richards, personal interview, Melbourne, 15 October 2011.

Nick and Audrey. Interviewed by Stuart Richards, confidential interview, San Francisco, 9 July 2011.

Polly and Alex. Interviewed by Stuart Richards, confidential, San Francisco, 11 July 2011.

Sam. Interviewed by Stuart Richards, confidential, San Francisco, 8 July 2011.

Whitham, Alexis. Interviewed by Stuart Richards, personal interview, San Francisco, 8 July 2011.

CHAPTER 5

# The Space of the Film Festival

The festival bar plays a key part to the festival and I would hate to see it disappear. It's the one time of the year where our audience, which is really disparate and eclectic, can actually get together and mix in the lounge. We get people turning up at 6:00 pm and I would ask 'what are you seeing tonight?' and they would respond 'oh nothing I'm just here to hang out with friends.' I get gay guys saying 'oh it's the one time of year where I can have drinks with my lesbian friends in a queer context.' You can't do that at the Laird or wherever.[1] That social aspect is crucial but it's *really* crucial for people like me to talk to punters and find out what they like and don't like and what's working and not working. It's a central part of the festival and I really hope we can keep using it at ACMI (interview with Lisa Daniel 2011).

The queer film festival was born out of a need for a space to exhibit and experience queer cinema with a community. Given this, it is imperative for us to interrogate the space of the festival itself. As outlined above by former MQFF director Lisa Daniel, the festival bar plays a crucial role in establishing the space of the festival. These surrounding areas are pivotal in the formation of one's experience. The queer film festival is more than just about cinema; it is a festival of encounters (Siegel 1997). In Chap. 2, I outlined how the queer film festival can play a key role in the development of a creative city, as film festivals can be "a catalyst for urban renewal, attracting tourists and capital investments, enhancing a city's image and creating new jobs" (Crespi-Valbona and Richards 2007, 106). This analysis was concerned with the value produced by the queer film festival. As an identity-based film festival, these events can also develop counter-public

© The Author(s) 2016
S.J. Richards, *The Queer Film Festival*,
DOI 10.1057/978-1-137-58438-0_5

spheres. Drawing on Michael Warner (2002) and Nancy Fraser (1997), Ragan Rhyne (2007) analyses how the development of the queer film festival shaped a continuously changing queer counter-public sphere. These subordinate counter-publics circulate counter-discourses and resist the values of dominant publics. Ultimately, Rhyne's dissertation outlines how changes in fund-raising practices resulted in the queer film festival being driven by a neoliberal discourse on self-management, as I have also done in Chap. 2. This chapter seeks to explore the influence the surrounding space has on the spectator in the queer film festival's counter-public sphere. This will be done through two very different case studies. First, I shall focus on the Castro neighbourhood and Frameline. While commonly known as the gay district in San Francisco, where Pride festivities are regularly held, this neighbourhood also engages in exclusionary practices that are subverted during the film festival. Second, I will explore how the effect the HKLGFF's screening location of shopping malls has for the spectator. The aim of this chapter is to emphasise the need to consider the screening locations when analysing the meaning generated by a film festival.

## The Castro as a Carnivalesque Space

Frameline performs a transgressive role within the conservative space of the Castro District in San Francisco. For the 11 or so days of the festival, the white male-dominated space is infiltrated by a whole plethora of identities not accustomed to being comfortable in this street, which is lined with bars, sex shops, and clothing retailers aimed at a distinctly wealthy gay male clientele. I will argue that this transgression is carnivalesque in nature. This signals a modification in methodology and approach for my investigation of Frameline. The examination moves beyond representational analysis to the environment where these films are exhibited. Audience responses in Chap. 4 highlight the stark difference in perception of the Castro versus the neighbouring Mission District. In light of this, the theatre locations where these films are programmed greatly alter reception. For instance, the Bruce LaBruce documentary *The Advocate for Fagdom*, which was screened in the grungy Roxie Theatre for Frameline 35 in 2011, created an intimate feel for both the duration of the film and the Q&A that followed with LaBruce. If this same film were to be screened in the expansive Castro Theatre, this intimacy would be lost. Furthermore, screening films with content that oppose the hegemony present in conservative gay and lesbian politics *in* a male-dominated neighbourhood warrants further investigation. While there is the possibility that this environment may dilute the dissident qualities of these films, fieldwork research presented in this chapter highlights the carnivalesque transgression that takes place. The following examination of the Castro neighbourhood is supported by spatial analysis of the district and interview responses from both staff and audience members. This data will be analysed within the conceptual framework of the carnivalesque theory, as employed most notably by Bakhtin.

Like all festivals, Frameline has a beginning and an end. A key text on festivals is Mikhail Bakhtin's *Rabelais and His World* (1984), which is a dissertation on French Renaissance writer Francois Rabelais. It is his analysis of Rabelais's work that Bakhtin isolates in the theory of the carnival. We see a collective social institution that is born out of folk humour. In the Middle Ages, "a boundless world of humorous forms and manifestations opposed the official and serious tone of medieval ecclesiastical and feudal culture" (5). This was folk carnival humour. It is my hypothesis that the queer film festival is carnivalesque in manifestation. Like Robert Stam, in his article "Film, Literature and the Carnivalesque" (1989), I choose to use the carnivalesque as an "exploratory device" (96). By looking at the queer film festival as a carnival, we can see how this social empowerment functions. Like Bakhtin's carnival, the more general Pride festivities in June in the San Francisco Bay Area are the "people's second life, organised on the basis of laughter. It is a festival life" (8).

The carnival sees a suspension of hegemonic relations through the ritual spectacles of folk carnival humour. Carnival time "abolishes hierarchies, levels, social classes, and creates another life free from conventional rules and restrictions. In carnival, all that is marginalized and excluded—the mad, the scandalous ... takes over the centre in a liberating explosion of otherness" (Stam 1989, 86). Those that usually don't have a voice are allowed to shout loudly. We can apply this conceptualisation of the carnival to Frameline as an explosion of queerness in the Castro.

The carnival space creates a "second life outside officialdom" (6) influenced heavily by the culture/politics of laughter. The carnival space is seen as an escape into the "realm of community, freedom, equality and abundance" (9). The social hierarchy of official public society is suspended and subverted in this second world. This sense of equality for all participants is particularly significant as this creates a unique type of communication impossible in daily life. Pieties and social ranks are overturned by normally suppressed voices. Thus, fools become kings and kings become beggars. Stam argues that the "carnival is not a spectacle seen by the people; they live in it, and everyone participates because its very idea embraces all the people" (7). All participants vibrantly experience the carnival. It is important to note, however, that this suspension and subversion of hierarchical rank is only temporary as there is always a beginning and an end to the carnival.

The temporality of the carnival is especially significant to my analysis of the queer film festival. In terms of queer films, once a year during the festival, they are given the spotlight as opposed to simply being niche DVDs watched at home. Umberto Eco (1984), in his contribution to the book *Carnival!*, states that for a carnival to be successful, "(i) the law must be so pervasively ... interjected ... at the time of its violation; (ii) the moment of the carnival must be very short ... an entire year of ritual is necessary to make the transgression enjoyable" (6). The multitude of queer content exhibited by a queer film festival can be seen as a transgression of the normal lack of queer images in everyday life. For Eco, this transgression must be authorized and short, which most contemporary queer film festivals are. As such, according to Eco's theory (1984), carnivalisation is not *real transgression* as it reminds us of the existence of the rule that was broken in the first place. The carnival space offers limited rebellion within the constraints set by the ruling class. If we are to play the devil's advocate, how socially transformative can such an event be if it is permitted and ultimately licensed by the contemporary hierarchy of social relations? (Stallybrass and White 1986). Penney (2010) interprets Eco not as highlighting "an inherent powerlessness within the structure of the carnival" but as an event that can be used to "reinforce the idea that the mainstream, when exposed to counterculture, offers the possibility for expanded consciousness" (151).

The participants in a queer film festival have a release from the "burden of socially imposed sex roles" (Stam 1989, 93). This release from burden can be said for any environment that is queer. This allows the participants to be comfortable to visibly express their queerness, such as public displays of affection. Thus, a queer festival can be carnivalesque. In his analysis of the Sydney Gay and Lesbian Mardi Gras as carnivalesque, Kates (2003) examines an event that has grown from being a rioting mob to one of Australia's hallmark events. Much like Frameline, Mardi Gras is a contested event that is "an analogous merging of the commercial, artistic and political arenas and the Mardi Gras to develop as a polysemous and syncretic consumption phenomenon that embraces meanings from the political, artistic, and commercial realms" (6). The carnival is the locus of togetherness with the community bridging the gap created by these political, artistic, and commercial realms (Bakhtin 1968, 94) bridging the gap created by these. This invokes the relationship of the film festival with the imagined queer community. Hence, going to these events makes me feel part of this queer community, that I am not really a minority in my own life, but one of many. For some screenings at queer film festivals, Stam's writings are relevant, which describe a "rejection of social decorum entailing a release from oppressive etiquette, politeness and good manners"' (Stam 1989, 94). Recent films that have encouraged a rejection of movie-going decorum would include *Leave It on the Floor,* which saw audience members dancing in the aisles; the response to cheesy sex comedies of the *Eating Out* films and the booing, hissing, and name-calling during screenings. Stam's final point is the erasure of the boundary between spectator and performer. Film festival attendees are not just spectators but participants in the experience of the film screening.

In light of this, we can identify three major conceptual elements of the carnivalesque for our discussion of Frameline. First, as outlined by Eco, this transgression reminds us of the existing social norms and rules. So, what are the hierarchies and social restrictions for queer identities in the Castro District? Second, how does attending Frameline break and transgress these marginal subject positions? Finally, and perhaps the most importantly, attending a screening can be a performative role. Queer audience members are active participants in the social experience of the film festival. It is this active experience that creates a social empowering transgression.

The queer film festival as a carnivalesque space has recently become a topic for discussion. As discussed at length in previous chapters, the queer film festival has been born out of an unruly past. Penney (2010) contends that the queer film festival is a countercultural space for transgression, and Zielinski (2009) argues that the queer film festival is indeed an endorsed transgression:

> Current interpretations of Bakhtin's concept of the carnivalesque place emphasis on transgression, namely the transgression of social norms, within a tightly circumscribed space for a finite duration. What is permitted was already permitted in advance. Laws, permits, agreements, and less directly, the policy of funding agencies, all perform this. It is in this way that these film festivals might be understood as participating in the carnivalesque, however limited and minor in degree, and this degree is firmly relative to local norms and mores (205).

Particular transgressions are context specific as highlighted by Zielinski. This chapter argues that the performative function of attending Frameline disrupts the white gay male homogeneity of the Castro. It must be clarified that this analysis addresses the carnivalesque transgressions of queer diversity disruption of the white male *homonormative* space. The Castro District is a visibly gay neighbourhood. As such, it would be difficult to argue that the space is heteronormative to begin with.

### *The Hegemonic Castro*

A popular term for the men that frequent the Castro District is the "Castro clone." This is a result of the dominance of both whiteness and gay men in the area. The gay male clone is a rejection of male effeminacy and age-old stereotypes of what it means to be gay, where "liberation turned *Boys in the Band* into doped up, sexed-out, Marlboro Men" (Levine 1998, 7). Signorile (1997) explores the gay clone's obsession with hyper-masculinity:

> A key factor in the formulation and promulgation of the cult of masculinity that also dismayed the gay liberationist was that the dominant gender style was now super-masculine. It was as if the 1960s and the counter culture androgyny never occurred. Gay male culture was still reeling from the crisis of masculinity that had affected homosexuals for decades. Gay men, attracted to the masculine ideas they'd cultivated in the furtive days prior to Stonewall, seemed now to institutionalize and exaggerate a heterosexual-inspired, macho look. The 1970s clone was born. (52–53)

Quite often in my interviews, a parallel arose between the Castro and the Mission with a rigid view of gay masculine dominance and a more fluid queerness.[2] The neighbouring Victoria and Roxie theatres in the Mission District definitely had more hipster credibility attached to them—although this is rapidly changing given the recent influx of tech employees forcing the neighbourhood to undergo dramatic gentrification. Opinions of the Castro Theatre and surrounding space were surprisingly unanimous. The Castro Theatre is grand and beautiful and adored. This is in spite of the ambivalent surroundings, as the dominance of white cisgendered men made many feel unconformable. In two separate interviews, subjects recounted experiences of how they were personally asked to leave clubs. While out bar-hopping in the Castro area with my dear friend Jeannie, I also experienced this blatant discrimination. While everyone was lovely to me, Jeannie had blunt, rude service in the first bar, was blocked entry to the female toilets and asked to leave in the second club, and blatantly refused entry in the third. To clarify, these were not strictly male-only clubs. Those that do not fit the desirable gay identity are simply unwelcome. When interview subjects were asked about the neighbourhood, most answers were the same. First, an audience member who identifies as a lesbian highlighted the apparent differences between the use of the terms gay and queer between the two neighbourhoods:

> (It's) predominantly gay male. It is just such a different culture than I am usually immersed in. I don't even think they would define themselves as queer. They would call themselves gay. It's very stylised and everyone is such gym bunnies. They all look like clones sometimes (Interview with "Polly," 2011).

An individual who identified as genderqueer concurred:

> People who live in the Castro tend to be middle upper class or upper class. The Castro also has a history of being dominated by white gay men. I know there are issues at certain bars where there were extra ID checks for men of colour so the Castro does have a history of exclusionary practices. It sucks (Interview with "Sydney," 2011).

A transgender male recounted a story of being harassed by a gay man when he used to live in the Castro:

> I have mixed feelings about it. I just moved from this area a month ago. I see a lot of gay people but not a lot of trans people in this area so I don't have a huge connection to it. Even in the gay community a gay man in this area could still harass me. It's happened before. This guy could tell I was trans and when he found out he kept on saying "oh my god! I didn't know." He kept on saying really inappropriate things about it and even when I told him I was uncomfortable he kept on at it. People who self-identify as queer often have mixed feelings about it here so they will go to other bars where people like that congregate (Interview with "Sam," 2011).

Volunteer intern from Frameline 35 Nissa Poulson recounted a personal experience of being kicked out of a gay bar in the Castro:

> I went with a group of girls to a Castro bar once and we were asked to leave. It's fine if I go with gay men and I'm the one 'fag hag.' They said I was 'invading a male space' or a 'gay male space.' They said that to my friend and we were then asked to leave the bar. It wasn't even by the staff but by the clientele (Interview with Nissa Poulson 2011).

In the same group interview, volunteer coordinator Lares responded to Nissa's story stating that this exclusivity has a history.

> There is definitely exclusivity at the bars and there's a history to that. It's a space that was made out when there wasn't one. I feel that history is very important to acknowledge but that's also kind of whack. A group of young women who may or may not be queer being kicked out of a gay bar is really 'effed' up (Interview with Feliciano 2011).

This exclusionary nature greatly contrasts the "gay index" posited by Richard Florida in his analysis on the creative class. As highlighted in Chap. 2, Florida argues that a city's gay population stands as a "reasonable proxy for an area's openness" (2002, 245). Ultimately, if a city has a developed gay community, then that city displays openness to different types of people and ideas. While there may indeed be a correlation between dense gay populations and a city's high-tech growth, Florida's logic between openness and the gay population is flawed. San Francisco (and the Castro specifically) in the 1970s was a gay Mecca and refugee camp for homosexuals across America (Wittman 1970) but has since developed into a neighbourhood that privileges hyper-masculinity (Signorile 1997). The Castro's privileged exclusionary practices result in an environment that is very far from this open, innovative, and almost utopian creative city Florida describes. This romanticised portrayal of gay men and their role in urban gentrification fail to unpack the very inequalities and exclusionary implications of this trend.

Whitham ties this male dominance to economic inequalities of gender. This is not an actual measurement of socio-economic gender inequality; this is about cultural perceptions of gender inequality in consumer culture, where "the gay male community have a lot of money" (Chura 1999, 3):

> At the end of the day most American businesses have to deal with making money and it's more financially beneficial to cater to a male demographic in that area then to cater to a female demographic because you wouldn't always be able to pay your rent the same way because of the perceived spending habits of gay men versus gay women. Unfortunately that's just how it plays

out. It would be awesome to have ten lesbian bars out there, I would *personally* enjoy that but I just don't see that happening (Interview with Whitham 2011).

The recent relationship between the Castro and the Mission has given us a spatial map of homonormativity. Sender (2004) notes that lesbian, bisexual, and transgender consumers are often ignored when advertisers and businesses choose to advertise to the gay community. Much like Florida's work on the creative class (2002), these gay villages are agents for urban regeneration. Not surprisingly, much of the imagery and branding evident in "gay villages and neighbourhoods" prioritise profit over community development (Hunt and Zacharias 2008), such as the resistance against the shelter for homeless youth for fears of the plan affecting local property value.[3] Not only is a myth created in this mindset that gays and lesbians are on a double income with no kids (Yaksich 2008; Gudelunas 2011), but also how this consumerism can lead to so-called liberation when this culture of consumption is based on distinct gender inequalities (Chasin 2000). "Gay ghettoes," such as the Castro, are a visibly male space with lesbian communities seemingly invisible (Podmore 2006).[4] Urban entrepreneurialism in gay villages has created sexualised spaces that are homonormative (Bell and Binnie 2003). The Castro was born out of structural racism, sexism, and elitism creating hierarchies of belonging, which still operate today (Reck 2009). This hierarchy of belonging in the Castro space creates the Castro Citizen, a "person embodying a homogenous white, adult, middle class, gay male identity and performance" (7). Indeed, those that don't fit the mould of the Castro Citizen are sidelined as a sexual other. This sexual other is defined in terms of the pink economy discourse, which is also a contributing factor to contemporary gay ghettoes. Gay villages are culturally gated with exclusionary practices in operation (Phelan 2001). Ultimately, debates on the Castro youth shelter and the interview responses in this work are indicative of systemic power and sexual normalisation.

There is truth to these observations from my interviews. The majority of the Frameline audience has traditionally been made up of older, white gay men. Here is an overview of the demographics taken from the audience survey in 2010 (Fig. 5.1):[5]

This is a dramatic over-representation of older white gay men. Development coordinator Jennifer Kim addresses this in her interview:

Gender Identity and Sexual Orientation

| Male | 54% |
|------|------|
| Gay | 47.2% |
| Female | 39% |
| Lesbian | 31.6% |
| Queer | 21.5% |
| Bisexual | 5.3% |
| Straight | 3.4% |
| Transgender | 1.7% |
| Genderqueer | 1.4% |

Race

| Caucasian | 79% |
|-----------|------|
| Latino | 9% |
| Asian American/Pacific Islander | 7% |
| African American | 4% |
| Multiracial | 3.4% |
| Arab/Middle Eastern | 1.4% |
| Native/Indigenous | 0.8% |

Age

| 18 - 24 | 2.2% |
|---------|------|
| 25 - 34 | 7% |
| 35 - 44 | 22% |
| 45 - 54 | 34% |
| 55 – 64 | 28% |
| 65+ | 5% |

**Fig. 5.1** Frameline's Audience Demographics for 2010

I feel that our audience is aging. Definitely if you go to a big sold out screening on a Friday at 7 or 6:30 it's going to be older and a lot of couples. I don't know how programming would change that or bring younger people. People don't go to the theatre or cultural events as much as their parents did, so people don't want to commit to a subscription because it's just too hard (Interview with Kim 2011).

This thought is continued in Price's interview, where the perception of elitism of the audience is a direct result of increasing professionalism:

One thing that you have to remember is that many of the core audience do tend to be a highly educated group of people. There is always the question of 'is Frameline a grass roots organisation?' It used to be in its early days but this is less so now. It was. It did have a lot of grassroots qualities about it but now it is trying to be a bigger, major film festival. The criticism it would get as a result of moving into this professionalised festival is that it was no longer going to be grass roots and therefore more elitist. One of the things that we realised when having the word elitist thrown at us in place of grass roots, is that our audience is more than 50 % has a second college degree. The very nature of showing high art film can be that way (Interview with Price 2011).

Is there evidence of resistance to these audience dynamics at Frameline as highlighted by Kim and Price? Kates's (2003) discussion of Mardi Gras, and the push and pull relationship between resistance and an appropriation of this resistance, reminds us that "these types of events may reflect, reinforce, exploit, and help constitute existing oppositional tendencies and meanings co-existing in the larger society" (7). In other words, is Frameline, to some extent, reinforcing dominant ideologies of race, gender, and age existent in wider society? In terms of the carnivalesque, is the festival merely reinforcing the social norms that are supposedly being challenged?

### *Transgression*

Male whiteness is diluted with the variety of festival patrons who wouldn't normally feel comfortable in the Castro, drinking in the nearby bars. Q Bar across the road is designated as the festival bar and is often frequented by Frameline staff, directors, actors, programmers, and audience members. When asked if they would go to the Castro outside of the festival time, those that did not fit into the Castro clone image stated that they would never do so. A previously mentioned, audience member who identified as genderqueer gave a response representative of the many who did not have any desire to be in the Castro:

> Would I ever go to the Castro? I haven't spent much time in the Castro outside of the festival period. There are some restaurants I might go to. It's a tourist place; if I had a friend visiting I would probably take them there, otherwise no (Interview with "Sydney," 2011).

Another audience member who did not fit the gay male clone persona had a response that mirrored the above-mentioned:

> I feel invisible most of the time. I don't really hang out in the Castro unless I am going to the Castro theatre for a film. That's the only reason why I go to the Castro because I feel there is not a lot of stuff catered towards me there. There are a lot of expensive shops and clothes stores that are not catered to me. It's not that I don't feel welcome, it's just not the top place for me to go. I am more pulled to the Mission and that scene (Interview with "Audrey," 2011).

During the period of the film festival, the Castro sees a suspension of previously held social hierarchies of sexual identity. As Bakhtin states "this temporary suspension, both ideal and real, of hierarchical rank created during carnival time a special type of communication impossible in everyday life" (10). Different identity groups of the queer community come together during the festival. This is an opportunity for communication and integration offered within the Frameline space. While of course there are screenings that individually cater to gay men, lesbians, S/M community, and so on, there are many centrepiece events that see a coming together of all the queer community. According to Whitham, the Castro is a great flagship location for the festival. This is an acknowledgement that the space of the festival is incredibly important. Planned for the Pride festival, Frameline is designed to *be* an actual festival:

> The Castro is in a location where it can be awesome and problematic depending on the day. It's in the centre of everything, and it holds such a large number of people that it just always has a feeling of grandeur, and then if you go to the Roxie or the Vic it may be a different ambiance but there it's still about independence and it's still a good festival vibe. It's really hard going to festivals or working at festivals that take place in a mall or Cineplex... It just gives you a different vibe; it feels like you are going to the movies. I think that

by using these theatres, filmmakers and film festival goers feel like they are at a festival. Everything revolves around Frameline and nobody there is also buying tickets to see *Cars 2* and that's really nice (Interview with Whitham 2011).

Whitham's response definitely reinforces that the Castro and Mission theatres are indeed their own space managed by Frameline and not shared with non-festival filmgoers.

> The Castro neighbourhood is amazing, it really helps Frameline be a great gay and lesbian and queer, LGBT destination for guests and filmmakers because they are not only motivated to come to the festival and see this film but they feel as though they are in a queer world. When you step out onto that street it's its own entity. You can see many things that you simply wouldn't see a mile away in the civic centre. Queer people are allowed to be much more forthright. And I think that helps Frameline to be more of a community event (Interview with Buford 2011).

With the films mentioned in the previous chapter, we are seeing a plethora of queer characters with fluid sexual orientations and an increase in films that challenge dominant film form. The festival is inherently a joyous experience for everyone. It is a time of laughter and a time for the "foregrounding of social overturning and the counter-hegemonic subversion of established power" (Stam 1989, 93). While this queer diversity may not permanently dismantle the homonormativity of the Castro, we are seeing small moments of resistance opening up.

This queer carnivalesque space becomes an imagined community that exists in opposition to the Castro's community outside of festival times. While the festival is a social enterprise that must interact with economically profitable yet politically problematic films such as *eCupid*, a resistant imagined community is formed. Coined by Anderson (1983), the imagined community advocates that each member will not necessarily meet face-to-face but still have a shared collective identity. While Anderson argues that the rise of nationalism was aided by the increased equitable access to print media, Frameline uses its own media (being its film screenings, website, programmes, and so forth) to create its own sense of the 'San Francisco Bay Area LGBTQ film loving community.' Here there are two different communities being imagined. First, the diverse queer community that envisions utopian ideals of everyone coming together. Second, there is a subaltern community of Frameline patrons who otherwise wouldn't feel comfortable in the Castro. It is this second community that is carnivalesque in nature. Sustained social empowerment occurs when the transgressive nature of this secondary community begins to infiltrate and change the configuration of the primary community.

## *The Film Festival as a Party*

For many who attend a Frameline screening, the film festival *is* an actual festival. The carnival sees a rejection of "social decorum entailing a release from oppressive etiquette, politeness and good manners" (Bakhtin 1984, 94). Frameline film screenings are unique in their rejection of traditional movie-going etiquette. I remember attending the shorts programme entitled "Sazon y Sabor" for Frameline 35, which featured a diverse array of short films from Latino filmmakers. My experience in the Victoria Theatre that afternoon was very different to that of a film with MQFF at ACMI. I could barely hear the movie over the hissing, booing, and clicking from audience members. My chair was actually rocking from the guy next to me constantly standing up yelling support to the characters on screen and clicking his fingers repeatedly yelling "fierce!" Watching a film at Frameline is a participatory experience. One does not simply attend a screening in a passive mindset. Frameline has the unruly festivity of the carnival as outlined by Berliner below:

> A big group of people who all identify within the community coming together is pretty awesome. You feel excited about watching the film. It's like a party. You are more amped up to party. I love it during the film festival because it's more than just tourists going there. I love seeing people lined up to see a film on the street. That is pretty awesome. It just makes me happy being there part of the numbers (Interview with Berliner 2011).

Frameline constructs a party-like atmosphere for its audience members. Alexis Whitham specifically stressed throughout her interview that Frameline caters to both "your party queers and your pensive queers." The film festival sees a breakdown of the barrier between spectacle and spectator while still being a cultural experience. This is a culture of trans-gression in a communication with official culture as "in the carnival, dogma, hegemony and authority are dispersed through ridicule and laughter" (Lachmann 1989, 128). This performative transgression is the process by which we move from a socially acceptable cinema-going state to an unruly festive one. The space of the festival allows for this transgression. For

Foucault, the transgressive subject is constantly in a process of self-definition in relation to "the other." The transgressive audience is neither unified, stable nor rational. Transgression constantly crosses boundaries of social decorum in that it "has its entire space in the line that it crosses" (Foucault 1977, 34). The boundaries of self and culture are illuminated by acts of transgression. This constructed dichotomy of self/other and appropriate/ inappropriate is a constant spiral reaffirming our own subjectivity. Attending these screenings, while sometimes more serious than full of debauchery, allows us to engage in self-exploration both internally and through physical acts of cinematic norm breaking.

## Hong Kong and Neoliberal Spaces

In discussing space and HKLGFF, I would like to focus on the ramifications of a film festival screening in commercial movie theatres in shopping malls. As highlighted in previous chapters, HKLGFF 2014 primarily held sessions in art-house venue Broadway Cinematheque (BC), which is located in Yau Ma Tei, and then shopping malls The One and Palace IFC, which is in the International Finance Centre in Central.

The space within which HKLGFF inhabits further adds the festival to being a commercial organisation. In Chap. 4, it was demonstrated that HKLGFF's programme is primarily determined by economic value rather than programming content that would not be commercial viable. This is a demonstration of neoliberal programming. Furthermore, this is indicative of an increasing neoliberal, cosmopolitan Chinese culture. In analysing how Hong Kong lesbians create spaces of resistance, Tang argues that it is imperative to take into account Hong Kong's status as a capitalist city and neoliberal economy (2011). Hong Kong's decolonisation is embedded within a "nationalistic discourses of 'return (huigui) to the grand narrative of Chinese history" and that this is embedded within "the global framework of capitalist modernity" (Lo and Pang 2007, 349). Hai Ren argues that China's reunification with Hong Kong has transformed the country into a neoliberal one (2010). In her analysis of neoliberalism in emerging markets, Aihwa Ong (2006) notes that the development of market-based strategies is not tantamount to Americanisation. Instead, this contemporary Asian neo-liberalism is a local phenomenon, where neoliberalism is "conceptualised as a new relationship between government and knowledge through which governing activities are recast as non-political and non-ideological" (3).

With HKLGFF taking place in shopping malls, the management of a social movement is primarily market driven.

BC aside, this movement away from the Hong Kong Arts Centre to the upmarket shopping malls upholds the neoliberal ideal of a cosmopolitan lifestyle and market mobility. The venue is surrounded by high-end boutique brands, such as Chanel, as opposed to bars or lounges for festival patrons. Having screenings within a shopping mall further commercialises the attendance of this festival. Anthropologist Daniel Miller (1987) argues that consumption of material goods has replaced a direct relationship to other people. Frameline, MQFF, and BC in Yau Ma Tei offer space for festival patrons to converge and form a temporary public. The One and Palace IFC do not. When attending these screenings, festival attendees would enter the space to see the film and leave, sometimes without uttering a word to anyone else. The spatial dynamics of films being exhibited in shopping malls are significantly different to singular theatres (Frameline) and Film Centres (MQFF at ACMI and HKLGFF at BC). There is an economic dimension to the political act of attending an LGBTI-themed event. Much like Miller's pessimistic views on consumption, these economic dynamics mask the potential for social connections. The social dynamics of attending the screenings at The One and Palace IFC are very different to that of BC, which was highlighted in my interview with Gary Mak:

> BC is more for the art house film buff and so they can accept difficult films, even though they might not know anything about the country or genre. Maybe the synopsis would be interesting or if they follow a particular director or actor. The audience is more accepting of any kind of film. It's a more local audience as well because it is in Yau Ma Tei, which is an old district on the Kowloon side. It's more for the locals.

> IFC is in Central and is more for the expats and also those living in mid-level or work in Central in finance or banking. The audience is more affluent, more English speaking. They talk more about consumption, lifestyle, and parties, instead of sharing about film. For more BC, people are more interesting in talking about films. For IFC they don't really give a shit about what the director says. Most of the time, if there were a director they would just go (Interview with Gary Mak 2014).

Art-house films and more challenging genres, such as documentaries, are exhibited in Yau Ma Tei for primarily working class and local audiences while Central sees predominantly expat and affluent audiences. I personally found this difference palpable when attending. Films with Chinese subtitles being popular with local audiences are also added to this "local versus expat" division. One could follow Postman's pessimistic critique of consumerism (1985), where we are amusing ourselves to death, whereby just seeing films has a debilitating effect on social interaction. Where Postman argues that politics and religion are diluted into packaged commodities, the political ramifications of tongzhi spaces are diluted within the shopping mall. These spaces highlight the tension between the appeal of shopping in the controlled setting of the mall and the supposed pretentiousness of such spaces, "a tension which we relate to people's concerns about the materialism and artificiality they have come to associate with shopping as much as with the transformation of nature in the commodity form" (Jackson 1999, 37). This controlled space is a commodity, which is evident by these screenings taking place next to other non-HKLGFF films. During HKLGFF 2014, promotional posters for *The Maze Runner* (Wes Ball 2014) were more prominent than HKLGFF material. This is not unique to HKLGFF, however, as many film festivals have to cope with the economic reality of only renting out singular theatres of a Cineplex. MQFF has also held screenings at Hoyts at Melbourne Central and the now non-operational Greater Union Cinemas on Russell Street. This is largely due to the availability and pricing of other theatres within their respective cities.

This pessimism implies, however, that festival attendees are passive in their consumption. These consumers could be engaging in postmodern politics of difference (Featherstone 1991). Popular gay screenings in these spaces could be a form of "demand-led capitalism" resulting in change (Miller 1995, 8). Rather than being passive dupes being shaped by neoliberalism, these festivalgoers could in fact be creating shifts in the symbolic social structures of elite shopping malls. Perhaps having promotional material of the festival alongside mainstream titles could rupture the existing social fabric of these elite spaces. This is akin to Frank Mort's (1995) analysis of the changing nature of Soho, London, in the 1980s, which was a product of the different masculine communities in the region. HKLGFF's presence in the International Finance Centre has the power to subvert pre-existing hierarchies of identity in these spaces. While HKLGFF is very much assimilated in this cosmopolitan arena, this does not discount the progressive potential of screening LGBTI-themed content in a mall.

## CONCLUSION

This chapter has examined the importance space plays when considering the progressive potential of a film festival. A significant finding in this chapter is the carnivalesque nature of the experience of attending Frameline in the Castro District. The carnival space allows for social empowerment through transgressing dominant social norms and subverting hierarchies that were previously in place. The social space created by Frameline in the Castro neighbourhood challenges the privileged hyper-masculine identity of the Castro clone. By creating Frameline an actual festival—go see a film and then have a drink with your friends at the festival lounge at Q Bar—the space of the Castro is subverted to allow for social empowerment to occur. This creates the attendance of a film festival a politically active deed. This is perhaps the quintessential aspect of Frameline's social empowerment as, ultimately, the empowerment that occurs through film spectatorship can transcend the physical boundaries of the film theatre. HKLGFF also employs a neighbourhood divide. While the more art-house film are screened at the BC screenings in the working-class Yau Ma Tei, more upmarket screenings occur in Central, which are predominantly attended by expats and locals that work in the banking district. Here, the environment is just as important as the films themselves.

## NOTES

1. The Laird is a male-only gay bar in Richmond. It's like most other gay bars in Melbourne that are predominantly male, including Sircut and The Peel, the latter of which militantly enforced these discriminatory entry practices.
2. Since conducting this fieldwork and writing this monograph, the Mission District has undergone a significant gentrification process. The neighbourhood has been experiencing socio-economic change for some time. However, the recent influx of Silicon Valley "techies" has fed an economic boom that has made the neighbourhood unaffordable for many. The area is now considerably different from the neighbourhood my interview subjects described in 2011. The Castro neighbourhood remains the same, however.
3. Jennifer Reck's PhD dissertation (2009) examines how this debate around the Castro LGBTQQ Youth Shelter resulted in a hierarchy of

belonging and further reinforcement of the "Castro Citizen," which is arguably the epitome of homonormativity.

4. Podmore's article "Gone 'Underground?' Lesbian visibility and the consolidation of queer space in Montreal" is highly recommended for its extensive literature review on gay male and lesbian spaces.

5. I am in great debt to Jennifer Kim, Frameline's former director of development, for these figures.

## WORKS CITED

Anderson, Benedict. 1983. *Imagined Communities: Reflections on the Origin and Spread of Nationalism*. London: Verso.

Bakhtin, Mikhail Mikhaïlovich. 1984. *Rabelais and His World 341*. Bloomington, IN: Indiana University Press.

Bakhtin, Mikhail. 1968. *Rabelais and his World*. trans. Helene Iswolsky. Bloomington, IN: Indiana University Press.

Bell, David, and Jon Binnie. 2003. Authenticating Queer Space: Citizenship, Urbanism and Governance. *Urban Studies* 41(9): 1807–1820.

Chasin, Alexandra. 2000. *Selling Out: The Gay and Lesbian Movement Goes to Market*. New York: Palgrave.

Chura, Hillary. 1999. Miller Reconsiders Gay-themed TV Spot: Commercial for Genuine Draft Would Be a First for Beer Category. *Advertising Age* 70(29):3. Accessed online at: http://adage.com/article/news/miller-reconsiders-gay-themed-tv-spot-commercial-genuine-draft-a-beer-category/61784/

Crespi-Valbonna, Monstrerrat, and Greg Richards. 2007. The Meaning of Cultural Festivals: Stakeholder Perspectives in Catalunya. *International Journal of Cultural Policy* 13(1): 103–122.

Eco, Umberto. 1984. The Frames of Comic Freedom. In *Carnival!* ed. T. Sebeok. Berlin: Mouton Publishers.

Featherstone, Mike. 1991. *Consumer Culture and Postmodernism*. London: Sage.

Florida, Richard. 2002. *The Rise of the Creative Class. And How It's Transforming Work, Leisure and Everyday Life*. New York: Basic Books.

Foucault, Michel. 1977. *The History of Sexuality: An Introduction*, vol 1. New York: Vintage.

Fraser, Nancy. 1997. Rethinking the Public Sphere: A Contribution to the Critique of Actually Existing Democracy. In *Justice Interruptus: Critical Reflection on the "Postsocialist" Condition*. New York: Routledge.

Gudelunas, David. 2011. Consumer Myths and the Gay Men and Women Who Believe Them: A Qualitative Look at Movements and Markets. *Psychology and Marketing* 28(1): 53–68.

Hunt, Mia, and John Zacharias. 2008. Representing Montreal's (Gay) Village. *Canadian Journal of Urban Research* 17(1): 28–57.

Jackson, Peter. 1999. Consumption and Identity: The Cultural Politics of Shopping. *European Planning Studies* 7(1): 25–39.

Kates, Steven M. 2003. Producing and Consuming Gendered Representations: An Interpretation of the Sydney Gay and Lesbian Mardi Gras. *Consumption, Markets and Culture* 6(1): 5–22.

Lachmann, Renate. 1989. Bakhtin and Carnival: Culture as CounterCulture. *Cultural Critique* 11(winter): 115–152.

Levine, Martin P. 1998. *Gay Macho: The Life and Death of the Homosexual Clone.* New York: New York University Press.

Lo, Kwai Cheung, and Laikwan Pang. 2007. Hong Kong: Ten Years After Colonialism. *Postcolonial Studies* 10(4): 349–356.

Mak, Gary. 2014. Interviewed by Stuart Richards, personal interview, Hong Kong. 21st September.

Miller, Daniel. 1987. *Material Culture and Mass Consumption.* Oxford: Basil Blackwell.

———. 1995. *Acknowledging Consumption.* London: Routlege.

Mort, Frank. 1995. Archaeologies of city life: commercial culture, masculinity, and spatial relations in 1980s London. *Environment and Planning D: Society and Space* 13(5): 573–590.

Ong, Aihwa. 2006. *Neoliberalism as Exception: Mutations in Citizenship and Sovereignty.* Durham, NC: Duke University Press.

Penney, Renee. 2010. *Desperately Seeking Redundancy? Queer Romantic Comedy and the Festival Audience.* Vancouver: The University of British Columbia.

Phelan, Shane. 2001. *Sexual Strangers: Gays, Lesbians, and Dilemmas of Citizenship.* Philadelphia, PA: Temple University Press.

Podmore, Julie A. 2006. Gone 'Underground'? Lesbian Visibility and the Consolidation of Queer Space in Montréal. *Social & Cultural Geography* 7(4): 595–625.

Postman, Neil. 1985. *Amusing Ourselves to Death: Public Discourse in the Age of Show Business.* New York: Penguin.

Reck, Jen. 2009. Homeless gay and transgender youth of color in San Francisco:"No one likes street kids"—even in the castro. *Journal of LGBT Youth* 6(2-3): 223–242.

Ren, Hai. 2010. *Neoliberalism and Culture in China and Hong Kong.* London: Routledge.

Rhyne, Raghan. 2007. *Pink Dollars: Gay and Lesbian Film Festivals and the Economy of Visibility.* PhD Dissertation. New York: New York University.

Sender, Katherine. 2004. *Business, Not Politics.* New York: Columbia University Press.

Signorile, Michelangelo. 1997. *Life outside: The signorile report on gay men, sex, drugs, muscles, and the passages of life.* New York: Harper Collins Publishers.

Signorile, Michelangelo. 1997. *Life Outside: The Signorile Report on Gay Men, Sex, Drugs, Muscles, and the Passages of Life*. New York: Harper Collins Publishers.

Stallybrass, Peter, and Allon White. 1986. *The poetics and politics of transgression*. London: Methuen.

Stam, Robert. 1989. *Subversive Pleasures: Bakhtin, Cultural Criticism, and Film*. Baltimore, MD: Johns Hopkins University Press.

Tang, Denise Tse Shang. 2011. *Conditional Desires: Honk Kong Lesbian Desires and Everyday Life*. Hong Kong: Hong Kong University Press.

Warner, Michael. 2002. *Publics and Counterpublics*. Cambridge: Zone Books.

Wittman, Carl. 1970. *Gay Manifesto*. New York: A Red Butterfly Publication.

Yaksich, Michael J. 2008. Connoisseurs of Consumption: Gay Identities, and the Commodification of Knowledgable Spending. *Consumers, Commodities and Consumption* 9(2). Accessed online at: http://csrn.camden.rutgers.edu/newsletters/9-2/yaksich.htm

Zielinski, Gerald J.Z. 2009. *Furtive, Steady Glances: On the Emergence and Cultural Politics of Lesbian and Gay Film Festivals*. PhD Dissertation. Montreal: McGill University.

### Interviews

Buford, Des. Interviewed by Stuart Richards, personal interview, San Francisco, 7 July 2011.

Daniel, Lisa. Interviewed by Stuart Richards, personal interview, Melbourne, 5 August 2011.

Feliciano, Lares, Sam Berliner and Nissa Poulson. Interviewed by Stuart Richards, personal interview, San Francisco, 7 July 2011.

Kim, Jennifer. Interviewed by Stuart Richards, personal interview, San Francisco, 7 July 2011.

Nick and Audrey. Interviewed by Stuart Richards, confidential interview, San Francisco, 9 July 2011.

Polly and Alex. Interviewed by Stuart Richards, confidential, San Francisco, 11 July 2011.

Price, K.C. Interviewed by Stuart Richards, personal interview, San Francisco, 7 July 2011.

Sam. Interviewed by Stuart Richards, confidential, San Francisco, 8 July 2011.

Sydney. Interviewed by Stuart Richards, confidential, San Francisco, 12 July 2011.

Whitham, Alexis. Interviewed by Stuart Richards, personal interview, San Francisco, 8 July 2011.

CHAPTER 6

# Conclusion

This book highlights the possibility for social empowerment to occur within the neoliberal framework of the contemporary queer film festival. The queer film festival boom throughout the 1990s was a result of community organisations engaging in the economically minded creative industry paradigm. At surface level, the queer film festival is structured according to a conservative ideology that privileges the ideal gay consumer. However, I have argued that while indeed some elements of the programming are homonormative, the very essence of attending a queer film festival is a communally empowering act. The queer film festival is inherently different from the general international film festival. The two spaces are entirely different. The fieldwork presented in this research substantiated that the queer film festival is so much more than *just* a space for film exhibition.

The Frameline San Francisco International LGBTQ Film Festival has the distinction of being the world's first queer film festival, although, of course, underground film screenings occurred prior to this collective of experimental film works. The festival was born during a tumultuous and exciting time for gay liberationist politics in San Francisco. Queer cinema during this period was greatly tied with the experimental genre and the political world of the gay rights movement. Fast forward 36 years and Frameline has grown into not just a community arts festival but also a professional organisation that has courted the pink dollar and attained financial sustainability.

The changing regulation of aesthetic creativity has been a driving force behind Frameline's growth. Once Frameline began to receive NEA

© The Author(s) 2016
S.J. Richards, *The Queer Film Festival*,
DOI 10.1057/978-1-137-58438-0_6

funding, the festival grew in its status as a community event that promoted social inclusion. This was the sole function for Frameline in its earlier years: to provide a space for queer film and to aid in the social inclusion of the Bay Area's LGBT community. While Frameline still serves this purpose today, the management of the festival has altered. With the growing rate of the pink dollar throughout the 1990s (Chasin 2000; Sender 2004), Frameline's funding became less reliant on grants and philanthropic gestures and more evenly on ticket sales and corporate sponsorship (Rhyne 2007). This saw Frameline adopt creative industries logic. This conceptual shift highlights that community art not only provides social inclusion but also reaps other forms of value. Creativity can be financially self-sufficient with careful management. Adding value to a creative aesthetic highlights a key concept in cultural studies today:

> That no object, no text, no cultural practice has an intrinsic or necessary meaning or value or function; and that meaning, value, and function are always the effect of specific (and changing, changeable) social relations and mechanisms of signification (Frow 1995, 145).

Through this network of institutions and stakeholders, the non-economic value of a community art event can be evolved into a marker of status. The contemporary queer film festival is very much a product of these "changing social relations and mechanisms of signification" (145).

The Melbourne Queer Film Festival (MQFF) began at the very beginning of this surge in wider commercial interest in the pink dollar. With the support of Midsumma's pre-existing contacts, MQFF was able to survive with a balance of grants, tickets sales, and sponsors (albeit shakily at first). The queer film festival in the age of the traditional cultural industry was primarily concerned with providing the audience value in terms of both social and cultural capital. The queer film festival framed in the creative industries paradigm highlights the potential for this value to be used for economic sustainability. There is an increased professionalism from the early days of a community event. Investors supporting these organisations are not engaging in social altruism but a new innovative means for exposure and profit.

The Hong Kong Lesbian and Gay Film Festival (HKLGFF) was on the forefront of the wave queer film festivals in East Asia. The festival is emblematic of Hong Kong's neoliberal cosmopolitanism, with economic value being the primary determinant of the film's programming. While the festival has a vibrant Asian focus, the festival is at the mercy of global inequalities in filmmaking, with many films unable to be screened with Chinese subtitles. The East Asian queer film festival circuit has been strengthened, however, with the formation of an Alliance amongst several festivals, including Queer Screen in Sydney.

This book has examined this balancing act of financial and social values through the conceptual framework of the social enterprise. The queer film festival is a non-profit organisation that relies no longer just on others' good will but on an increasingly complex economic outlook to increase their financial sustainability. Throughout my analysis of Frameline and MQFF as social enterprises, I highlighted six ongoing themes evident in scholarly literature on the social enterprise. First, the organisational leaders are seen not only as community leaders but also as business heroes that make innovative choices. Lisa Daniel, Dillan Golightly, and Spiro Economopoulos from MQFF, and the various departmental leaders at Frameline are often in the local queer press. This positions these individuals as subcultural celebrities within their respective communities. The second significant social enterprise factor demonstrated that the festival addressed gaps in the current market. While for audiences in San Francisco, Melbourne, and Hong Kong, there is an increasing amount of queer narratives in the mainstream media, characters in television and commercially released films are predominantly white, gender appropriate, and male. There are also very few *authentic* self-representative narratives by queer writers and directors. This significant hole in the market is filled annually by the queer film festival's programme. This gap remains, however, in Hong Kong, with minimal lesbian and transgender content being programmed. Interview responses identified three key needs that the queer film festival addresses. First, the film festival is an alternative distribution network outside of the hegemony of Hollywood. Second, the festival provides an identity-affirming experience, and finally, the festival space allows for interaction with one's community and experiences this collective identity in a safe environment.

The third key theme addressed the innovation of these festivals. In order for the festivals to produce sustainable social change, the "business heroes" must provide innovative solutions to complex issues with both programming and management. For Frameline, this was seen with specific programming choices and strategies for ticket sales. Their initiative Frameline Voices provides a viable exhibition space for marginalised identities within the queer film market. For MQFF and HKLGFF, this innovation was also seen in specific curatorial decisions, such as MQFF's travelling festival to Bendigo and Yarraville or HKLGFF's accompanying art exhibition.

The fourth key theme analysed social empowerment, in terms of both the audience and the sustainability of their social empowerment. Social empowerment saw the expansion of the organisation's size to allow for more beneficiaries to be affected; this was demonstrated in each case study's history. There was as increase in the variety of activities undertaken. Finally, there needs to be an impact on both the beneficiaries directly and other like-minded community organisations to continue similar work. We can clearly see this in Frameline's position as a world leader in the queer film festival circuit. MQFF engages in this third aspect differently. While it does not have many visiting stakeholders, it supports Australian filmmakers with its cash prizes and has positive relationships with local businesses. HKLGFF is now part of an alliance with other East Asian queer film festivals.

The fifth key element identified the festivals' relationship with corporate sponsorship. While there can be apprehension when a non-profit organisation courts sponsorship, very little was discovered in my fieldwork research. Interviews with both case studies almost unanimously agreed over the important role sponsorship plays with the festival's financial viability. For Frameline, its involvement with the Israel's pink washing campaign remains an issue that causes tension within the Bay Area LGBTI community.

The final key characteristic of the social enterprise is the evaluation of the festival's success. Evaluating a festival's success on ticket sales alone is an improper approach. The Blended Value Proposition (Emerson 2003) establishes the importance of financial, social, and environmental worth being considered at equal measures. The qualitative social change generated from the social enterprise is just as important as economic viability. A key aspect for both festivals to consider is the sustainability of this success. What measures are they going to implement to ensure continuance of this success?

This detailed classification of the queer film festival as a social enterprise has noteworthy implications for community arts events. Sustainability is a key concern for non-profit organisations, particularly when it comes to developing a tolerant union between social legitimacy and fiscal management. These six characteristics of the social enterprise make this research an important addition to community arts scholarship, especially when dealing with possibly fragmented communities such as the audience of the queer film festival.

By defining the queer film festival as a social enterprise, an association is made between the organisation existing within a neoliberal framework and the need to programme homonormative films. Born out of heteronormativity and neoliberalism, an analysis of homonormative subject matter takes the critical weaponry of Warner's heteronormative discussion in *Fear of a Queer Planet* (1991). Duggan (2003) defined homonormativity as not contesting "dominant heteronormative assumptions and institutions, but upholds and sustains them, while promising the possibility of a demobilized gay constituency and a privatized, depoliticized gay culture anchored in domesticity and consumption" (50). This is a result of the polarity between economic and cultural politics, where one's socio-economic status is a great determinant of one's access to an equitable standing in society. This new homonormativity and normalising trends in contemporary LGBT politics see a yearning for assimilation rather than dismantling the status quo of identity politics. The association between sexual norms and a wider hegemony is a key area under discussion for current queer theory. The queer film festival engages in homonormative politics through its focus on economic value.

This research highlighted three distinct dichotomies evident in the manifestation of homonormativity in the films programmed. First, how do the narratives engage in contemporary politics? A distinct trend of gay male romantic comedies, such as *eCupid*, all displayed a clear lack of engagement with contemporary politics. Homonormativity shows a "demobilized gay constituency and a privatized, depoliticized gay culture anchored in domesticity and consumption" (Duggan 2003, 50), and these films throughout the analysis of the programmes highlighted that. On the other side of this spectrum were films heavily imbued with an awareness of the hegemonic relations of contemporary identity politics. Films also positioned on this spectrum were decidedly not anchored in consumption by having an art-house aesthetic, being experimental or a genre hybrid. These films were decidedly less "bums on seats films" (as the saying goes) and exhibited a keen awareness of contemporary identity politics.

The second binary under discussion in the analysis of the film programmes concerned domesticity. A collection of films, such as *The Green*, privileged the domestic space and the normative familial relationships. In some examples, queer sexuality was positioned in alienation to the traditional family, while others exhibited domestic settings that attempted to mimic the nuclear family. In opposition to this were films that flaunted subversion of the above norms. While non-heterosexual identities traditionally existed independently from familial settings (Cook 2010), films presented "families of choice" that were explicit politicisations of kinship

(Weston 1991). A distinction needs to be made between the union in films such as *The Green* that yearn for assimilation and refrain from overt displays of their sexuality and films such as *Drool* that present a "family of choice" and celebrate in their alternative sexualities. *Drool* presents two queer women and their kin forming a network that is beyond the nuclear family. The queer family of choice exists in plurality and on their own terms.

The final dichotomy at play in the programming examines how identity in the narrative plays out. While some films exhibited a clear hierarchy of sexual identity that privileged whiteness, gender appropriateness, and masculinity (amongst other categories), other films celebrated their queer diversity. While the former reinforces pre-existing hegemonic identity constructions, the latter selection of films gives space for identities traditionally marginalised by the homonormative gay mainstream. While we can problematise this joy of queer diversity and question whether this actually creates *sustainable* change, we can also use this to highlight a distinct difference between the two case studies. While Frameline is *still* an LGBTQ film festival, thus reinforcing anachronistic rigid identity categories, MQFF has been queer for most of its existence. A queer label allows for a greater fluidity in identities that an LGBTQ festival may hinder.

Following on from this discussion on Frameline and MQFF's relationship to homonormativity, HKLGFF was discussed in relation to the influence of a global gay aesthetic. This is, of course, not to say that the other queer film festivals are immune from the global gay image. Both Frameline and MQFF exhibit a high proportion of commercial films with the image of the white, masculine gay male in their programmes. This influence of the global gay figure results in fewer local productions and films with transgender and lesbian protagonists.

The final question that needs to be asked is thus: Is there a connection between the homonormativity evident in the programming and space of the festival and the social empowerment generated when attending? The carnivalesque theory was employed to analyse the space of the Castro during Frameline. Throughout the duration of the festival, the Castro District is transformed from being a male- and white-dominated neighbourhood to being full of various identities that don't fit the "Castro clone." HKLGFF's move to shopping malls was identified as being representative of the influence of neoliberalism in the region. The difference between the screenings at Broadway Cinematheque in Yau Ma Tei and the screenings at Palace IFC in Central creates a local versus expat divide. The element of space is a quintessential aspect to the positive nature of the queer film festival. While yes some films that are exhibited are conservative, these politics do not transcend to the experience of attending a queer film festival, being in a room full of other filmgoers whom you share a connection with. In this respect, programming a film such as *eCupid* brings significant value to the festival. It will get bums on seats and aid the financial sustainability of the festival. At first thought, the very idea that anything homonormative could manifest a socially empowering experience seemed incomprehensible. However, when taken all aspects of the organisation into account, it is evidently possible.

This research has significant conceptual implications for queer film studies. This research is founded upon there being a distinction between two spectrums in queer cinema market; that there is a different audience intended for *Brokeback Mountain* and *The Kids Are Alright* as opposed to *Drool, Sasha,* or *Fig Trees.* What this research reveals, however, is that this latter market is far more complex than what the label "by/for/about" allows. Films such as *Shelter, Another Gay Movie,* and the plethora of *Eating Out* films exist in a market that embodies different exhibition and distribution strategies than what *Fig Trees, The Advocate for Fagdom,* or *Maggots and Men* inhabit. This research highlights the importance of alternative distribution networks for those films intended for the LGBTI community that are not commercially viable outside of the queer film festival.

The queer film festival has transformed from its underground, grassroots beginnings to a commercial creative industry. By using the theory of the social enterprise as a critical tool, this research has established that economic and social values *can* coexist. In fact, for a socially legitimate queer film festival to function at the height of Frameline or MQFF, the harmonious synthesis of both empowering and homonormative films in the programming is imperative. Even though Friday and Saturday night film screenings might be filled with romantic comedies with gender-appropriate, attractive, upper middle-class, white (and so on) lovers, there is the possibility for the social experience of attending these events to outweigh any socially conservative programming. This pilgrimage is an important one for any socially aware queer.

## WORKS CITED

Chasin, Alexandra. 2000. *Selling Out: The Gay and Lesbian Movement Goes to Market.* New York: Palgrave.

Cook, Matt. 2010. Families of Choice? George Ives, Queer Lives and the Family in Early Twentieth-Century Britain. *Gender & History* 22(1): 1–20.

Duggan, Lisa. 2003. *The Twilight of Equality: Neoliberalism, Cultural Politics, and the Attack on the Democracy*. Boston, MA: Beacon Press.

Emerson, Jed. 2003. The Blended Value Proposition: Integrating Social and Financial Results. *California Management Review* 45(4): 35–51.

Frow, John. 1995. *Cultural Studies and Cultural Value*. Oxford: Clarendon Press.

Rhyne, Raghan. 2007. *Pink Dollars: Gay and Lesbian Film Festivals and the Economy of Visibility*. PhD Dissertation. New York: New York University.

Sender, Katherine. 2004. *Business, Not Politics*. New York: Columbia University Press.

Weston, Kath. 1991. *Families We Choose*. New York: Columbia University Press.

# Index

Note: Page numbers followed by "n" refers to notes.

© The Author(s) 2016

S.J. Richards, *The Queer Film Festival*, DOI 10.1057/978-1-137-58438-0